THE FALLEN WOMAN IN THE NINETEENTH-CENTURY ENGLISH NOVEL

The Fallen Woman in the Nineteenth-Century English Novel

George Watt

CROOM HELM
London & Canberra

BARNES & NOBLE BOOKS
Totowa, New Jersey

© 1984 George Watt
Croom Helm Ltd, Provident House, Burrell Row,
Beckenham, Kent BR3 1AT
Croom Helm Australia Pty Ltd,
28 Kembla Street, Fyshwick,
ACT 2609, Australia

British Library Cataloguing in Publication Data

Watt, George
    The fallen woman in the nineteenth-century
    English novel.
    1. English fiction—19th century
    2. English fiction—History and criticism
    3. Prostitution in literature
    I. Title
    823'.8'09352042   PR830.P/

    ISBN 0-7099-2781-9

First published in the USA 1984 by
Barnes and Noble Books
81 Adams Drive
Totowa, New Jersey, 07512

Library of Congress Cataloging in Publication Data

Watt, George.
    The fallen woman in the nineteenth century English
    novel.

    Bibliography: p.
    Includes index
    1. English Fiction—19th Century—History and criticism.
2. Prostitutes in literature. 3. Women in literature.
4. Social problems in literature. 5. Moral conditions
in literature.   I. Title.
    PR878.P73W37 1984   823'.8'093520692   83-22316
    ISBN 0-389-20443-9

44,036

Printed and bound in Great Britain

CONTENTS

For Jessie

PREFACE

I would like to thank Dr Robert Dingley of The University of New England for his help with the better disciplined sections of this book and Jacki Gray for her quiet, enthusiastic work with the manuscript. Belated thanks also go to Gordon Thomas, Paul Thomas and Sandy Thomas for their well-remembered and well-loved influence.

G.W.

'They were only women; they were not regular labourers; they were not particularly required anywhere; hence they had to hire a waggon at their own expense, and got nothing sent gratuitously.'

Thomas Hardy, *Tess of the d'Urbervilles*, Ch. 52

INTRODUCTION

To what extent can nineteenth-century reform novels or novels of social consciousness actually accept credit for affecting social change? The Victorians themselves 'never doubted that the art of literature was an art of power'.[1] Despite this assurance the question is still difficult to answer. Perhaps the most accurate measurement can be found through a study of particular reformers and their relationship to the novels they read. One such reformer is Josephine Butler, a strong-minded, zealous woman who gave the women's movement sufficient unity, strength and purpose to mount its first head-on collision with the establishment, the male world of Victorian England. After a protracted struggle the movement experienced its first major success in the repeal of the discriminatory Contagious Diseases Acts in 1886.

It was a novel read by Mrs Butler some thirty years before 1886, which prompted her to make an effort to help women, especially those who suffered. The developing sense of indignation she experienced was brought to a climax when Mrs Gaskell's bestselling novel *Ruth* shocked a prudish reading public in 1853, because it was the story of an unmarried mother who had to survive in a hostile world and raise her bastard son in it. Josephine was appalled at the unexpectedly pompous response from her husband's narrow-minded Oxford acquaintances, most of whom were fellow dons. Taking into account the male role in the fall of young girls like Ruth, Josephine could not accept the injustice. On finding a girl pregnant and discovering the father was an Oxford don, she visited one eminently wise scholar (by repute) for help. Her aim was to force the offending gentleman to accept fair responsibility. 'She was shattered by the professor's reaction to her approach. "It would only do harm to open up in any way such questions as this", he told her. "It's dangerous to arouse a sleeping lion".'[2]

Social awareness, sharpened by the sensitivity of Mrs Gaskell, was to take her on the long road which had never been traversed by any woman prior to this date. Her early attempts were amateurishly philanthropic. She helped fallen women by taking them into her own home in the late 50s. In the 60s she became president of a society, the aim of which was to provide higher education for women. She formed and led the Ladies' National Association which fought for seventeen years, on a national and international level, for the repeal of the Contagious Diseases Acts mentioned above. These Acts gave the police power, in garrison towns, to subject any woman they suspected to compulsory and regular hospital checks for venereal disease. Their aim was to cut down the incidence of venereal disease in the armed forces. The members of these forces were not inspected at all. In effect, Josephine felt, the Acts legalised prostitution and placed all the responsibility on the women themselves. Their repeal was largely the result of a *de facto* understanding between working-class men in the unions and middle-class women under Josephine's banner.[3] Although Josephine Butler was not the women's movement she was the first to unify the voice which challenged the male world's 'moral reality'—immorality is not in the act but being caught at it. Most of her life's work was with the victims of this iniquity.

   The central point is that the reading of *Ruth* inspired Josephine to work with prostitutes and non-professional fallen women, the latter being victims of one mistake or simply male craft. The novel is certainly not overtly about prostitutes or prostitution. Its heroine, though ultimately more noble than some of her literary compatriots, is fairly typical of the women studied in this book. She is a single, innocent, unprotected young girl who is seduced by a corrupt visitor who throws her off when it suits him. She must then survive as an outcast in her own land; she may be forced to become a prostitute to survive. Mercy Merrick in *The New Magdalen* and Nancy in *Oliver Twist* have to enter the oldest profession for some time at least. Tess, although never considering prostitution, is forced to be a kept mistress. From the twentieth-century perspective there is a difference, and a distinct one, between a prostitute and a girl who makes one mistake. An element of Victorian society did not allow for such a distinction.

   Mr Bradshaw is the church-going, middle-class neighbour of Ruth who discovers the secret of her past—she has never been the Mrs Denbigh she purports to be; her son is illegitimate. Prior to this discovery Ruth is a favourite of Bradshaw's. She is the governess of his young children and the companion to his eldest daughter. He sends Ruth presents, symbols of his patronising wealth, which are to make her his property in a chaste and economic sense. On discovering Ruth's lie this is his reaction:

'If there is one sin I hate—I utterly loathe—more than all others it
is wantonness. It includes all other sins . . . '
   'I was so young.'
   'The more depraved, the more disgusting you . . . '

He uses the opportunity to teach his own daughter a moral lesson,
interrupting his tirade against Ruth to point out that

> 'She has turned right into wrong, and wrong into right, and
> taught you all to be uncertain whether there be any such thing as
> Vice in the world, or whether it ought not to be looked upon as
> virtue . . . '[4]

Bradshaw is, no doubt, related to those paternal academics who
frequented Mrs Butler's home—his is a mind which admits the
existence of only two kinds of women, the virtuous and the fallen.
He cannot or will not recognise the forces social, economic or
psychological which shape the fate of the fallen. As such he
becomes the voice of middle-class male respectability. Josephine
Butler knew that while the collective voice was mouthing moral
platitudes its hand was under the supposedly inviolate petticoat.
But because the latter was not often seen, and the former was often
heard, the dichotomy of the two classes of women persisted
throughout the century.

   Novelists like Gaskell, Collins, Hardy and, to a lesser extent,
Dickens, tried very hard to change this convention. Unfortunately
many other novelists felt it their duty to uphold it in their fiction.
Nowhere had it a more popular voice than in the novels of Mrs
Henry Wood. Joan Pomeroy, the attractive but virtuously haughty
heroine of *Pomeroy Abbey* who is admired by her creator, belongs
to the ancient Pomeroy family who inhabit the gothic house that
gives the book its title. Despite her pride she has befriended the
poor Sybilla Gaunt, daughter of her father's gentleman game-
keeper. This friendship horrifies the *nouveau riche* tenant living in
the other large home on the Pomeroy estate. (Not wishing to offend
the gentle sensibilities of her plentiful middle-class readers, Mrs
Wood takes pains to point out several times that Sybilla's lack of
status is ameliorated by her line of descent from none other than
John of Gaunt.) Joan's flaunting of convention has its limits, however, as does Mrs Wood's, when it is rumoured that Sybilla is not
very well. That her spirits are down encourages gossip. Her father

claims that she suffers from the heat. Joan suspects something is wrong when she encounters Sybilla wearing a copious shawl. Ironically her father is correct—she does suffer from the heat, but it is the heat of passion. The shawl tries to cover that which society sees as the wages of sin. In the novel Sybilla is spirited away, only to enliven the turgid plot at a later moment. Mrs Wylde (the widowed, wealthy tenant) has the following conversation with her daughter shortly before the 'fallen' disappears:

> 'How very beautiful she is!'
> 'Who, child?'
> 'Sybilla Gaunt, mamma.'
> 'Oh', said Mrs. Wylde, scornfully. 'A homely saying my old mother sometimes used is a very true one. "Handsome is as handsome does." Sybilla Gaunt had better have been born ugly enough to frighten the cows.'[5]

From this moment the outcast is *persona non grata*. She is rejected by Joan because she will not give her the name of the father. The maids, farmers' wives, and menservants all discuss her in low tones, with quiet, but persistent relish. Even though Mrs Wylde is not totally supported by Mrs Wood, there is no doubt that the novelist feels the immediate rejection of the fallen is justifiable. She takes this stand more directly in the novel which was to sit beside *Pilgrim's Progress* and The Bible in hundreds of thousands of pious households throughout the Empire—*East Lynne*. The novel's popularity was such that Parsee and Hindustani translations were considered economically worthwhile: 'Indian readers will gather a large circle of Hindus around them, and read the book to them in their own tongue; seated on the ground, the listeners rock themselves to and fro and laugh and weep by turns.'[6] 'In Australia', writes a newspaper critic on her death, 'the sale of her works vies with that of Charles Dickens's books.'[7]

Novelists like Mrs Wood could well be more entitled to the nomination as the 'moral' voice of the middle classes than is Bradshaw in *Ruth*. Her son comments on her influence in terms of the number of volumes published:

> praise at this hour could neither add nor take from her fame. To one whose works, in the words of Mr. Bentley have sold only less, if less than those of Scott and Dickens, more praise or the

contrary can avail little.[8]

In *East Lynne* Mrs Wood has her almost too perfect Mr Carlyle refuse to hear his wife's name mentioned after she allows herself to be whisked off by the melodramatic cad, Captain Levison. She is convinced that her husband is giving too much attention to an attractive client of his legal business. True to expected form, Levison plays with her for a while, then leaves her after the conception of her child. The deserted Mr Carlyle even changes his daughter's name because it is her mother's. The mother has to face the fate worse than death. But what is more interesting and strange to the twentieth-century mind (or the enlightened one of Mrs Gaskell) is that the fall is completely irreversible. The heroine herself never feels her lot is to be anything but one of misery. She knows on 'the very hour of departure' what she has done. She accepts that she can never go back: 'the guilt, whose aspect had been shunned in perspective, assumed at once its true, frightful colour, the blackness of darkness, and a lively remorse, a never-dying anguish, took possession of her soul for ever'.[9] Very few writers would have the courage to write 'the blackness of darkness', yet Mrs Wood obviously used her poetic licence to popular effect. Permanent darkness mixed with 'never-dying' and 'for ever' characterise effectively, if not impressively, the attitude of Mrs Wood to her fallen heroine. No doubt feeling a zeal equal to evangelical fervour she foretells a similar fate to any woman who succumbs to temptation: 'O reader, believe me! Lady—wife—mother! Should you ever be tempted to abandon your home, so will you awaken! The alternative to endurance against such ill . . . if you rush on to it, will be found far worse than death!'[10] The representative of the moral voice reminds us that there is no doubt: the fall, when it comes, will be final.

It was this 'great' moral sense, combined with a rather juicy fall which makes Mrs Wood's fiction a popular mixture of sensation, melodrama, and moral rectitude. Other writers, however, sensed there was something about it which would not wash, something quite unconvincing. Thus Mrs J.H. Riddell: 'Mrs Wood is simply a brute; she throws in bits of religion to slip her fodder down the public throat.'[11] What ought not to be forgotten where the dichotomy of the 'two women' is concerned, is that the popular writer both influences her public's attitude and provides for it—she knows what they want. I do not, of course, wish to argue for the existence of a homogeneous middle-class attitude, nonetheless, the set of attitudes which underlies the acceptance of the 'two women' was shared by a sizeable number. What is astonishing is that the dichotomy of the 'two women' persisted despite common police corruption, an obvious parliamentary hypocrisy which perpetuated sexual licence, and a pragmatic stand adopted by non-working-class males who felt they had an inalienable right to use women as chattels. 'Walter', whose pornographic, eleven-volume 'autobiography', *My Secret Life*, contains as much fiction as fact, is one of the best known Victorian despoilers of the innocent. His work is the most vulgar expression of middle-class pragmatism. On the sexual use and abuse of the poor he reminds his readers that a 'Gentleman had better fuck them for money than a butcher boy for nothing . . . '[12] It is ironic that Walter and Mrs Wood belong to the same class. This brief comparison of their writing does much to stress the heterogeneous character of the Victorian milieu.

Despite this diversity the conventional acceptance of the mythical 'two women' remained the norm. As a result many women suffered—the fallen woman had no power to assert herself; she had few rights, if any. Acceptance of the norm, fortunately, was not to go unchallenged, but it was not challenged by the social scientists of the age. Most, with the exception of Acton, and, to a lesser extent, Tait, did their best to ensure the conventional attitude to fallen women remained unchanged. The most energetic challenge came from the artists and novelists of the age. Nina Auerbach in her short and general survey of Victorian fallen women in *19th Century Fiction* includes one of the most remarkable visual challenges to the dichotomy of the two women, the painting by Ford Madox Brown 'Take Your Son, Sir'. Here the fallen woman possesses strength of character. She is given the air of an angry but virtuous woman. A full figure (her size allows for very little background) she is painted in a mock-Renaissance style as a Mary figure holding her bastard son. A mirror hangs on the wall behind her head giving the impression of a halo. Her indignant expression is combined with beauty and pain. The victim is drawn in what Auerbach calls a monumental style: 'For not only is she free from the conventional posture of abasement, but the viewer is abased before her.'[13] The mother rises through her fall—gains power from her isolation—increases in strength as she belittles the male world which both worships and condemns her. Brown's challenge was timely but too fierce. The work was never finished or exhibited contemporaneously.

The great writers of the nineteenth century joined Brown in his protest; fortunately they did not hide their art till a better time made it safer to publish or exhibit. Dickens, Eliot, Gaskell, Collins, Gissing, Moore and Hardy each have, in at least one major work, questioned the absolute nature of the two groups of women—the pure and the fallen. They proved there was no one fall, no single disgrace, no automatic placing in categories of purity or prostitution. Through the study of the sexual fall these novelists are able to highlight the intense and complex problems of Victorian women from all classes, expose the sham respectability which personifies the patriarchy, and give themselves the role of social reformer in the process. Concurrent with this revaluation of the fallen woman is an exposition of the crisis of the urban revolution, the unfeeling dogma which made the Christian church anything but purely Christian. Morality of the type represented by Mrs Wood had to face an opposition which ultimately helped to shape attitudes of the twentieth century, while the outdated conventionality of Mrs Wood gathers dust in older libraries of the western world.

That this conventionality refused or failed to see the difference between a pure woman like Ruth and a prostitute seems absurd to the twentieth-century mind. It seems even more incongruous when it is realised that a large but hidden number of Victorians accepted the presence of a large body of prostitutes, not as a force against the *status quo* but rather as a supporter of it. Before her rigged trial in the late 1880s, when justice managed to turn a blind eye, the wealthy madame, Mary Jeffries, was quite adamant that she had nothing to fear: 'Nothing can be done as my clients . . . are of the highest social order.'[14] She was very lightly dealt with. A related attitude to this tacit acceptance of prostitution was the ridiculous belief that men had a natural sexual energy which women did not possess. Women must, therefore, be perverse who sell themselves. A man could vent his sexual passion on someone other than his wife, often managing to keep the purity of his wife intact: 'In absorbing the destructive excess of intemperate and overwhelming male sexuality, it was sometimes argued, the prostitute not only prolonged the marriage relationship, but created conditions as a result which favoured the smooth transfer of property through unbroken inheritance and the stable family.'[15]

Few historians accept the exaggerated figure of 80,000 prostitutes resident in late-Victorian London, but even if this number were to be halved, and kept mistresses not included, there still has to be a very large clientele to support business on such a large scale. It is precisely this large number combined with consistent male rationalisation which furthered the myth of the 'two women'. To many middle-class Victorian males there were, indeed, two women: the pure one to be married, the other to be used. It was essential that there should be no meeting of the two. He could put one foot in one nation and one in the other with sophisticated ease, a pragmatic colossus who could bridge the gap that women were not even allowed to discuss in public.

Keeping the two worlds apart was essential for the preservation of the *status quo*. If a woman transgressed this represented a threat to the whole system—this threat could not be tolerated. We can even detect a double standard in the lives of the men who fought for reform. Stead, the newspaper magnate who supported Mrs Butler and who printed a sensational exposé of the white slave trade, was a moral giant in the enlightened public eye. He kept a mistress. Had his wife been discovered in a similar relationship she would have been plucked from one female category and permanently plunged into the other.

Even the passage of the law reinforced common, unwavering attitudes on the permanence of the fall. Howard Vincent, after he had retired as the head of the CID, was quite adamant in his support of police officers who did not rush to a scene when a suspected rape was taking place, screams notwithstanding. There was little use in intervening. The victim could not prosecute. 'Who is she to prosecute? She does not know her assailant's name . . . Even if she did, who would believe her? A woman who has lost her chastity is always a discredited witness . . . and the woman would be condemned as an adventuress who wished to levy blackmail.'[16]

When the male profligacy of the upper and middle classes was quietly accepted as part of the order of things, the very uneasiness caused by the hypocrisy is sufficient to encourage a convention which protects the sanctity of their homes. After all if one father and husband is on the prowl after others' wives and daughters, is there not every chance that another prowler will be doing his best to ravish the deserted nest? So the rejection of Sybilla Gaunt by the Pomeroy society, the self-rejection of Lady Isabel Carlyle, the damnation hurled at Ruth by Bradshaw, whilst being reprehensible in the context of twentieth-century sexual enlightenment, are quite understandable when the attitudes and norms of the mainstream culture are explored.

The number of fallen women who feature in nineteenth-century fiction is so large that it makes choosing them difficult, especially in a short work. I have chosen Dickens, Mrs Gaskell, Collins, Moore, Trollope, Gissing and Hardy because they examine a similar type from differing social and aesthetic perspectives. The figure studied is a young girl whose corruption is related to her feminine weakness, her poverty or her isolation. She is an outcast because of her sin. The results of the fall differ—Nancy is a prostitute whose only place is with the low life of London; Ruth is an innocent who is saved from prostitution by a kindly couple who rescue her; Mercy Merrick, the heroine of Collins's *The New Magdalen*, finds herself forced into prostitution and a life in women's refuges as a result; Tess falls in the same manner as Ruth but social pressures force her to become the mistress of the man who corrupted her in the first place. I have included Trollope's *An Eye for an Eye* which is an excellent study of the fallen woman and her relationship to economics and the purity of the aristocratic tradition. George Moore's naturalist novel *Esther Waters* is an important contribution to fallen-women fiction, as is Gissing's *The Unclassed*, and their respective individual voice builds on the foundation set by the mid-Victorian novelists.

A sympathetic view of fallen women in Victorian England begins in the novel. The creation of Nancy in *Oliver Twist* marks the beginning of a new type. She is not simply the criminal's moll of the commercial Newgate Novels written by Ainsworth and Lord Lytton. She is not the means of satirising high society as we find in *The Beggar's Opera*, nor is she the fleshy celebration of sexual, picaresque life to be found in the eighteenth-century novel. I hope to show that she is, amongst other things, a direct response to the new society of the nineteenth century, that she is the first in a long line of sympathetic creations which clash with many prevailing social attitudes, and especially with the supposedly accepted dichotomy of the 'two women'.

Notes

1. Keith Hollingsworth, *The Newgate Novel 1830—1847* (Detroit: Wayne State University Press, 1963), p. 229.

2. Michael Pearson, *The Age of Consent* (Newton Abbot, Devon: David and Charles, 1972), p. 59.

3. *Prostitution in the Victorian Age: Debates on the Issue from 19th Century Critical Journals*, Introduction by Keith Nield (Westmead, Hants: Gregg International,

1973), pp. 9-11.

   4. Elizabeth C. Gaskell, *Ruth* (London: Smith, Elder, 1906), pp. 334-7.

   5. Mrs Henry Wood, *Pomeroy Abbey* (London: Richard Bentley, 1890), p. 40.

   6. Charles W. Wood, *Memorials of Mrs Henry Wood* (London: Richard Bentley, 1894), pp. 248-9.

   7. Ibid., p. 318.

   8. Ibid., p. 184.

   9. Mrs Henry Wood, *East Lynne* (London: Collins, 1954), p. 265.

  10. Ibid.

  11. Malcolm Elwin, *Victorian Wallflowers* (London: Jonathan Cape, 1937), p. 241.

  12. 'Walter', *My Secret Life*, quoted in Pearson, *The Age of Consent*, p. 12.

  13. Nina Auerbach, 'The Rise of the Fallen Woman', *19th Century Fiction* (1980), p. 36.

  14. Pearson, *The Age of Consent*, p. 100.

  15. Nield, 'Introduction', *Prostitution in the Victorian Age*, p. 1.

  16. Pearson, *The Age of Consent*, pp. 135-6.

1 NANCY

A sympathetic approach to fallen women in the nineteenth century, an approach which encouraged a revaluation of popular misconceptions, really begins in the novel. One of the earliest is Dickens's treatment of Nancy in *Oliver Twist*. This work was part of a fictional trend which liked to have crime and low life as its central interest. The 1830s saw a rise in interest about crime which was to become the Newgate novel in fiction. Bulwer Lytton and Harrison Ainsworth took advantage of the trend in their work, and were popular as a result. The fame of the former rests on *Paul Clifford* (1830), and that of the latter on *Rookwood* (1834) and *Jack Sheppard* (1839). Dickens's novel preceded *Jack Sheppard* by a few months, and was never quite so popular as it. *Oliver Twist* can only be considered a type of Newgate novel, but there is something in the spirit of the convention which is important when Nancy and her role are considered. In both *Paul Clifford* and *Jack Sheppard* the romantic hero is the criminal. The large numbers of supporting characters come from the slums of London. They can never match the courage, innate nobility and panache of the hero. The criminals in *Oliver Twist* are not romanticised to the same extent, nor are they the central interest of the novel.

The spirit to which I refer above is something to do with the penchant the Newgate novel had for reform and for questioning. *Paul Clifford* sets out to reform 'two errors in . . . [our] penal system; vis., a vicious prison discipline, and a sanguinary Criminal Code,—the habit of corrupting the boy by the very punishment that ought to redeem him, and then hanging the man, at the first occasion, as the easiest way of getting rid of our own blunders.'[1] Paul's life of crime, the novel argues, is as much the fault of society as the fault of the hero. *Jack Sheppard* argues similarly, centring its ideas on Lytton's argument that 'Circumstances make guilt . . .'[2] Absolutes of right and wrong, good and bad, justice and injustice are all questioned by Ainsworth and Lytton. Neither, however, use this to highlight the social problems and the extenuating circumstances which ought to colour the attitude towards the fallen woman, prostitute or otherwise. This was left for Dickens to do. He applied the questioning spirit not to the male criminals in *Oliver*

Twist but to Nancy and her plight. It is not surprising that a prostitute should ultimately figure in a type of novel which gleaned its
host of characters from the low life of London—they were not at all
scarce. What Dickens challenges through Nancy's presence in
Oliver Twist is the mistaken idea that a woman is either fallen or
not, either totally corrupt or pure. Paul Clifford may well be the son
of a harlot, but he can still be noble. Nancy might be a harlot, the
companion of murderers and thieves, but she can still be essentially
good. This germ of relativity was to grow in the minds of Mrs
Gaskell, Collins and Hardy as the century progressed. Understandably and sadly it was always questioned.

By looking at two incidents from *Sketches by Boz* Dickens's
sensitivity can be realised as it feels for all social outcasts. We can
also know the figures who are Nancy's precursors. In 'A Visit to
Newgate' Dickens describes a hardened prostitute. A recognition
of the power of circumstances surrounding the woman reduces the
condemnation he may have felt, and heightens his sense of charity:

> The girl belonged to a class—unhappily but too extensive—the
> very existence of which should make men's hearts bleed. Barely
> past her childhood, it required but a glance to discover that she
> was one of those children, born and bred in neglect and vice, who
> have never known what childhood is: who have never been
> taught to love and court a parent's smile, or to dread a parent's
> frown . . . They have entered at once upon the stern realities
> and miseries of life, and to their better nature it is almost hope
> less to appeal . . . [3]

The compassion Dickens felt to the type is further developed in a
later sketch, 'The Hospital Patient', which was to provide the
embryo for the Nancy–Bill relationship. Dickens always insisted
that Nancy is true to life. He records accompanying a magistrate
whose job it was to try a man charged with brutality. The object of
his brutality was hospitalised and could not attend the trial. The
court came to the hospital ward to question the victim. The woman
did her best to hide the wounds, and insisted that the clearly guilty
offender was innocent:

> 'Oh, no, gentlemen', said the girl, raising herself once more, and
> folding her hands together, 'no, gentlemen, for God's sale! I did
> it myself—it was nobody's fault—it was an accident . . . '[4]

Despite being warned that he would be convicted in any case, and despite the fear of perjury, being so close to death herself, the girl continued to be loyal to her man:

> 'Jack', murmured the girl, laying her hand upon his arm, 'they shall not persuade me to swear your life away. He didn't do it, gentlemen. He never hurt me.' She grasped his arm tightly, and added, in a broken whisper, 'I hope God Almighty will forgive me all the wrong I have done, and the life I have led. God bless you, Jack. Some kind gentleman take my love to my poor old father. Five years ago, he said he wished I had died a child . . . '⁵

Perhaps the vocabulary used by the dying woman was 'edited' by Dickens, and this may make the scene a little implausible. It remains, nonetheless, an effective interpretation of a heart-rending scene, effective because it encourages allowance for the fact that the fallen woman is capable of self-sacrifice.

Nancy follows the example of the woman in the hospital bed. But whilst Dickens includes this idea in *Oliver Twist* he does move beyond it to challenge another of the fallen-women myths which managed to gain a great deal of credence—this was the idea that women were the source of disease, moral pollution and degradation. In sexual matters men acted from natural impulse. That the Contagious Diseases Acts, mentioned in the Introduction, only allowed for venereal checks on women, confirms the existence of a legislative or political manifestation of the attitude mentioned above. A woman had to prove that she was a virgin, and that she was not a prostitute before she could refuse to undergo the compulsory, degrading tests. 'Literally and figuratively', writes Walkowitz in her fine study of Victorian prostitution, 'the prostitute was the conduit of infection to respectable society'. The world from which she came provided 'cheap labour and illicit pleasure', but at the same time led to common 'deep seated social fears and insecurities, most vividly expressed in the images of filth and contagion associated with the Great Unwashed'.⁶ Dickens does his best to reverse the attitude which blamed women for the corruption, by making her a pawn in the hands of Fagin and Sikes. Nancy was ruined before she had a chance to understand the meaning of the word. Nancy knows this when she meets Rose Maylie:

> 'Thank heaven upon your knees dear lady . . . that you had

friends to keep you in your childhood, and that you were never in the midst of cold and hunger, and riot and drunkenness, and—and—something worse than all—as I have been from the cradle. I may use the word, for the alley and the gutter were mine, as they will be my deathbed.'[7]

Nancy lives as she does, not because of innate depravity, but because Fagin's craft is too much to withstand. Corruption in *Oliver Twist* is male-engendered. To the modern reader this idea would not normally seem to be very important. The prevailing attitude which Dickens had to counteract suggests otherwise. Common reaction to the subject included ostrich-like avoidance (Lord Shaftesbury when questioned on prostitution 'knew little of it, and wished to know less'[8]), to evangelical ranters like William Bevan and J. B. Talbot who saw every sexual transgression as a threat to civilised living. Ironically these Christian leaders ought to have been the prostitutes' best friends. Talbot saw every fallen woman as one 'who seduces innocence and . . . [by] assuming appearances the most honorable paralyses authority and spreads with impurity the most frightful contagion and immorality the most flagrant'.[9] Men are seldom mentioned by Talbot.

The newness of Dickens's claim through fiction that virtue and vice can mix in one character can be more easily realised by comparing Nancy's goodness with the common type of gangster's moll in another Newgate novel. Ainsworth, for instance, in *Jack Sheppard* confirms the idea that women are the source of moral pollution. It is subtly done, perhaps not even realised by the writer himself. Jack Sheppard's mother is very poor. His father was hanged early in Jack's life. The mother is too weak to withhold her son from the influence of the world of crime and poverty. The early crisis point in the novel comes when Jack is lured to the thieves' den. Mrs Sheppard follows him, intent on forcing him home, but is unable to do so. Poll Maggott and Edgeworth Bess, both women of questionable virtue, have a literal hold on the fifteen-year-old Jack. Their sexual wiles combine with the influence of alcohol to ensure Mrs Sheppard's lonely return home without her son. The source of Jack's corruption in the novel can be traced from this moment, when the two molls are 'the conduit of infection':

The agonized mother could scarcely repress a scream at the spectacle that met her gaze. There sat Jack, evidently in the last

stage of intoxication, with his collar opened, his dress dis-
arranged, a pipe in his mouth, a bowl of punch and a half-
emptied rummer before him,—There he sat receiving and
returning the blandishments of a couple of females, one of whom
had passed her arm round his neck, while the other leaned over
the back of his chair, and appeared from her gestures to be
whispering soft nonsense into his ear.[10]

In this context Ainsworth and Talbot meet, the latter quite sure that
'Once a woman has descended from the pedestal of innocence, she
is prepared to perpetrate every crime.'[11] When Jack finally sees the
tragic end to his adventures, when he accepts there can be no
reformation he recognises the women who were partly to blame for
his downfall. 'Would I had never seen either of you!'[12] laments Jack
when they profess their love and loyalty to him. Ainsworth's treatment of the fallen woman is the antithesis of Dickens's, who ultimately sees Nancy as a saving influence, not a corrupting one. Even
the enlightened Tait, who was one of the first social scientists to
study prostitution, could not see the possibility of change or reformation in the prostitutes' condition. He published *Magdalenism:
An Inquiry into the Extent, Causes, and Consequences of Prostitution*, two years after *Oliver Twist*. He knew that the lack of
reasonably paid work combined with overcrowding resulted in an
increase in prostitution, but still felt that once fallen every woman
'abandoned the prerogatives of civil liberty'.[13] It was not until 1857,
nearly twenty years after *Oliver Twist*, that a social scientist tried to
disagree with some of the myths Dickens questions in the novel.
The permanence of the fall was the fallacy Acton tried to disprove in
Prostitution Considered etc. Like Dickens he argues that the following were not always (or often) the case:

(1) Once a harlot, always a harlot.
(2) There is no possible advance, moral or physical, in the
condition of the actual prostitute.
(3) The harlot's progress (decline) is short and rapid.[14]

In other words Acton questioned the prevailing myth of the 'two
women' purported by writers and moralisers like Talbot and Mrs
Wood. That this error is challenged by Dickens twenty years earlier
makes it clear how advanced a social observer he really was. When
he hoped 'to do great things with Nancy'[15] he may have had the

intention of dispelling the falsehoods Acton deplored. All three are questioned by Dickens.

   A look at the first meeting between Nancy and Rose Maylie gives an indication of the comment Dickens makes about the 'two women'. Some would see the meeting between Rose and Nancy as a meeting of representatives of the two types of women. Instead of stressing the virtue of one and the impurity of the other he wonders at the self-sacrifice of Nancy whose life had been 'squandered in the streets and amongst the most noisome of the stens and dens of London'. (*Oliver Twist*, p. 368) Whilst Dickens allows for the power of the forces around her, Nancy does not. She understands the forces of poverty and want but still feels a distinct sense of shame in front of Rose. Her shame is in itself dated—it reflects the conventional moral stance of the mainstream culture in middle-class Victorian England. The hotel servants are quick to notice Nancy, and quick to judge her with 'virtuous disdain' and an 'audible expression of scorn'. (*Oliver Twist*, p. 360) The ignorance of the 'chaste' housemaids annoys Dickens. They have no right to judge Nancy's case, and their placing outside the room where Rose and the prostitute meet accentuates their inability to see the truth of the matter. Nancy's shame and honesty make her more noble, and the errand of mercy she undertakes makes her virtuous. The 'two women' become one—Nancy is both pure and corrupt at the same time, although her corruption is a residue from the past. That Nancy sees herself as the opposite to Rose ('If there were more like you there would be fewer like me.') is another irony which pleads for an acceptance of Nancy's basic goodness. The idealisation of the character is one way of emphasising his point—to make her a symbol of goodness despite her history is an effective way of doing so. Thackeray, amongst others, objected to the idealisation, and felt that since Dickens 'could not be able to paint the whole portrait, he has no right to present one or two favourable points as characterising the whole; and therefore, in fact, had better leave the picture alone altogether . . . '[16] Dickens could not paint the real character—that he could invent an idealised character and still make his point is a compliment to his ability as an artist. His idealised portrait was a means to an end. It was a realisation of this end which prompted Wilkie Collins to say that Nancy was his favourite Dickensian character. By way of satire Thackeray wrote *Catherine*, a novel in which the bad are really bad, especially the heroine after whom the novella is named. He idealised nothing. It is very hard to read, and even harder to admire. After the unrelieved horrors of *Catherine, Oliver Twist* is an exceptionally readable book, perhaps because of Nancy's idealisation rather than despite it.

Nancy's murder, argues Hollingsworth, 'is by no means a necessity of the plot'.[17] That may be true—the plot may have survived without it. Not so the meaning of the novel, as far as Nancy's role is concerned. For Dickens to effectively challenge the prejudice inherent in 'once a harlot, always a harlot' it is necessary to see a reformed prostitute dying a pure woman. Nancy dies in the act of saving, not in the act of destroying or corrupting. Her death also brings about the defeat of Bill and Fagin, so has a power in its passivity. Nancy's last meeting with Rose has particular importance. Rose wishes to give Nancy money, but the latter asks for something of Rose's own which cannot taint of corruption. The gift given, a white handkerchief, becomes the ritualistic means of passing purity from one soul to another. It is the unification of two types of virtue. Nancy's death is the ultimate fall, yet she rises through it. It is the confirmation of her moral advancement denied in the myth Dickens and Acton challenge.

Working out his attitude to Nancy may well have prepared Dickens for his active work in the reclamation and reformation of prostitutes, a work which began in 1840 with the planning of Miss Coutts's 'Home for Homeless Women'. The very choice of the name indicates the sympathy he felt for the so-called fallen who took refuge there. On interviewing potential inmates he felt it was desirable to 'repress stock religious professions and religious phrases; to discourage shows of sentiment, and to make their lives practical and active. ' "Don't talk about it—do it!". . . '[18] This was the motto for the girls—it was a wise one. But it was also Dickens's motto for himself. Dickens's sensitivity is so much part of *Oliver Twist*, but when his belief becomes action he is so much more impressive and Nancy so much more important.

Notes

1. Right Hon. Lord Lytton, *Paul Clifford* (London: C.J. Howell, 1840), p. vii.
2. Ibid., p. 501.
3. Charles Dickens, 'A Visit to Newgate', *Sketches by Boz* (London: J.M. Dent, 1968), p. 178.
4. Charles Dickens, 'The Hospital Patient', *Sketches by Boz*, p. 213.
5. Ibid.

6. Judith R. Walkowitz, *Prostitution and Victorian Society* (Cambridge: Cambridge University Press, 1980), p.33.

7. Charles Dickens, *Oliver Twist* (London: Penguin, 1971), p. 362. Subsequent quotes from the text of the novel will be marked in the body of the chapter.

8. Lord Shaftesbury, *Amberley Papers*, ed. Bertrand Russell (1937), Vol. II, p. 117, quoted in Phillip Collins, *Dickens and Crime* (Bloomington: Indiana University Press, 1968), p. 94.

9. Walkowitz, *Prostitution and Victorian Society*, p.34.

10. W. Harrison Ainsworth, *Jack Sheppard* (London: Richard Bentley, 1839), Vol. II, p. 37.

11. Walkowitz, *Prostitution and Victorian Society*, p. 39.

12. Ainsworth, *Jack Sheppard*, III, p. 67.

13. Walkowitz, *Prostitution and Victorian Society*, p. 39.

14. For an effective summary of Acton's research and conclusions see Walkowitz, ibid.

15. Collins, *Dickens and Crime*, p. 96.

16. William M. Thackeray, 'Going to See a Man Hanged', *Fraser's Magazine*, August 1840, XXII, pp. 154-5.

17. Keith Hollingsworth, *The Newgate Novel 1830–1847* (Detroit: Wayne State University Press, 1963), p. 124.

18. Charles Dickens, quoted in Collins, *Dickens and Crime*, p. 103.

2   RUTH

A shared concern for the fallen woman possibly brought Mrs Gaskell into contact with Dickens for the first time. There is some evidence to suggest that the first letter the authoress received from her future editor was in response to a request for advice on the wisdom of organising a refuge for fallen women in Manchester, along the lines of Miss Coutts's home, of which Dickens was the patron.[1] Certainly the earliest surviving item of correspondence between the two writers is a letter from Dickens, dated 9 January 1850. This was in the form of a reply to Gaskell's call for help. A certain Miss Pasley's fallen state demanded that the unfortunate lass be shipped to Australia, so that she could start life afresh. Sharps recalls the parallels between Ruth and the young lady mentioned in the letter:

> Coming from respectable families, Ruth was an orphan and Pasley virtually so; both were apprenticed to dressmaking, having mistresses who paid scant attention to the real moral well-being of their charges; pretty and not seventeen, each was seduced by a man socially her superior. Ruth attempted suicide, Pasley confessed to having hoped for death; later each encountered her seducer in unexpected circumstances.[2]

These likenesses are not difficult to trace. To intimate, however, that *Ruth* is simply an attempt by Mrs Gaskell to record the plight of someone like Pasley would be to ignore the larger social meanings of the novel as they relate to the development of the heroine. Ruth and Pasley were innocent young victims—a common type. There could be fewer more pathetic victims than Pasley, a weak and exposed patient who was seduced by her vulpine physician. In contrast, the whole movement of the novel is to see Ruth progress from victim to tragic heroine. By the close of the novel, Ruth's death is the culmination of her growth as an individual of some stature. It is then very difficult to see her as belonging to the same world as Pasley. Ruth's life of suffering, her selflessness, and her resulting death, imbue her with an almost monumental stature. Her life and death as a new type of heroine was to be the confirmation of a new force in literature, and a new force in the liberation of women. Gaskell is trying to do more in *Ruth* than simply record the downfall of a fallen woman. It is by tracing the development of the heroine that the reader can come to grips with the novel's meaning.

It is easy to forget how completely new *Ruth* was. There had been many fallen women in the novels of the age, but none like *Ruth*. Mention of the following will bear this out. Pasley's type features in *Mary Barton* in the form of Aunt Esther. As the prostitute, Butterfly, her vulnerability is given slight prominence. She remains very much outside the major concerns of the work, reminding the reader what Mary might have become should the temptation Carson provided hold ultimate sway. 'Lizzie Leigh', Gaskell's second work which includes a fallen woman, is really a story about the effect the daughter's fall has on her mother. The young heroine does not die. Instead she spends the rest of her life tucked away from the rest of society, dwelling on the child as the physical embodiment of her sin.

Dickens includes the type in his work. Alice Marwood in *Dombey and Son* died painfully, seeking a state of forgiveness. Nancy's death in *Oliver Twist* foreshadows the fate of Alice. Their destruction is part of the cleansing of the society which produced them. The frequent appearance of these women would indicate that many Victorian readers were ready to accept the type:

> But there is no denying that there are literary conventions and expectations to be satisfied. Sexual irregularity is acceptable if it is history, or treated with reticence or humour, or secondarily; prostitutes can appear if idealised or good-hearted, or if they die, and almost any topic and its implications can be examined if the actual event does not happen . . . or if we are left in some uncertainty . . . One feels that the mid-nineteenth century in its fiction could stomach fallen women, illegitimate children . . . profligates of both sexes, provided that certain rules were observed: that, if present in large quantities they are peripheral, that there is no reward for vice, or if there is, it is condemned . . . [3]

Ruth included the fallen woman as the major concern of the work. That in itself was shocking to some. Not only did Mrs Gaskell ignore some of the other conventions alluded to above, she positively questioned the very definition of vice itself. George Henry Lewes was pleasantly surprised: 'The author of *Ruth* has wisely done what few authors see the wisdom of doing—opened a new mine instead of working the old one'.⁴ Mrs Gaskell, however, questions the wisdom of opening new literary territory. To say that she wrote the novel in spite of her misgivings, would perhaps be a temptation for a critic, and certainly be an exaggeration. Nonetheless, she had misgivings. It is interesting to see the psychological reaction of an artist doing something quite new. She did not like the fuss which she did not expect. 'I hate publishing because of the talk people make.'⁵ After publication she wrote to her good friend, Elizabeth Fox, discussing some very small part of the fuss she feared—

> I think I must be an improper woman without knowing it, I do so manage to shock people. Now should you have burnt the 1st. vol. of *Ruth* as so very bad? even if you had been the very anxious father of a family? Yet two men have; and a third has forbidden his wife to read it; they sit next to us in chapel and you can't think how 'improper' I feel under their eyes. (150)

Despite her determination to be loyal to her own work she admitted that 'it was not a book for young people, unless read with someone older'. (148) One irony which arises out of Mrs Gaskell's own comments on the scandal caused by *Ruth*'s publication, is the rather surprising fact that more women objected to the book than men. 'I am surprised to find how very many people—good kind people— and *women* infinitely more than men, really & earnestly disapprove of what I have said . . . ' (153) This is especially sad when it is accepted that amongst the many moral purposes of the novel, freeing women was not the least important. Charlotte Brontë felt the importance of the work lay in its ability to restore hope and energy to a class of women who previously felt alienated from society and were, like Lizzie Leigh, doomed to a life of misery.

Making a 'sinner' heroic is essential to the newness of the novel. It is to Mrs Gaskell's credit that she can make an heroic figure out of an innocent, poorly-educated young girl whose nascent sexuality and natural gullibility combine to make her easy prey for a young man who finds her an attractive challenge. By the end of the novel she has more in common with the distinguished fallen madonna painted by Ford Madox Brown in 'Take Your Son, Sir', than she does with the innocent young girl who falls to a worldly male. Both Ruth and the subject of Brown's painting are ultimately aggran- dised through their reaction to their sin. The quiet, submissive Ruth is ultimately freed from the cowed posture of debasement she adopts as her fate throughout most of the novel.

The development of the heroine's stature is all the more impressive when the powerlessness of her early life is taken into account. Mrs Gaskell takes great pains to stress Ruth's early plight. The young girl seems unable to exert any influence on the trials she must face as a child. Her mother was the daughter of a penniless clergyman, her father an unpretentious farmer of modest means. After their marriage 'everything seemed to go wrong'.[6] Ruth's mother is one of a common type, the invalid who takes to her bed, not so much from diagnosed complaints, as from a general inability to cope with life on a day-to-day basis. After the early death of this weak but dear mother, Ruth's father undergoes a mental decline. Ruth's lack of early education which helps isolated individuals survive is stressed by Gaskell when we see Ruth unable to do anything to help support herself when living with the Bensons. It ought to be pointed out, however, that she is not allowed to work in society after her secret is known. Her later occupation in nursing is a calling rather than a job; it is one of the ways she expiates her sin. Gaskell was well aware that the education of many young ladies was not well balanced between the refining arts and practical skills. Ruth's guardian, after the death of her parents, was such a 'hardheaded man of the world' that he looked to rectifying this inadequacy in her education with a minimum of inconvenience. The respectable sweat shop run by Mrs Mason was one of the few options open to a guardian who needed to place an unwanted ward. When George Gissing wrote *The Odd Women* in 1893, the situation had not changed a great deal. The poor conditions, the naivety of some of the girls, the worldliness of others, the long hours, the lack of nourishment—all are described by Gissing with the same care characteristic of Gaskell's treatment. The latter is sufficiently understanding to record the extenuating circumstances responsible for Mrs Mason's harshness. That woman is a victim, an isolated mother, one of the odd women so well drawn in all Gissing's work, albeit much later in the age. Mrs Mason is embittered by the difficult task of bringing up a family without her husband. Her eldest son, without the care of a father figure, is a very troublesome young man. Mrs Mason is a hard worker. Gaskell takes care to point out that she works as hard as the girls. The only benefit Ruth is to gain from her experience in the workshop is the ability to make her son's clothing.

Early in the work Ruth is surrounded by incomplete individuals. Her mother and father are loving but incapable. Her guardian and Mrs Mason are capable but unloving. Ruth's inability to influence the adult world, her tractable nature, her vulnerability, are all captured in the symbol of the ride in the cart. She is the passenger who is driven. She is carried off by her cold guardian to the workshop. Later in the novel Bellingham takes her on a ride. The journey to Wales is the journey she makes into her own awakening womanhood. Even when the Bensons take her to Eccleston she is still the tractable and weak soul. Her powerless state when first travelling to the workshop is further stressed by the fact that she cannot even express her deepest emotions, having to wait for the darkness of the night: 'When she took her seat in the gig, she was little able, even if she had been inclined, to profit by her guardian's lectures on economy and self reliance; but she was quiet and silent, looking forward to the night time, when, in her bedroom, she might give way to all her passionate sorrow . . . ' (*Ruth*, p. 38) The irony that she should be lectured on self-reliance, at the very time when she is incapable of it, is one of the small, but effective ways Gaskell's sympathy for her heroine is conveyed.

Gaskell gives herself a daunting task—to build her heroine out of a seemingly weak creature. Brontë managed to do the same thing in *Jane Eyre*. The point is similar in both: if the heroine can triumph over her own weakness and the oppressions of the society which tries to destroy her, then the novel itself becomes the vindication of a truly feminine strength. The difference between the young Jane and the innocent Ruth is that the former has an inner strength and determination which our heroine does not. 'Something spoke out of me over which I had no control.'[7] This is Jane's innate spirit which helps her to defeat the Reeds, and to survive Brocklehurst's vicious hypocrisy. When he places Jane on a pedestal in order to debase her, he confirms her status as heroine. We then expect great things from her, and are not disappointed. It is her living force which will make it possible for Jane's novel to be ultimately comic in its conclusion. The essential difference between the development of the two women is that Jane's novel records the development of spirit, whereas Ruth's highlights the discovery of it. In both cases, the initial impotence of the orphan is the context in which her rise will be seen, and as a result it will seem all the more impressive.

Ruth's innocent state has a great deal to do with the first adventure she has with Bellingham in Wales. Like many heroes in western literature, the adventure which is to be her lot draws her into a relationship with forces which she does not fully understand. Ruth travels to Wales. She also experiences a mystical journey into her own nature. The second part of her metaphoric journey is into the mores and norms of 'respectable' society. Initially she does not see her sexual relationship with Bellingham as anything other than an expression of her love for him. She does not 'sin' until she is rejected. It is interesting that the progress of her adventure from the workshop to Eccleston follows the pattern of the often repeated primitive initiation rite—separation, initiation, then return. Ruth is initially separated by her abduction. This act brings about the death of her innocence. The descriptions of Ruth's innocent joys in the beauty of the natural world give her an almost Eve-like character: 'Ruth was up betimes, and out and away, brushing the dew-drops from the short crisp grass; the lark sung high above her head, and she knew not if she moved or stood still, for the grandeur of this beautiful earth absorbed all idea of separate and individual existence. Even rain was a pleasure to her.' (*Ruth*, p. 64) That this world, so blissfully beautiful, should be the gateway to a kind of purgatory for Ruth is another of the ironic moments which Mrs Gaskell uses to convey a deal of sympathy for her creation.

In addition to using the rite of passage tradition to play a role in the shaping of her heroine's fate, Gaskell uses an inversion of the Beauty and the Beast archetype at the same time. In this story, the heroine, always the central figure, is faced with the terrors of reconciliation to the Beast (the great symbol for the animal in man). By submitting to the horrors of kissing him she finds true fulfilment. He often takes the attractive form of a young prince. The archetype almost seems to be propaganda to convince young maidens that acceptance of male sexuality promises great things.

The young man who is going to seduce Ruth appears anything but a beast. Likewise, the men who are attractive to Little Em'ly and Hetty Sorrell appear as the reverse of the beast figure. Bellingham is a mixture of youthful exuberance and native cunning. Both of these act to control his every move as he awaits his prey: 'By no overbold admiration, or rash passionate word, would he startle her; and, surely, in time she might be induced to look upon him as a friend, if not something nearer and closer still'. (*Ruth*, p. 33) The beast usually has to use stratagem to convince the heroine that she ought to treat him with some care, but usually it is to her benefit. In the long run, the reward she earns outweighs the trials she has to endure. The trials Ruth has to endure make it impossible for her to live happily ever after. Gaskell seems to realise that by presenting Bellingham as an out and out rogue he would become rather two-dimensional. By making him more human she makes her tale more realistic. George Eliot does the same thing with Arthur Donni-thorne, the father of Hetty Sorrell's murdered baby. She gave Arthur a rather bad conscience during his courtship of Hetty. The loss of innocence in women is, therefore, partly due to the foibles of youth. Gaskell touches Bellingham's scheming with a modicum of excuse, though she is not quite so forgiving as is Eliot in *Adam Bede*: 'he first saw Ruth Hilton, and a new, passionate, hearty feeling shot through his whole being. He did not know why he was so fascinated by her . . . It would be an exquisite delight to attract and tame her wildness, just as he had often allured and tamed the timid fawns in his mother's park.' (*Ruth*, p.33) The beast is hiding something, but it is not a noble youth trying to get out. To make matters difficult for timid fawns like Ruth and playful kittens like Hetty, the beast with whom they have to come to terms looks quite the reverse. In accordance with many myths and tales the perpetrator of evil takes the disguise of an attractive form. Bellingham is no exception:

'Don't you remember your promise to consider me as a brother?' (*Ruth*, p. 41)

'Tell me everything, Ruth, as you would to a brother . . . ' (*Ruth*, p. 37)

'I might be able to befriend you through my mother, . . . ' (*Ruth*, p. 37)

'[I] would go through fire and water for you.' (*Ruth*, p. 57)

These are particularly cruel lies. They appeal to the weakest part of Ruth—the pain caused through the loss of her family. He takes advantage of the same loss when he organises the walk to her old home. Old Thomas can certainly see through Bellingham's kindly front.

The images Gaskell uses throughout the novel to present Ruth and her abductor are particularly apt. Bellingham is the powerful young horseman who dashes into the swiftly flowing river to rescue the child in distress. (It is another of the intentional ironies of the novel that Ruth attempts to throw herself into the river after she finds her lover has deserted her.) Bellingham is the capricious youth who acts on impulse, saving and destroying as his impetuous desires will. Jemima Bradshaw is both attracted and repelled by Bellingham, then named Donne. He is seen as a horse-like animal by the astute Jemima. In the following scene she is discussing her reactions to the man. Her mother is the second party in the conversation. Jemima looked at Donne with the 'curious observation which a naturalist bestows on a new species of animal':

> 'Do you remember our stopping at Wakefield once, on our way to Scarborough, and there were horse races going on somewhere, and some of the racers were in the stables at the inn where we dined?'
>
> 'Yes, I remember it; but what about that?'
>
> 'Why, Richard, somehow, knew one of the jockeys, and, as we were coming in from our ramble through the town, this man or boy asked us to look at one of the racers he had charge of.'
>
> 'Well, my dear?'
>
> 'Well, mamma! Mr Donne is like that horse! . . . Brutes are sometimes very beautiful mamma. I am sure I should think it a compliment to be likened to a racehorse, such as the one we saw. But the thing in which they are alike, is the sort of repressed eagerness in both.' (*Ruth*, pp. 260-1)

The horse is, of course, frequently a symbol for the uncontrollable instinctive drives which form part of the animal nature of man. If the horse is the *alter ego* of Bellingham then Ruth's nature will be understood through the delicate images which Gaskell associates with her. Ruth was 'white as snow' and 'snow pure'. Ruth's room at Eccleston had the 'colouring and purity of a snowdrop'. The fall of her character and her self-debasement were to be reflected in the colour grey which was to be her chosen shade for clothing. Gaskell's use of colour and image is effective. When the dark horse figure is pitted against the snowdrop, it seems that the latter has no chance.

But Bellingham is not only the horse figure. He is something more elemental and sinister. He is the bringer of darkness. When Ruth considers her proposed visit to the old home with Bellingham, she can see no 'shadow' throwing its gloom over the preparations. That the shadow exists which she cannot see, is an irony which would not escape the reader. Her grey dress almost reflects the work of the shadow on her innocent snow-white state. It is most appropriate that Donne's reappearance in Ruth's life should be accompanied by shadow. The day he appears with Bradshaw, on the sands at Abermouth, is very dull. The 'sun did not show his face'. The sea is 'leaden'. The sand even changes from yellow to 'dull brown'. These are Donne's heralds. The two men make their entry when the evening is 'fast closing in the dark and sunless day'. (*Ruth*, pp. 264-5)

Ruth as lightness and Donne as darkness give the novel an internal conflict very much like the innocence-experience battles in Blake. It is one of the novel's archetypal bases. It is the eternal struggle between light and dark, good and evil. By superimposing a contemporary social theme on this universal conflict, Gaskell gives her moral purpose more weight, and the novel potential greater poetic depth. Herein lies much of the novel's power. By aligning the conventionally fallen with light and ultimately truth, and the so-called respectable with dark and falsehood, Gaskell forces any reader to a re-evaluation of both stereotypes.

The physical placing Gaskell assigns Bellingham (then called Donne) and Ruth on their visit to the church at Abermouth further develops the elemental struggle. Bellingham

> followed them in, entered himself, and shut the door. Ruth's heart shrank as she saw him there; just opposite to her: coming between her and the clergyman who was to read out the word of God . . . She durst not lift her eyes to the bright eastern light— she could not see how peacefully the marble images of the dead lay on their tombs, for he was between her and all light and peace. (*Ruth*, p. 279)

Bellingham and his influence are often given a background of mountains, rocks and crags. Ruth's discovery of the sexual is accompanied by an awakening to new, more powerful vistas:

> It was opening a new sense; vast ideas of grandeur and beauty filled her mind at the sight of the mountains, now first beheld in full majesty. She was almost overpowered by the vague and solemn delight; but by-and-by her love for them equalled her awe . . . (*Ruth*, p. 64)

In one sense her relationship to the mountains follows the same pattern as her short life with Bellingham. She holds him in great awe, then tempers this awe with love and devoted admiration. When he leaves her stranded, at his mother's suggestion, Ruth sees them in the distance. She runs after them in a most poignant and pathetic manner, trying to reach them before they arrive at the summit of the hill over which they are travelling. Her only thought is to catch him and appeal to that which she thought was his love for her. 'If she could only gain the summit of that weary, everlasting hill . . . ' (*Ruth*, p. 92) The situation is symbolic of her need to understand the innermost thoughts of Bellingham himself. He is as unapproachable and cold as the mountains and hills. Earlier in the chapter it is difficult to separate her relationship with him and the mountains themselves. The disappearing mountains seem to echo his sickness:

> Out beyond, and the calm sky, veiled with a mist rather than with a cloud, rose the high dark outlines of the mountains, shutting in that village as if it lay in a nest. They stood, like giants, solemnly watching for the end of Earth and time. Here and there a black round of shadow reminded Ruth of some 'cwm' or hollow, where she and her lover had rambled in sun and in gladness. She then thought the land enchanted into everlasting brightness and happiness; she fancied, then, that into a region so lovely no bale or woe could enter, but would be charmed away and disappear before the sight of the glorious guardian mountains. Now she knew the truth, that earth has no barrier which avails against agony. It comes like lightning—like down from heaven, into every mountain house and town garret. (*Ruth*, p. 83)

When Ruth leaves Wales the memory of the mountains and the memory of Bellingham merge together.

By the time he returns as Donne the references in the setting are not to grand mountain scenes which fill with awe, but to sharp, jutting, craggy outcrops of rock. The awe is gone but the danger remains. When Donne returns, the governess is playing with the two girls on the beach. She is a child again: 'in all this [play] Ruth was as great a child as any'. Once Ruth recognises one of the three figures 'near the rocks', the elemental struggle begins again, when the 'sands heaved and trembled beneath' her. It seems that Ruth has to expose herself to the elements of night, in a mock battle of defiance. What follows is one of the most impressive moments in the book. She throws open the window to the raging storm outside, an act that is reminiscent of King Lear's own elemental struggle with the dark powers of the universe as they mirror the turbulence of his own soul. Ruth

> threw her body half out of the window into the cold night air. The wind was rising, and came in great gusts. The rain beat down on her. It did her good . . . The wild tattered clouds, hurrying past the moon gave her a foolish kind of pleasure that almost made her smile a foolish smile. (*Ruth*, p. 271)

This time Ruth seems to know the powers of that which she must face. She is no longer the innocent in the garden who does not know good from evil. Donne's visit is a temptation to her, but she has the strength to change from one rock to another. 'My God I pray thee to be my rock and my strong fortress, for I am nothing.' (*Ruth*, p. 272) In their subsequent meeting, he is described as the 'figure moving in the direction of the great shadow made by the rocks'. The defeat of Donne by Ruth is almost a *fait accompli*, even though it is still the source of some agony to our heroine. After he tries to bribe her with marriage and do the respectable thing, he leaves her exhausted. We are not surprised to see her revived by a 'ruddy blaze of light' which gave her 'strength and courage'. This moment of mystical, divine intervention is to be repeated at her death when the 'light' comes to claim her.

It would have been very difficult for Gaskell to aggrandise her heroine without this almost cosmic, archetypal level in the work. Instead of detracting from the didactic moral purpose of the theme, it gives it greater importance. It is a remarkable combination. On one hand we see the quiet, submissive, devoted mother, sewing for her son, on the other, a participant in a heroic struggle.

The other means employed by Gaskell to lift her central character from the problems caused by her lack of motivation, and her powerless state, is a method which is as old as story-telling itself. The authoress provides Ruth with two or three active helping figures. The helping figures in *Ruth* are not difficult to identify. The most important one is Thurstan Benson, a crippled dissenting minister whose physical deformity belies the great soul which lives within it. He has a large role to play in the development of the heroine. Gaskell seems to go to some pains to show Ruth's dependence on him, once he is introduced.

His early appearance in the novel is certainly tinged with mystery. When he turns out to be a loving little minister we are probably a little surprised, if not a little disappointed. His first appearances are amongst the most striking aspects of the novel, certainly on the first reading. He is closer to a dwarf or the Welsh equivalent of a leprechaun than a man: Ruth 'looked up and saw a man, who was apparently long past middle life, and of the stature of a dwarf; a second glance accounted for the low height of the speaker, for then she saw he was deformed'. (*Ruth*, p. 66) Thurstan is one of Mrs Gaskell's inversions in the novel. He looks weak, yet he is strong. He looks incomplete, yet he is whole. Bradshaw, the upstanding pillar of the church, and the embodiment of morality in the community, appears strong and dominating, yet as the novel progresses his insecurities become more obvious. Ruth who is, in conventional terms, immoral, becomes the major moral force in the novel. Benson's is the first inversion to make itself clear. He becomes a gauge for other characters. Mrs Gaskell lets us know through her creation of Thurstan that we will have to reevaluate our concepts of beauty and goodness. Ruth is able to see beyond the crippled façade. She feels that his face is 'quite beautiful'. She is struck by the 'mild beauty of the face' which reflects 'something of a quick spiritual light in the deep set eyes . . . ' (*Ruth*, p. 67) Ruth's reaction to the fine spirit within the dwarf tells us something about her fine spirit. Bellingham, on the other hand, is curt and cruel in his remarks. To him Benson is the little hunchback who looks like 'Riquet-with-the-Tuft'. Ruth asks her lover if he has seen his face. Bellingham replies that he has not, but that he has seen his back. This is consistent with Bellingham's presentation throughout the novel. He is initially attracted to Ruth only by her physical beauty.

Benson seems to follow Ruth, knowing that she faces some danger. He reappears when Ruth is being attacked by the aggressive child who has been told how evil Ruth is. He appears later, quite mysteriously, like the fairy godmother of the Cinderella tale, or like the stranger in the Pardoner's moral tale who tells the revellers where they might find death. He appears at the very worst moment for Ruth. She runs towards the raging mountain torrent, apparently with the intention of committing suicide. It is a reminder of the first time the two met. Ruth was having trouble crossing the water. He helps her, in an act that is to foreshadow his role in the novel. He saves Ruth, not by force, but by his human weakness. He falls, cries out, and attracts Ruth's attention with the cry, something which touches the sympathetic chord within her nature: 'the tender nature was in her still, in that hour when all the good angels seemed to have abandoned her'. (*Ruth*, p.46) Benson is the good angel in disguise, having what seems to be a superhuman power which helps him to be on the scene at the right time. He has a dream where he sees Ruth in a 'deep, black pool'. We have seen her near such a pool with her lover, when he was crowning her with the white lilies.

Benson has another role to play in the novel which is not connected with his mysterious initial appearances. He is the personification of the new morality Gaskell would have her readers accept. His unconventional Christianity is best seen in his discussions with his sister, whom he asks to come to Wales to help look after the ill and deserted young girl. Mrs Gaskell would argue that Thurstan's beliefs are very close to God's intentions. If Benson represents the true moral stance, then Faith represents the converted. Her first reaction on discovering Ruth's sin is to respond in a Victorian cliché—'It would be better for her to die at once . . . ' (*Ruth*, p. 117) None the less Faith, who does have a good heart, agrees to help Ruth whilst she is ill. The discovery of the baby is certainly a trial to her faith. She is shocked at the pregnancy, but even more surprised that Ruth does not react adversely to the discovery. She seems almost pleased. Faith has trouble telling Thurstan. The fact is too shocking. 'She [Faith] was allowed to make noises unnoticed for a few minutes. Her brother did not speak. At last she wanted his sympathy. ' "Isn't it shocking, Thurstan? . . . I'm afraid she is very depraved." ' (*Ruth*, p. 117) Ruth thanks God for the child. That is the depravity to which Faith alludes. In conventional terms the child ought to be considered a blighted creature, a badge of shame. Faith does not mind looking after a fallen woman, but to see her offspring in a positive or even divine light is too new. It is very difficult to gauge exactly how the illegitimate child or his mother would have been treated in the Victorian society. There would have been more down-to-earth acceptance of her in the working classes. The members of the moral middle class typified by Bradshaw would have been difficult to sway. That Faith has trouble accepting her brother's argument, combined with Bradshaw's refusal to listen at all, would indicate that Mrs Gaskell had a difficult and unenviable task to perform.

Faith tells Thurstan that she is going to wash her hands of the girl, and any similar cases in the future. She cannot see beyond the badge of shame:

> 'Faith, Faith! let me beg of you not to speak so of the little
> innocent babe, who may be God's messenger to lead her back to
> Him. Think again of her first words—the burst of nature from
> her heart! Did she not turn to God and enter into a covenant with
> Him— "I will be so good?" Why, it draws her out of herself! If
> her life has hitherto been self-seeking, and wickedly thoughtless,
> here is the very instrument to make her forget herself, and be
> thoughtful for another. Teach her (and God will teach her, if
> man does not come between) to reverence her child; and this
> reverence will shut out sin,—will be purification.' (*Ruth*, p. 118)

That the reader is aware of Ruth's essential goodness makes him go
one step further than Benson in his acceptance of the child, and
Ruth's right to have it. His final criticism of Faith is that she
confuses the consequences of the sin with the sin itself. It is not
surprising that such unconventional theory leaves Faith bewildered
and softened. Her conversion to the new way of thinking is slow but
definite, and the relish with which she embellishes the fictitious
history of Mrs Denbigh is the confirmation of her change of mind.

For the most part, the Bensons do Ruth's thinking for her, the
heroine not being a decisive individual. She becomes decisive
shortly before her death, but the action is the result of the one talent
she knows is within her—the ability to minister to the sick. It is not
only her method of earning a slight living, it is the way she can be
loyal to herself. It is the final admission of self-worth. The number
of incidents where the Bensons' help is invaluable to Ruth needs
little emphasis here. It is the way Mrs Gaskell keeps her character
consistent with the young girl early in the novel. One example
occurs when Ruth wants to return Bradshaw's gift to the new baby.
Benson feels it ought to be retained. On Benson's quiet suggestion
that it ought to be kept, Ruth acquiesces—'I will do what you wish
me'. (*Ruth*, p. 157) Later in the novel, Benson explains this aspect
of Ruth's character to the interested Farquhar, who wants to send
Leonard to school at his expense. Farquhar was confused by her
vague refusal, so sought a foothold through Benson's influence.
Farquhar wonders what the boy is going to do in the future. Benson
replies, 'I don't know. The wonder comes to my mind sometimes
but never hers, I think. It is part of her character—part, perhaps, of
that which made her what she was—that she never looks forward

and seldom back.' (*Ruth*, p. 416)

By giving Ruth such helping figures as the truly moral Benson, the energetic Faith, and the indomitable Sally, Gaskell is able to give her heroine a vicarious strength she does not initially have. She helps her to survive in a world which rejects weak victims like Ruth. This leaves the authoress free to draw her heroine as a type almost above trivial mortal concerns, and to imbue her with a passive sensitivity which rarefies her personality. She is mostly feeling and emotion, blessed with a minimum of rationality. Without the inclusion of the Bensons, it would have been difficult for Gaskell to make the main character and her predicament realistic, yet sufficiently unusual to warrant building a novel around her. The Bensons help Ruth face the trials which the world feels wont to offer.

In *Ruth* the heroine has to face what Gaskell calls the 'labyrinth of social ethics' (*Ruth*, p. 116), a complex network of interacting traditions, habits and individuals. This force takes on a set of physical forms, such as Mrs Mason, Mrs Pearson, and Bradshaw. It appears in minor characters—the boy who hits Ruth outside the hotel and the gossip in front of the hospital who has heard Ruth is a great sinner. It takes the abstract form of cruel social mores which demand scapegoats in the forms of fallen women and their cursed offspring. That this force demands sacrifice is borne out in the novel not only by Ruth's potential destruction but by the inclusion of a victim by the name of Thomas Wilkins, a young man who discovers his illegitimacy late in life. He does not play a large role in the novel, but his example does. The Bensons remember him when they are still unsure of what they should do with the young pregnant girl they hope to rescue. The example is sufficient reminder to the reader that it was very difficult to live with the disgrace of a blighted birth. Faith alludes to Ruth: ' "Poor child!" she said at length—"the poor, poor child! Do you remember Thomas Wilkins, and the way he threw the registry of his birth and baptism back in your face? Why he would not have the situation; he went to sea and was drowned, rather than present the record of his shame." ' (*Ruth*, p.120)

It is this memory which prompts Benson to agree to the lie which is to plague him for many years. The minister had been haunted by the bitter look on the young man's face, and his ensuing untimely death. His face had demonstrated a 'wild fierceness . . .as the registry told him he must go forth branded into the world, with his hand against every man's and every man's against him'. (*Ruth*, p. 121) In all Mrs Gaskell's novels the thing which seems to bother

her most is the barrier man sets up to keep himself in and/or others out. In *Mary Barton* the barrier is between the worker and the master. It is the fear and loss of Wilkins which seems to hurt Benson most; the rejection of one human being by another is the theme of *Ruth*. Of especial horror is the exclusion of one quiet innocent by the larger group—a human sacrifice to the god of legitimacy.

Fear of loss of character (really a synonym for being discovered) seems to worry more than one person in the novel. When Ruth has her first Sunday at Eccleston, Sally senses that Mrs Denbigh is not all that she appears. Although it is part of her general chatter, she does express fears of a potential shame on the chapel house. This would affect her standing in the community. 'I suppose I must stand by you and help you through with it; I only hope I shan't lose my character—and me a parish-clerk's daughter!' (*Ruth*, p. 147) She complains that Benson is 'always picking up some one or other that nobody else would touch with a pair of tongs'. (*Ruth*, p. 147) She then feels it best to remove Ruth's long hair, ostensibly because she ought to look like a widow. On another, deeper psychological level Sally seems to be putting Ruth through a ritualistic trial and sentence. When she cuts Ruth's hair it is the latter's quiet patience which makes her feel uneasy. As a mark of some penitence, Sally hides the hair away in a dark corner of a drawer in her room. The guilt she tucks away in a dark corner of her memory, only allowing it to resurface many years later when Ruth dies.

Mrs Mason's fear is not so subtle. She is well aware of the potential loss of revenue incurred by a commercial house which suffers a loss of character. The desire to vent her frustrations caused by her son's restlessness on some other scapegoat is only part of the reason Mrs Mason rejects Ruth. It is also an aggressive attack based on the need for self-preservation:

> Mrs Mason was careless about the circumstances of temptation into which the girls entrusted to her as apprentices were thrown, but severely intolerant if their conduct was in any degree influenced by the force of those temptations. She called this intolerance 'keeping up the character of her establishment'. It would have been a better and more Christian thing if she had kept up the character of the girls by tender vigilance and maternal care. (*Ruth*, p. 53)

Gaskell's point is obvious. Girls fall, not because of an innate perversity, but because they are just not looked after. That society rejects a fallen woman it helped to create through sins of omission is, Gaskell suggests, where real perversity lies. The other point Gaskell stresses through Mrs Mason's rejection of Ruth is the fact that the expulsion causes the downfall of the girl; the downfall was not the reason for the expulsion. Punishment can cause the very thing it is trying to destroy. Girls may then be driven to the streets, not by their sin, but by others' reactions to that which they consider sin. Gaskell feels that human sin cannot be considered in absolute terms.

Gaskell is able to criticise a societal attitude through the presentation of one character, as in the example of Mrs Mason mentioned above. Mrs Bellinghams's refusal to accord any of the blame to her son for the affair with Ruth is an effective way to comment on a Victorian demand for purity on the part of women, and discretion on the part of men. On discovery, the woman falls; the man is embarrassed for a while, but may move freely in society. Because women fall they must be rather weak and depraved creatures. It is ironic in the novel that a woman's voice upholds this stance. Mrs Bellingham accepts that Ruth must be the cause of her son's indiscretion. The mother is representative of a larger attitude shared by many. Ruth's loss of virtue must be borne by the girl herself. She is the source of corruption. Mrs Bellingham's stand is best seen when she listens to the 'ludicrous' manner in which Ruth thanks God for sparing the life of Bellingham. Mrs Bellingham 'did not imagine the faithful trustfulness of [Ruth's] . . . heart'. It is more than the desire to protect her son from the scandal which prompts her to ignore the possibility of Ruth's innocence; it is the result of habit and convention. Her great fear is that Henry may wish to make more of the relationship. A fallen woman of a lower class was more than Mrs Bellingham could accept: 'it was my wish to be as blind to the whole affair as possible, though you can't imagine how Mrs Mason has blazoned it abroad; all Fordham rings with it; but of course it would not be pleasant, or, indeed, I may say correct, for me to be aware that a person of such improper character was under the same [roof]'. (*Ruth*, p. 88) It is astonishing that Ruth must be considered 'improper' and Bellingham not so. And when Bellingham's loyalty to Ruth speaks of his guilt in the affair, the Mother silences the admission. 'I do not wish to ascertain your share in the blame: from what I saw of her one morning, I am convinced of her forward, intrusive manners, utterly without shame, or even common modesty . . . A more impudent, hardened manner, I never saw.' (*Ruth*, p. 90) Ruth remains in Mrs Bellingham's mind, a 'degraded girl', a 'vicious companion' who, with her 'artifices', leads Henry astray. Ruth's weak pliability, her simple nature, and her innocent devotion, cry out against the unfairness of Mrs Bellingham's conventional voice. In showing Mrs Bellingham as she is, Gaskell is able to present the conventional voice as it operates for selfish ends. In her letter to Ruth, which was to 'do the thing handsomely', her façade of moral outrage tells us more about the writer then the receiver: 'before I go, I wish to exhort you to repentence, and to remind that you will not have your own guilt alone upon your head, but that of any young man you may succeed in entrapping into vice'. (*Ruth*, p. 91)

The weight of social opinion aligns to destroy youth. Without the Bensons' help, as mentioned above, that may have been imminent. The very best she could have hoped for was the penitentiary to which Mrs Bellingham directed her. By blaming Ruth, Mrs Bellingham tries to cleanse her son. It is almost as if society needs a supply of outcast figures as a constant reminder of its own purity and essential goodness. The fallen woman in fiction is so pervasive a figure that she must owe her existence to a larger, more elusive cultural obsession. Why did Victorian society choose the particular kind of scapegoat figure it did? A study of Bradshaw, the most socially powerful figure Ruth has to face, may not answer that question completely. His presence in the novel, however, will give a clue to an answer. One Victorian attitude represented through Bradshaw is the one which expects women to be submissive, gentle, clinging, uncomplicated and, above all, pure. Bradshaw is an old hand at shaping his wife to fit his expectations, rather than her nature. She fits the picture mentioned above, but also has 'been trained to habits of accuracy very unusual in a woman'. (*Ruth*, p. 220) That woman must copy models designed by their male superiors is a most common theme in Victorian literature. Mr Bradshaw, Mr Gradgrind, and Mr Murdstone have something in common. Mrs Gradgrind is even more of a caricature of the stereotype of the submissive wife than is Mrs Bradshaw: 'Mrs Gradgrind, a little, thin, white, pink-eyed bundle of shawls, of surpassing feebleness, mental and bodily: who was always taking physic without effect, and who, whenever she showed any symptoms of coming to life, was invariably stunned by some weighty piece of fact tumbling on her . . . '[8] All real sense of individuality is lost in the frightened little heap of remnants. Mrs Gradgrind and Mrs Bradshaw are popular examples of the victim whose individuality is sacrificed to the male demand for the stereotype. Sexuality is not conventionally associated with the stereotyped ideal. Repression of an overt acceptance of female sexuality seems to be very much part of the reason for the expulsion of women who are discovered to be sexual creatures.

The attempt by Bradshaw to shape the behaviour and character of his daughter, Jemima, broadens Gaskell's treatment of this theme. Mr Bradshaw is convinced that Jemima is a manageable and marriageable prospect for Mr Farquhar, even though he admits that she does have a fair amount of spirit. He compliments himself on the ability he has to handle this aspect of her personality, and is confident that he can teach Farquhar how to get the best out of her by handling her correctly. As can be expected, Bradshaw's thoughts of his partner's potential marriage to Jemima do not allow for sexual considerations. Passion and impulse are to be feared.

The marriage will be a good one. A furnished house already exists. Mr Farquhar has no near relatives who would be bothersome, or make claims on the family fortune. Mr Farquhar's age would 'unite paternal and conjugal affection', and her dowry can be reinvested in the business.

Mr Farquhar has trouble accepting Jemima's frank, spirited and passionate nature. She does not fit the conventional image of the trouble-free Victorian wife. It is for this reason that the apparently quiet and gentle Ruth is considered a better choice when Jemima's internal conflict is destroying her external beauty, and her chances of marriage. 'His character was to bask in peace; and lovely, quiet Ruth with her low tones and quiet replies, her delicate waving movements, appeared to him the very type of what woman should be—a calm, serene soul, fashioning the body to angelic grace.' (*Ruth*, p. 305) This repeats a similar thought expressed in an earlier chapter: 'her shy reserve, and her quiet daily walk within the lines of duty were very much in accordance with Mr Farquhar's notion of what a wife should be'. (*Ruth*, p. 239) It is not surprising that Jemima suspected manoeuvring in every action of her father and Farquhar. Her fears are well-founded, when men like her father demand the sacrifice of her self to convention.

It is a major part of Gaskell's intention (and achievement) to place her heroine at the centre of a discussion on Victorian marriage and the expectations which surround it. It is only when the norms and expectations of Victorian marriage are taken into account that attitudes to fallen women can be understood. Mrs Gaskell characterises Ruth as a girl who fits in every way the conventional ideal of womanhood, and for this very reason, is all the more easily seduced by someone like Bellingham.

When Bradshaw discovers Ruth's duplicity, his own troubled conscience over the election bribery, when he tried to turn wrong into right, makes him unconsciously project his own sin on the weaker Ruth. She becomes the scapegoat not only for Bradshaw's repression of sexuality in women, but for his own wrongdoing:

> His uneasy, fearful conscience made him stricter and sterner than ever; as if he would quench all wondering, slanderous talk about him in the town by a renewed austerity of uprightness; that the slack principled Mr Bradshaw of one month of ferment and excitement, might not be confounded with the highly-conscientious and deeply-religious Mr Bradshaw, who went to chapel twice a day, and gave a hundred pounds a-piece to every charity in the town, as a sort of thank offering that his end was gained. (*Ruth*, p. 304)

Ruth's exposure could not be more timely. It corresponds exactly with the need Bradshaw has to project his inadequacies on another human being. It is Ruth's sin of pretence, of turning wrong into right, which raises most of his ire. Ruth also proves him wrong. She is not the perfect creature he has judged her to be. When Mrs Gaskell finally shows his change of mind through his acceptance of Leonard and the building of the monument, she presents her final piece of evidence that the fall is not permanent nor ultimately degrading. Changing Bradshaw's mind may be a ploy to change the mind of her most emphatic critics. Mrs Gaskell has great faith in the fact that innate virtue will have its ultimate victory and reward, in this world or the next. Gaskell's 'villains', the so-called respectable, suffer the greatest fall. When Bradshaw is bowed and prematurely aged 'respectability' has tumbled. Ruth manages to transcend her own sin, but, more importantly, ultimately manages to transcend society's reaction to it. She can cure the sickness of the world around her, becoming one of the first feminine saviour figures in Western literature. She suffers the rejection of society, then gives her life to the root cause of her problems.

I am surprised that Brontë protested over Ruth's death when she read the plan of the novel, though I am aware that the cause of her death has little to do with the former action which precedes it. I cannot imagine the novel without it, and even though its presentation is somewhat melodramatic I cannot help but be moved. Ruth's death is a return to the world of her innocence and youth. It is a reunification with light, and as such is a permanent reminder that a human being can achieve a spiritual victory in a world where pragmatism, political corruption, petty vice and self-righteousness, all form the foundations of national institutions from the family to the parliament.

The interesting thing is that it is not Ruth herself who plays the major part in the ultimate rejuvenation of society; it is her fall. When her sin is not known, her influence is limited to domestic duties. Societal changes multiply after her fall is known. Farquhar marries Jemima. Bradshaw is faced with the truth not only about his son's crime but about his whole 'model' system. Ruth's fall is catalytic.

Ruth's power as a tragic heroine is best seen as it relates to Jemima. Jemima is the first person in the novel, other than the Bensons, to discover the truth about the past suffered by the young mother who becomes the object of her love and hate. Is it possible, Jemima wonders, that the fallen who sin can be as pure as she knows Ruth to be? Faith asks a similar question, though in different words. The question is the major point made by the novel. That the answer to the question is very clear would suggest that the novel's success is confirmed. Jemima's conclusion, so similar to Faith's, is that 'whatever Ruth had been, she was good, and to be respected as such now'. Her fear of Ruth turns to pity. After her father refuses to ask the question posed by Ruth's exposition, and he expels her from his house, Jemima touches her garment. This quasi-ritualistic act seems an attempt to repent of the hatred previously felt towards Ruth, but it is more than that. She wishes to gain some of Ruth's power, much like the woman who touched Christ's coat to be healed. Because it is an act of impulse, impulse is vindicated. Jemima also learns humility through Ruth's fall, which had initially been such a shock: 'standing, she had learnt to take heed lest she fall; . . . It showed how much her character had been purified from pride . . . ' (*Ruth*, p. 366)

It is typical of Mrs Gaskell's faith in both the individual, and the ultimate goodness of society, to include Jemima in the novel, a character who is able to assert her individual femininity without falling, whilst at the same time being a regenerative force in that society itself. Her victory is the triumph of earthly, feminine emotional sensitivity. Despite her painful emotions throughout the novel we still see their triumph over her father's male pragmatism. Ideas and philosophies about institutions, social conventions, class and power mean nothing when the heart suffers. Bradshaw finds this out.

The fallen woman is a complex creature. She is a dynamic force. She is the reassertion of femininity. Mrs Gaskell argues that a fallen woman can be the stuff around which a tragedy can be built. This is in itself a new idea. Mrs Gaskell also forces her readers to re-evaluate concepts of sin and morality. Ruth's fall ultimately heightens the stature of women. Mrs Gaskell's development of a noble heroine from a fallen girl was sufficient to cause a storm. And that reaction is easily explicable when we imagine the novel being read by hundreds of Bradshaws.

Notes

1. John Geoffrey Sharps, *Mrs Gaskell's Observation and Invention* (London: The Linden Press, 1970), p. 148.

2. Ibid., pp. 149-50.

3. W. A. Craik, *Elizabeth Gaskell and the Provincial Novel* (London: Methuen, 1975), p. 48.

4. George Henry Lewes, 'Ruth, . . . ', *Leader*, IV (22 January 1853), pp. 89-91.

5. J. A. V. Chapple and Arthur Pollard (eds.), *The Letters of Mrs Gaskell* (Manchester: University Press, 1966), No. 140. Hereafter the letter number will be placed in brackets in the text after a quote.

6. Mrs Gaskell, *Ruth* (London: Smith, Elder, 1906), p. 35. Hereafter textual references to the novel will be indicated by the title of the work and the page number in the body of the chapter.

7. Charlotte Brontë, *Jane Eyre* (London: Penguin, 1978), p. 60.

8. Charles Dickens, *Hard Times* (London: J. M. Dent, 1974), p. 13.

3　CARRY BRATTLE AND KATE O'HARA

Although Anthony Trollope did not claim his mother's novels were great works of art, he did gain from the career of Francis Trollope the idea that one can survive by writing novels. In addition he was influenced by the energetic, demanding, but sympathetic heart which 'was never comfortably complacent in the presence of human suffering'.[1] Both mother and son shared the suffering caused by the financial failure of Anthony's father. One novel, the theme of which is directly related to human suffering and its relationship to the New Poor Law, is *Jessie Phillips, a Tale of the Present Day*. The heroine shares much in common with Nancy in *Oliver Twist*. Both have to survive in an unsympathetic world made up of starving masses, criminals, pimps and factory workers. Both are fallen women. The main didactic thrust of the novel is a cry for the reform of prison-like workhouses. But Jessie also shares much with Ruth. Jessie is the village beauty, a seamstress who is led astray by the young village squire then abandoned by him. Helen Heineman feels Mrs Trollope's novel is unduly melodramatic, and quite improbable at times; the young man feels safe when he seduces Jessie because he is aware of the protection awarded him under the bastardy clauses in the New Poor Law which is the object of her scorn:[2]

> The terror that formerly kept so many libertines of all classes in check was no longer before him, the legislature having, in its collective wisdom, deemed it 'discreetest, best' that the male part of the population should be guarded, protected, sheltered, and insured from all the pains and penalties arising from the crime contemplated. 'No, No,' thought Mr Frederick Dalton, 'thanks to our noble lawgivers there is no more weaning away a gentleman incognito now. It's just one of my little bits of good luck that this blessed law should be passed.'[3]

Trollope worshipped his mother but was well aware of her faults as a novelist. 'She was neither clear-sighted nor accurate; and in her attempts to describe morals, manners, and even facts, was unable to avoid the pitfalls of exaggeration.'[4] The two novels Anthony Trollope devoted to the fallen woman and the injustice she had to tolerate can be seen as a continuation of the sympathy felt by his mother for the type, and can be regarded as an artistic vindication of the theme so clumsily, but well-meaningly developed by his mother. *The Vicar of Bullhampton* and *An Eye for an Eye* are singularly different in intention and execution. The first follows *Ruth* in that it is a novel about the country maiden's fall. It is a conventional look at the type. The second novel is not. Instead of looking at the woman's fall from her standpoint it examines the character of the man responsible, making specific statements about the whole concept of interclass marriage in Victorian society. This chapter will look at the two novels but will spend most of its time on the more original of the two novels. Before that, however, *The Vicar of Bullhampton* is sufficiently interesting to warrant some attention.

Carry Brattle

Anthony Trollope's adolescent loneliness and the fear he had of isolation, when combined with his acute memory of these miseries, made it easy for him to empathise with human suffering, especially the type of suffering caused by expulsion from society. The fallen woman was a type with which he could identify, despite the gap caused by his sex, his pecuniary success, and the social popularity which he experienced late in life. The memory of his early suffering kept him humble. When he writes of it in *An Autobiography* the former moments of rejection and frustration are still alive in his heart. 'My boyhood was,' he writes with some feeling, 'as unhappy as that of a young gentleman could well be, my misfortunes arising from a mixture of poverty and gentle standing . . . '[5] Added to the disgrace of poverty is the constant 'want on my own part of that juvenal manhood which enables some boys to hold up their heads even among the distresses which such a position is sure to produce'.[6] At Harrow, Winchester, and the lesser-known Sunbury, he was always in disgrace—to use his own word he was a pariah. The fear of being an outcast was one of his Achilles' heels throughout his life. His busy schedule, his numerous acquaintances, his close family life—all helped him to overcome the fear of isolation, but it surfaced from time to time in his adulthood, when the potential outcast would steep himself, for a moment, in the adolescent fear of being a pariah. His fallen women could well be anima figures from his own subconscious mind, a claim that is impossible to prove, but, none the less, an interesting speculation.

This becomes more possible to imagine when one considers that *The Vicar of Bullhampton* was written during one of the most depressing periods Trollope experienced in an otherwise relatively content life. He attempted to win the seat of Beverley, standing as a Liberal in 1868. He was so unpopular in the electorate that he did not attend Church, for fear of causing a storm. 'No Church of England church in Beverley would on such an occasion have welcomed a Liberal candidate.'[7] The pang of fear is reminiscent of his particular boyhood terrors—the fear of being part of a rejected inferior caste. 'I felt myself to be a kind of pariah in the borough, to whom was opposed all that was pretty, all that was nice, and all that was—ostensibly—good.'[8] He could be writing of the fate of the fallen woman, and at the time of the election, coincidentally or not, he wrote his work on the plight of Carry Brattle, a simple country girl whose wanton innocence and fulsome beauty bring about her total rejection by the family and society which loved her, envied her, and spoiled her. It is also interesting to note that both novels on fallen women were written within a very short time of each other. *The Vicar of Bullhampton* first appeared in monthly parts from 18 July 1869 to 18 May 1870 and was first published in book form in April 1870. Although *An Eye for an Eye* was not published until 1879, it was written very much earlier. Sadleir records that it was started in September 1870, just four months after the final number of *The Vicar of Bullhampton* appeared on the bookstalls.[9] Possibly thematic connection, or the fear of flooding the market, made Trollope withhold the publication of *An Eye for an Eye*. It is interesting, then, that one of the most negative periods of his adult career was related to rejection, and that that rejection resulted in two novels, the very themes of which are based on societal pariahs.

Although Trollope states that his main purpose in *The Vicar of Bullhampton* is to justify the regeneration of the fallen woman, he does not make her the central character of the novel. Instead *The Vicar of Bullhampton* follows George Eliot in *Adam Bede* when he makes Carry Brattle, like Hetty Sorrell, a secondary character, rather than the heroine of the story. Carry Brattle is the attractive country lass who is the toast of the village, and the apple of her father's eye. Unlike Hetty's seducer, the despoiler in Trollope's work is unseen. The results of his activities are not. Carry is forced to leave home by her indignant father; she becomes a prostitute because she has been trained for nothing better. Neither Carry Brattle nor her creator's reasons for including her in the novel are marked by their originality. The Preface to the novel could well have been written for *Ruth*, a work which preceded Trollope's by seventeen years. His moral stance is similar to Mrs Gaskell's: '*The Vicar of Bullhampton* was written chiefly with the object of exciting not only pity but sympathy for a fallen woman, and of raising a feeling of forgiveness for such in the minds of other women'.[10] Trollope then goes on to suggest that making the fallen woman the heroine of the story rather than the 'second-rate personage' on which he decided, would, in fact, have been 'directly opposed to my purpose'.[11] I confess to being a little confused by this. I fail to see why her inclusion in a work as the heroine would work against this purpose. He may, of course, have anticipated the same criticism levelled at *Ruth*, and made plans to avoid it by limiting the scope of Carry's role. Despite one or two memorable scenes, like the return home of the reformed prostitute and her relationship with her Bradshaw-like father, Carry never approaches the stature we sense in Ruth, nor does her plight have the same artisitic realisation which we see as characteristic of Mrs Gaskell's novel. She does not have the same life as Ruth does, partly because she is not given a major role to play in the novel.

The plot of *The Vicar of Bullhampton* is rather complex and delightful, as are the main characters therein: Mary Lowther who is forced to choose between the man she loves and the man others tell her she should love; Mr Fenwick, the young Anglican minister whose image of his own Christian nature is challenged when the nonconformist minister builds a huge church literally at the doorstep of the vicarage; Harry Gilmore whose life is destroyed by unrequited love; even Carry's brother Sam and her father Jacob Brattle seem to leave more of an impression than the fallen woman herself. Other themes seem to be more important in the novel than the reclamation of the prostitute. The whole question of marriage plays a dominant role in the novel. There is the Collins-like murder mystery, which, though it involves Carry Brattle in the peripheral sense, does not relate to fallen women at all. The decline of the power of the aristocracy is given some attention by Trollope through the inclusion of the Marquis of Trowbridge, one of the author's comic characters in the work, and certainly one of his most memorable aristocrats. He gives the land to the nonconformists to spite the Vicar whom he sees as an enemy. To his horror it is discovered that the land he bestowed on the dissenters actually belonged to the Vicarage. He is a man out of touch, an anachronistic monument from another age, whose very blindness to change makes him comic yet symbolic of the out-of-touch aristocrat, who appears to have missed the great nineteenth-century changes. With all this thoughtful, entertaining content I find it hard to believe Trollope, who tells us after the novel is written that the major reason for the novel's being is to argue for the reclamation of the fallen woman. The spirit of the novel's broad canvas belies the dictum of the Preface. I suspect that the novel was written, not with the specific didactic purpose claimed by the writer in retrospect, but out of the pure joy of plot, character, community diversity, and life itself. It surprises me that Trollope continued to insist that the 'hero and heroine with their belongings are all subordinate'.[12]

Had he deliberately submerged the character to ward off potential criticism, then he could claim some success. Donald Smalley, in *Trollope: The Critical Heritage*, summarises the critical response to the novel which Trollope felt was 'meeting a new and difficult challenge by trying to create sympathy for the fallen woman':[13]

> The novel received no very cordial welcome from the Press. There was not much protest, and there was even some approval, at Trollope's rehabilitating Carry Brattle; but critics found much to complain about in the monotony of large parts of Trollope's story. [I wonder if this response is one result of the novel's lack of artistic unity in terms of content and theme?] *The Athenaeum* (30 April 1870) judged on the whole Trollope had brought off his story of Carry Brattle's reinstatement, but had 'not unnaturally' sheered away from the history of her fall.[14]

If Carry Brattle is meant to be the centre of attention then both Mrs Oliphant in *Blackwood's* and the unsigned reviewer in *The Times* were misled by the appearance of Mary Lowther's problems, giving most of the attention in their respective reviews to that character.[15] *Harper's Magazine* was annoyed by what it saw as a novel which lacked a noticeable centre of attention: it is an example of Trollope's habit of playing off one lover against another in his usual style 'through three hundred pages of what is called romance, probably for the all-sufficient reason that it contains neither history nor philosophy nor poetry enough to give it a right of classification any where else'.[16] The *Saturday Review* felt that the novel is 'a story without a plot, and not only without a plot, but one showing no connexion whatever between the two trains of events and two groups of characters which occupy its pages'.[17]

Despite these unenthusiastic responses, Henry James liked the novel, not because it is a great novel but because there exists in it a certain vividness of character which gives an otherwise relatively formless work some deliberate life. One of the most memorable characters is the miller, Jacob Brattle, the father who treats his daughter's fall as Bradshaw does Ruth's, though there is a quietness about his rejection which makes the personality deeper and more complex. Mr Fenwick

> knew well that an edict had gone forth at the mill that no one should speak to the old man about his daughter. With the mother the Vicar had often spoken of her lost child, and had learned from her how sad it was to her that she could never dare to mention Carry's name to her husband. He had cursed his child, and had sworn that she should never more have part in him or his. She had brought sorrow and shame on him, and he had cut her off with a steady resolve that there should be no weak backsliding on his part. Those who knew him best declared that the miller would certainly keep his word, and hitherto no one had dared to speak of the lost one in her father's hearing.[18]

The two prevailing mistakes which fathers and others made are important when considering the extreme behaviour manifest above: the fall was permanent, and any who came in contact with the fallen were likely to be tainted and morally destroyed. Fallen women are as likely to corrupt as are books which contain material needing censorship. In fact one can look at twentieth-century censorship, which did not free *Lady Chatterly's Lover* until the fifties, as the last vestige of the state of mind which rejected fallen women because of their supposed power to bring about the moral fall of the nation. The attitude which censors books is related to the attitude which alienated fallen women. The Victorians often believed that any association with immoral people and immoral pages would change the contacted individual for the worst. They agree with Sheridan's Sir Anthony: 'Madame,' he lectures, 'a circulating library in a town is an evergreen tree of diabolical knowledge. It blossoms through the year; and depend on it, Mr Malaprop, that they who are so fond of handling the leaves will long for the fruit at last.'[19] Jacob Brattle fears the return of his daughter will corrupt the rest of his family and be a permanent sore on the face of his family life. Bradshaw fears that Ruth's presence will corrupt his children. The fallacy in the argument is obvious: if Ruth is of necessity an influence for ill why does she influence his daughters for good, and why does Bradshaw comment on her fine nature and accept the positive work she is able to do with difficult girls? Part of Bradshaw's temper comes from the fact that he is proven wrong. Part of Brattle's temper is his natural desire for revenge, even at the expense of his own daughter.

Mrs Gaskell and Trollope fight for the restoration of the fallen to the level of acceptable respectability. At the same time they argue for the freedom to write that which they feel demands saying. The Preface is Trollope's attempt to ward off undue criticism of his inclusion of a fallen woman in the novel. He wants to defend himself 'against a charge which may possibly be made against . . . [him] by the critics'.[20] That there was little major objection is as much to do with the times as with the Preface's argument. It ought to be stated that Trollope certainly did not wish to write a novel which needed to become a *succès de scandale*. Mrs Gaskell did do this, but really by accident. Dickens used the word 'prostitute' to describe Nancy in the Preface to *Oliver Twist*, but he did not leave it there for long when subsequent editions were forthcoming. Trollope is more careful in the first place. He writes of Carry Brattle as a 'castaway'. Despite his caution, his argument is determined and sound. The Preface almost does more for the fallen woman through logical argument than the novel does through pathos—this is one reason for dwelling on it at such length. He argues sensibly and fairly that ignorance of the fallen woman's fate amongst the young of both sexes is the main perpetrator of the continuation of the lack of justice the type must face—the punishment is disproportionate to the initial crime. Ignorance is more potentially dangerous than is the corruption which Bradshaw and Sir Anthony both feel is imminent:

> There arises, of course, the question whether a novelist, who professes to write for the amusement of the young of both sexes, should allow himself to bring upon his stage such a character as Carry Brattle. It is not long since,—it is well within the memory of the author,—that the very existence of such a condition of life, as was hers, was supposed to be unknown to our sisters and

daughters, and was, in truth unknown to many of them. Whether that ignorance was good may be questioned; but that it exists no longer is beyond question.[21]

Even in the 1870s I suspect the latter statement to be rather optimistic. Keeping the truth about sex from young ladies is bad enough, but it is worse when it is remembered that it causes an unawareness of the very thing which the respectable woman in society most feared. Not knowing the nature of what causes a fall, not knowing the male role, not knowing the social ramifications of it—all of these make for potential vulnerability because 'the punishment, which is horrible beyond the conception of those who do not regard it closely, is not known beforehand'.[22] Trollope's argument is sound: punishment exists as a deterrent and is retributive in nature. It is a deterrent to the would-be offender who recognises it is not worth the risk. It is retribution to the individual who knowingly sins. How can punishment for a sin which was innocently done make sense to the sinner? And if all potential sinners are not exposed to the punishment of others how can they know what to expect? Trollope prods at the senselessness of the convention of rejection and the attempt to keep young ladies in the dark for fear of their corruption. Half-truths which can be gleaned from some social observation are also dangerous. The young girl sees the bright clothing of the prostitute, but does not know of her total expulsion, and her difficulty experienced in trying to avoid venereal disease.

> Instead of the punishment [which cannot be understood without explanation and education] there is seen a false glitter of gaudy life,—a glitter which is damnably false,—of which, alas, has been more often portrayed in glowing colours, for the injury of young girls, than have those horrors, which ought to deter, with the dark shadowings which belong to them.[23]

Trollope is sufficiently cautious to only imply that the punishment should not happen at all, but therein lies the difference between the novel and its Preface. The punishment looms largely in the novel, but more important is the overriding feeling that it is unwarranted. It is, Trollope insists, true to life.

Ruth is rejected only by Bradshaw, at least in the framework of the novel's action. When Trollope repeats the expulsion in *The*

Vicar of Bullhampton he gives it greater coverage by having several relatives refuse to have anything to do with Carry from time to time throughout the story. In fact Trollope spends no time at all on the seduction which causes her fall—he is largely interesting on the way it changes the role the girl is allowed to play in the community. She is transformed from happy country wench to social leper. Her despoiler remains unimportant in the terms of the novel's reference. The sexual sin is deliberately distanced from the action, making the fall seemingly belong to a world outside the life of the novel. Her punishment, however, is the constant subject of reference and discussion. It is very much alive though the original sin is dead. The most devastating punishment is her father's refusal to see her, or to speak to her. He is a hard pagan character who is very much in love with his wife and family, though never admitting to it, nor perhaps even consciously knowing it. He is a sober, hard-working miller. His good points, which he does possess, are clouded by a moody, tyrannical disposition. To be meek is the ultimate defeat. 'He was a man with an unlimited love of justice,' writes Trollope, 'but the justice he loved best was justice to himself.' His dark, taciturn façade hid a quarrelsome interior which 'brooded over injuries done to him . . . till he taught himself to wish that all who hurt him might be crucified for the hurt they did to him. He never forgot, and he never wished to forgive.' (*Bullhampton*, p. 34) The greater the sin, the greater the blackness inside. Carry had been his favourite child. In her innocence she is 'such a morsel of fruit as men do choose, when allowed to range and pick through the whole length of the garden wall'. (*Bullhampton*, p. 34) Her early life gave him the same portion of joy that her fallen life gives him sorrow. Despite his decision to disown Carry there is no release of sorrow caused by her fall. He is eaten away with longing, yet he will not give his lonely suffering any respite. An angel announcing that his daughter was to be the second Magdalen would bring no relief, no comfort, no amelioration. Despite the father's constant desire to push his daughter's fallen image deeper into his own heart and try to bury her there, the Vicar does everything he can to find the outcast and restore her to her family.

Like Ruth and Nancy, Carry may not have known the ramifications of her sin with the anonymous amorous lieutenant, but she is well aware of her punishment which is not legally founded, but is part of a larger social law, the active duty of every citizen being to shun, reject, hound and insult in public, but to hire in private.

'Nobody loves me now,' she cries to the Vicar. 'I am bad.' Despite the promise from within the pure ethos of the national religion, that forgiveness is the key to making crooked things straight, Carry finds little hope. She can never face her father again. The Vicar spends a great deal of time finding Carry. He promises to do what he can for her, if she promises to leave her wicked life style. Jacob's reaction is predictable when Mr Fenwick tells him of his great find. To be told of his daughter by anyone is to have salt rubbed into his wounds of shame, sorrow and guilt. Each time the Vicar is rejected, Carry is further from finding a way out. The Vicar keeps trying to find a place with one of her relatives since Jacob Brattle even refuses to discuss her plight. George Brattle is Carry's brother, now a relatively successful farmer who is dominated by his wife. To him Fenwick journeys with his mission. At the mention of Carry's name 'there came upon the farmer's face that heavy look, which was almost a look of grief; but he did not at once utter a word . . . ' He is probably building his argument which he hopes will defeat the pangs of conscience which he feels. Although not as terse as his father he refuses to sympathise with her fate. 'She brought it on herself, and on all of us.' (*Bullhampton*, p. 280) To counteract his own pangs of conscience, and the Vicar's quiet condemnation, he offers money, then allows himself to agree to take the girl provided that his wife approves of the move. This is a safe offer, however, because he knows that his good wife would do no such thing. The wife's refusal is based on the so-called permanent nature of the fall—'They never leaves it.' (*Bullhampton*, p. 288) She cannot see that the life of a prostitute is often one of misery, starvation, illness, deprivation and sorrow. To her it is always a life of wealth, colour and dissipation. 'Would you have her starve or die in a ditch?' asks the sensitive Vicar who is well aware of the true answer. (*Bullhampton*, p. 289)

> 'There ain't no question of starving. Such as her don't starve. As long as it lasts, they've the best of eating and drinking,—only too much of it. There's prisons; let 'em go there if they means repentance. But they never does,—never, till there ain't nobody to notice 'em any longer; and by that time they're mostly thieves and pickpockets.' (*Bullhampton*, pp. 289-90)

Rejected himself, Fenwick continues his pilgrimage by visiting Mr Jay, Carry's prosperous brother-in-law. He is a merchant shopkeeper in a nearby town. It is deliberate that Trollope uses each relation to personify or represent one dominant attitude in his culture which is commonly accepted as the truth of the matter about fallen women. Jacob Brattle represents the group which sees the fall as permanent, unforgivable. George Brattle's wife speaks for those who see prostitutes as women who have sold their souls to the devil for a life of feasting and crime. Mr Jay agrees that 'she is a bad 'un' then proceeds to speak in terms of another well-accepted misconception—he reminds the Vicar that there isn't anything which a man can do which is 'nearly so bad'. (*Bullhampton*, p. 330) Trollope makes sure that Mr Fenwick has to face the shallowness of several aspects of conventional arguments for the expulsion of the fallen woman. The invention of these minor characters to do so dramatically makes his point more subtle, and at the same time gives more than an impression of Carry's rejection by the community. Mr Fenwick, deciding that Christian argument has failed to produce the desired result, plans to be unconventional by simply bringing the father and daughter face to face. He hopes this will shock them into reunification. In the meantime Carry tires of waiting in Salisbury lodgings with nothing to fill her time but attending church. This does not interest her for long. She decides to leave and search for an unknown quantity. Her feet take her homewards where Fanny and her Mother hide her for the night. The domestic scene is tense, convincing and memorable. Jacob hardly talks to her for two months, and when he does so the tone and content would be considered gruff even for the lowest servant. His implacability fights with his deep-felt love for his daughter, until he is forced to face the issue when Carry must attend the trial of two murderers as a witness. At last he breaks his silence, but not without much pain and excruciating volubility:

'It was a bad time with us when the girl, whom we had loved a' most too well, forgot herself and us, and brought us to shame,— we who had never known shame afore,—and became a thing so vile as I won't name it. It was well nigh the death o' me, I know.'
    'Oh, father!' exclaimed Fanny.
    'Hold your peace, Fanny, and let me say my say out. It was very bad then; and when she come back to us, and was took in, so that she might have her bit to eat under an honest roof, it was bad still;—for she was a shame to us as had never been shamed afore. For myself I felt so, that though she was allays near me, my heart

was away from her, and she was not one with me, not as her sister is one, and her mother, who never know'd a thought in her heart as wasn't fit for a woman to have there.' By this time Carry was sobbing on her mother's bosom, and it would be difficult to say whose affliction was the sharpest. 'But them as falls may right themselves, unless they be chance killed as they falls. If my child be sorry for her sin—'

'Oh, father, I am sorry.'

'I will bring myself to forgive her. That it was stick here,' and the miller struck his heart violently with his open palm, 'I won't be such a liar as to say. For there ain't no good in a lie. But there shall be never a word about it more out o' my mouth,—and she may come to me again as my child.'

There was a solemnity about the old man's speech which struck them all with so much awe that none of them for a while knew how to move or speak. Fanny was the first to stir, and she came to him and put her arm through his and leaned her head upon his shoulder.

'Get me my breakfast, girl,' he said to her. But before he had moved Carry had thrown herself weeping on his bosom. 'That will do,' he said. 'That will do. Sit down and eat thy victuals.' Then there was not another word said, and the breakfast passed off in silence. (*Bullhampton*, pp. 474-5)

There are aspects of this scene which Victorian readers would have enjoyed. It is the moment of reunification of the family. Its pathos and tension would have caused the odd tear to fall, and one can imagine Trollope himself feeling with it. But from the twentieth-century perspective, there is something of a defeat which the women suffer—after all there ought not to have been two months' silence which needed breaking. The refuge Jacob takes in the command 'Get me my breakfast, girl' is something which reconfirms the misuse of male power which was unquestioned by many in the nineteenth century, and rarely by Trollope whose conservative nature manifests itself in the atonement scene above. He intends it to be totally satisfying, but I have trouble accepting it so. Nonetheless it does solve one potential problem. Carry thinks she will run away from the unbearable tension at home. His attitude may well have forced her back into the way of life which causes him so much pain in the novel. Trollope points to another of the in-built absurdities in the social system as it reacted to fallen women. The prevailing hard-line stance was supposedly to prevent prostitution and moral decline, yet the very stubbornness of the reaction forced many to remain outcasts. In other words the very social system which set out to cure prostitution, lasciviousness and sexual sin actually managed to encourage that which it was trying to counteract. Carry's banishment by her righteous family is bad enough, but her situation in society makes her the lowest of the low. Even the drunken landlady of the filthiest public house can look down on Carry. Trollope makes his point (even though he tends to impose middle-class values on the suburban poor which often were not adopted by them at all), and that point is that the punishment does not fit the crime: when Mr Fenwick asked

> after Carry's present address the woman jeered at him, and accused him of base purposes in coming after such a one. She stood with arms akimbo in the passage, and said she would raise the neighbourhood on him. She was drunk and dirty, as foul a thing as the eye could look upon; every other word was an oath, and no phrase used by the lowest of men in their lowest moments was too hot or too bad for her woman's tongue; and yet there was the indignation of outraged virtue in her demeanour and in her language, because this stranger had come to her door asking after a girl who had been led astray. (*Bullhampton*, pp. 278-9)

Here Trollope sacrifices some truth to life by having the lowest working-class type respond like an outraged middle-class individual who fears for the moral wholesomeness of the community. In reality the poorer classes were 'perforce less hypocritical and more tolerant when it came to reacting on moral wrongdoing'.[24] High society, the other end of the economic scale, often bought itself out of trouble and responsibility, or used connections to minimise the troublesome effects of what the middle classes called scandal. It is not uncommon for other middle-class writers to impose prevailing middle-class consciousness on members of the aristocracy in their novels. Lady Dedlock, to quote one example cited by Margaret Wells in her introduction to the new edition of *Ruth*, is obsessed by the secret of her pre-marital sin and illegitimate daughter. It could be argued that as Trollope imposes middle-class values on his poor, Dickens does so with his aristocracy. Both, perhaps, lack some reliability.

Trollope's discussion of both sides of the argument on the middle-class habit of expelling the fallen woman certainly does not lack reliability. It is interesting that he manages to allow for the argument that the expulsion of the fallen woman is essential for the continuation of the moral wholesomeness of the whole community; then it is equally interesting to see him counteract it. Like Gaskell he is well aware of the fact that it must only be the woman who is sacrificed to keep society on an even keel. None the less he does not avoid the conventional argument: 'It may be said,' he writes in his Preface to *The Vicar of Bullhampton*, 'that the severity of . . . judgement acts as a protection of female virtue and deterring as all known punishments do deter from vice'.[25] Despite the obvious lack of sympathy Trollope feels for this argument it is one aspect of the fate of the fallen woman which, he felt, ought not to be ignored. After all it was in vogue for three-quarters of a century, and the most common argument to support the stock response. Trollope, Gaskell and Collins were adamant to point out that this habit does run contrary to the pure doctrines of Christian dogma. Other considerations, however, than the efficacious being of the tenets of Christian forgiveness were of vital concern to the mid-Victorian middle classes. Beatrice Curtis-Brown, in her fragmented and often inaccurate book which attempts to survey Trollope's literary life, at least effectively summarises the reasons for the middle-class fear of sexual freedom, resulting in that behaviour which we see as proud, hypocritical, unbending, unfair and unchristian. Early Victorians, she reminds, 'had known, or their parents had known the laxity of an earlier age, a laxity which could lead to a sort of brutal cynicism which could elbow out delicacy and tenderness'.[25] London was an aristocratic playground, a world of glamour, immorality and extravagance. The rise of the middle class in the nineteenth century made cities, including London, middle-class—it was necessary in their minds that the new order should replace the looseness and wickedness of the Regency with a strict, well-defined code of behaviour. In many ways the Victorian age was an age of systematising, organising, reorganising and categorising, and doing so with a measure of unbending determination. The reaction to Georgian immorality, lasciviousness and waste, was the moral equivalent of the reforms of industry, trade, civil service, parliament, health and education. The reaction was probably largely unconscious when they set up 'their white tents of purity'.[27] Memory of the French Revolution ('atheism in action' to the Victorian mind[28]) coupled with the ardent religious revival led by dissenting sects which had gathered momentum in the latter half of the eighteenth century and continued into the nineteenth century, to produce a schism between the established church and relatively new, very much less pragmatic religious institutions, a schism which was to become one of the landmarks of the nineteenth century. Here then are the roots of the new moral code which is known for its unbending stance, particularly when regarding the narrow sexual code which became the social norm. It could be argued that the unbending nature of the middle class was, in fact, part of a class struggle—the middle classes versus the aristocracy. As the century progressed it became clear that the relatively unified and determined middle-class front was continually gaining ground on their less unified, and certainly less numerous aristocratic counterparts. Brown quotes Bagehot as evidence:

> The aristocracy live in fear of the middle classes—of the grocer and the merchant. They dare not frame a society of enjoyment as the French aristocracy once framed it.[29]

Sexual promiscuity was seen as one of the most obvious examples of aristocratic privilege. A large part of Queen Victoria's long survival as monarch, often turbulent but never questioned seriously, lies in the fact that she and Prince Albert adopted the middle-class moral consciousness rather than the aristocratic code of values. The middle-class sexual code 'was, of course . . . a rather proud banner waved at the retreating upper classes by those who were pushing them from below: "We may not be elegant, but we are pure!" '[30] Bagehot again. That they went too far to ensure faithfulness to their code of purity is rarely questioned today, none the less it can still be understood by considering the historical perspective.

The roots of Victorian hypocrisy and cruelty lie, then, in an earlier age, and the Victorian relationship to that earlier age. A consideration of Walter Scott's *The Heart of Midlothian* highlights the former as they relate to the fallen woman. *The Vicar of Bullhampton* and *The Heart of Midlothian* do share something in common, despite the fact that Scott's novel belongs to an earlier age and is a romance in spirit. Still, Trollope's domestic social comedy has some of its literary roots in the Scottish romance. Effy Deans in *The Heart of Midlothian* is, as far as I can learn, the prototype for the largest number of fallen women in nineteenth-century fiction. She is responsible for the birth of the type as we know it, probably even more than the prostitute from the post-Newgate fiction of Dickens. Certainly Dickens's social consciousness played a dynamic role in all nineteenth-century fiction, but the relationship between plot and character type can be traced to Scott. Carry Brattle and Effy Deans have much in common. Effy is a rural lass possessing a very strict father, and a saintly sister who, like Fanny Brattle, plays the role of saviour to her fallen sister. Effy, like Carry, is the one person who in her attractive youth can soften her unbending Presbyterian father. The parallels between the two novels are fairly clear:

> [Effy] . . . was currently entitled the Lily of St Leonard's, a name which she deserved as much by her guileless purity of thought, speech and action, as by her uncommon loveliness of face and person.
>
> Yet there were points in Effy's character which gave rise not only to strange doubt and anxiety on the part of Douce David Deans, whose ideas were rigid, as may easily be supposed, upon the subject of youthful amusements, but even of serious apprehension to her more indulgent sister. The children of the Scotch of the inferior classes are usually spoiled by the early indulgence of their parents . . .
>
> Effy had a double share of this inconsiderate and misjudged kindness. Even the strictness of her father's principles could not condemn the sport of infancy and childhood; and to the good old man, his youngest daughter, the child of his old age, seemed a child for some years after she attained the years of womanhood, was still called the 'bit lassie', and 'little Effy', and was permitted to run up and down uncontrolled, unless upon the Sabbath, or at the times of family worship . . . With all the innocence and goodness of disposition, therefore, which we have described, the Lily of St Leonard's possessed a little fund of self-conceit and obstinacy, and some warmth and irritability of temper, partly neutral perhaps, but certainly much increased by the unrestrained freedom of her childhood.[31]

When this personality responds to an attractive young man who visits the neighbourhood, the results are predictable. She shares Carry's wilfulness. When her affair becomes known her father, like Jacob Brattle, unequivocally rejects the daughter, who is arrested for the murder of her illegitimate child which disappears shortly after it is born. Mr Deans is an elderly, unbending presbyterian, owing allegiance to the strictest branch of that tradition. His reasons for expelling his daughter are primarily religious. She is impure. He responds to her fall in scriptural terms, but mainly as they relate to his own guilt and the fact that he feels he has let down the congregation because he is one of the pillars of the church. 'I have yet been thought a polished shaft, and must be a pillar, holding . . . the place of ruling elder—what will the lightsome and profane think of the guide that cannot keep his own family from stumbling?'[32] But the wider social effects of Effy's fall also become the prototype for the Victorian fall. Jeanie Deans, the virtuous sister, feels that she cannot now marry the man she loves, a young presbyterian minister, because it would ruin his career. 'Jeanie felt herself lowered at once, in her own eyes, and in those of her lover, while she shed tears for her sister's distress and danger, there mingled with them bitter drops of grief for her own degradation.'[33]

So the negative social and personal ramifications which spread from the offender to her whole family circle, considered so typical of the Victorian moral code, are not a Victorian invention. The Victorians adopted a code which existed in the eighteenth century, but which was not part of the way of thinking of the then ruling class. A comparison of Scott's and Trollope's novels does show up one major difference which, though subtle, has far-reaching implications. Deans's rejection of his daughter had its roots in a new religious tradition which had grown out of calvinistic sects which were on the ascendancy during the eighteenth century. By the time Jacob Brattle rejects his daughter Carry, the rejection is based not on a spiritual code but a social norm. The perspective changed in the Victorian age; becoming more and more a social norm, it was difficult to avoid the social issues which arose from the girl's fall. Jacob Brattle belies his biblical name by being quite pagan. The rejection of the fallen woman in the Victorian age moves from a calvinistic passion to become a social concern. In a real sense the social code was more harsh because it did not have the softening influence of the kindly aspects of Christian charity. George Brattle's argument, you will notice, tends to lend itself to a social discussion rather than a dogmatic Christian one: 'The truth is, Mr Fenwick, that young women as go astray after that fashion is just like any sick animal as all the animals as ain't comes and sets upon immediately. It's just as well too. They knows it beforehand, and it keeps 'em straight.' (*Bullhampton*, p. 290) In his own way George

Brattle recaptures Beatrice Curtis-Brown's argument in précis. Trollope counteracts this social argument which allows for the undue persecution of a whole class simply by insisting that it does not work. Society is not protected at all when its individual female members remain unaware of the truth about love, marriage, sex and sin. By telling what he sees as the truth, Trollope hopes to counteract the cold social argument and soften the hard heart. After all it 'didn't keep poor Carry straight'. (*Bullhampton*, p. 299)

> But it may perhaps be possible that if the matter be handled with truth to life, some girl who would have been thoughtless, may be made thoughtful, or some parent's heart may be softened. It may also at last be felt that this misery is worthy of alleviation, as is every misery to which humanity is subject.[34]

In some ways Trollope successfully does this, but when the novel is compared with a more unified single-minded novel on the same subject, such as *Ruth* or *Tess of the d'Urbervilles* or *Esther Waters*, it does not come off well. The work moves the reader away from the fallen woman theme to look at such themes as the inter-church conflict, man-woman romance, aristocracy versus the middle classes, money and its role in marriage. Its ability to carry out its stated aim is very much limited by its diverse personality. Its aesthetic structure and content certainly work against its stated didactic purpose. As much as I find the characters delightful, the country scenes engaging and the plot relatively interesting, I do have to agree with *The Times*, 3 June 1870, when it suggests that 'we do not think that either in construction or development this novel will add much to Mr Trollope's reputation'.[35]

The work simply has no internal unity. That, more than anything else, reduces the potential power it has to make a definite comment on the persecution of the fallen woman.

Kate O'Hara

Trollope's second novel on the fallen woman, *An Eye for an Eye*, has a very definite unity between content, intent and theme—as a result it is a far more effective work. It is, unfortunately, not well known at all. For our purpose it is a fascinating book, though rarely read today, despite Anthony Blond's attempt to resurrect it in a new edition in 1966, along with other forgotten novels. Brown's survey of Trollope's work does not mention the novel at all. Sadleir, in his literary biography, writes only two or three sentences on it. The novel dwells on the fallen woman and her relations to the institution of non-working-class marriage in Victorian society. It includes little else. There exists no character who does not have a direct role to play in the literary discussion of this complex topic. The poor response of the reading public in the twentieth century has mirrored that of the nineteenth century when the novel was largely 'dismissed as another of Trollope's uncomfortable stories, devoid of his earlier charm'.[36] R.F. Littledale, writing critically in the *Academy*, suggested that Trollope is reviving the 'pre-eminently painful' mood of one other Irish story.[37] *The Illustrated London News* was disappointed in the tale of seduction and marriage which it saw as 'so very moderate a specimen of his great powers'.[38] One or two reviews disagree with the above, which represent the larger body of critics who express their displeasure, and they praise the novel in glowing terms. Some of their content will be included below when I study the text. In the meantime a short discussion on Victorian interclass marriage norms will provide a context for a discussion of the meaning of the novel itself.

A. J. Munby was not well acquainted with Anthony Trollope. Both lived in London at the same time and both were civil servants who wrote to supplement their income, though the latter was far more financially successful than the minor poet who spent so much time and energy on his voluminous private diary. Munby's diary records that he met Trollope a few times. If their relationship had little importance then why are they being drawn together now? The answer lies in the private life of Arthur Joseph Munby which has a great deal to do with the theme of *An Eye for an Eye*. The diary was not to be opened until 1950. This was the instruction of the writer. It lay in the British Museum, together with a massive collection of photographs and other material, not being edited and published until 1972. It will become well known as one of the most important and fascinating, informative diaries in the history of nineteenth-century England. Its writer is a man of his age, yet the diary reveals his secret life, his hopes, fears and fetishes, to make him one of the most individual of men to be met in writing. As a man about town he was a companion to such men as Rossetti, Ruskin, and Swinburne. He met Browning, Tennyson, Trollope, Thackeray, and once passed Dickens in the street. He helped to found the Working

Men's College where he taught Latin. He was, to all intents and purposes, a typical upstanding middle-class gentleman, but he had a most unusual secret, one which would have made Trollope and many others more interested in him. He ignored the boundary between classes by marrying a lowly working servant after having an affair with her for many years. This marriage would have been censured as a *mésalliance*, a disgrace, and a grave sin. The affair, had it remained as such, would have been perfectly acceptable if discreetly managed. The *mésalliance* would have fascinated Trollope who, so often in his work, deplores the pragmatic, sensible marriage for financial reasons, for family status, and for reputation and standing. Mary Lowther, the heroine of *The Vicar of Bullhampton*, is pressured, almost beyond endurance, to marry the man she does not love. She has been brought up by her poor but respectable aunt. They have a name but are quite penniless. Gilmore, the squire at Bullhampton, has a great deal of money and is quite in love with Mary. Her aunt tries to promote the marriage. Her few deeply respected friends join with the aunt to force the issue for the good of the girl. Two such friends are Mr and Mrs Fenwick with whom Mary spends a few months each year. All work towards the end which is for her own good. Unfortunately they see her good only in terms of position, wealth, reputation, comfort—they fail to see, as does Trollope, that loyalty to her own inner self is the first good. Trollope, despite some vestiges of prudish Victorianism in his character, would have probably admired Munby's private bravery, and his unusual determination to be loyal to his own desires. But Munby's bravery can only take him so far—he has to keep the affair and the marriage between the girl, Hannah, himself, and his beloved diary.

He probably met Hannah in about 1854. They often went out together, she walking behind him so that they would not be discovered. They sat in the 'gods' at the theatre in the cheap seats with the other commoners. He visited her regularly, and she him. They even went on holiday together to the Continent. His diary reveals the fact that his relationship with Hannah was part of a larger fetish. He loved to watch her work hard with her rough hands. In fact he had a fascination for all working girls, particularly those of the most common labouring kind: miners, mudlarks, farm workers, mill workers. He is very cross indeed when factory legislation takes some women away from the mines. Even though he spoke to hundreds, maybe thousands of these working girls, recording their conversations in his diary, he seems to have been very faithful to Hannah whom he married on 14 January 1873. The diary records the preparation a few days prior to the event:

> Wednesday, 8 January—Went to Gloucester Street Pimlico, to see my invalid colleague Digby Green. He was writing a note in his cosy sanctum, and a smartly drest young woman was sitting before him on the edge of a chair. She rose, seeing me, and retired with the note. 'Excuse me—she is only a servant' said D.G; 'she has been sent to bring me these grapes and this jar of—have some?' 'Only a servant'? I went home at seven to dinner, and was received by one who also is only a servant.[39]

One week later he married the servant to whom he went home. The passage above has very little importance, but it quickly captures the difference between the common way the middle class thought about a lower servant, and the way Munby thinks. Juxtaposed in the entry is the attitude that the girl is 'only a servant' and the unconventional stance of a human being who refuses in his heart to accept the prevailing attitude about class and marriage. It was certainly not uncommon for Victorian gentlemen to have secret lives. The number of prostitutes who unsuccessfully pester Munby in the pages of his diary is proof of that, if indeed proof is needed. It was uncommon for Victorian gentlemen to marry their secret life. Some four months prior to the marriage, Munby told his father of the affair, the paternal reaction being violent and fairly conventional. Munby's sin is in the telling of his relationship with a fallen woman:

> Monday, 26 August . . . Late at night, when the rest had gone to bed, I had a pathetic and terrible scene with my dear Father: for I had schooled myself at last, to tell him of my love for Hannah— begging him however not to tell my dearest Mother. What matters it that Hannah is pure, honourable, gracious, comely and intelligent, devoted to me now for 18 years? She is a servant: and the shame and horror of that fact, to me so simple, was to my honoured father so overwhelming, that I could not bear it; and comforted him, by crushing—not her, God forbid!—but my own hopes.[40]

On 3 September he wrote a long letter to his father, the content of which has been lost, but which we presume concerned Hannah. The editor of his diary feels that 'What he said in the letter can only be conjectured; he must have avoided a promise not to marry, but may have assured his father he would be no more troubled with the matter. The immediate effect of the painful scene was to postpone the marriage . . . '[41] He wrote the following sonnet to Hannah, which lay with thirty-five others in the strongbox in the British Museum, surrounded by hundreds of sketches, photographs, and many volumes of writing, until Derek Hudson made his timely discovery:

> How well I recollect our Wedding Day!
> She did her black work with a beating heart;
> Then wash'd herself, and own'd a servant's part
> Waiting on me, and then she went away
> Down to the kitchen bedroom, where she lay
> Among the pots, alone and quite apart;
> There doff'd her servile dress, and with meek art
> For once did make herself a little gay:
> Her long dark cloak: a red stuff gown quite new;
> Her black straw bonnet with white cap: Oh, no
> No gloves, no flowers! 'Massa, shall I do?'
> She cries; 'I have no looking glass, you know!
> Now, I am off! And mind you, all my life
> I shall be servant still to you, as well as wife.'[42]

Only on one occasion did Munby try to make his working-class girl into something grander. On the whole he was wiser than Gissing who married his working-class girl, set her up as the mistress of a sizeable middle-class establishment, then complained about her inability to cope with the running of such a household. Munby kept Hannah, for the large part, in her place. I have decided to introduce a chapter on Victorian marriage in *An Eye for an Eye* through Munby's experience, rather than through a more complex sociological study. From Munby's experience we can list the points necessary for a sound understanding of the theme in *An Eye for an Eye*. Classes are not to mix, especially through marriage; liaisons are acceptable if not public; *mésalliances* are regarded by patriarchs like Munby senior to be precursors to inevitable doom (one common argument suggests that Prince Albert's death at a relatively young age was hastened by the heir's indiscreet behaviour); severe psychological hurt can come to the offended parents (note

Munby's insistence that his mother must never hear of his relationship with Hannah); that Munby kept the marriage a secret is evidence enough to confirm the existence of a large social reaction which had potential power to wreck his image as a respectable man-about-town. Munby is not above the odd gossip about men who did not regard some or all of the above when they formed public relationships with girls of an inferior class. One such offender is Lord Robert Montagu, the second son of the Duke of Manchester, who made his *mésalliance* quite public:

Sunday, 11 January [1863] . . . Hannah came to me at five, and stayed till nine. From her I learn the other side of the Great Montagu Case. Robert Montagu—Lord Robert—whom I remember at Trinity, has positively gone and married a housemaid! [There is a deal of irony in his exclamation mark which I can't help feeling is a little comic.] Of which event one Davis, a nurse who knows the cook as lived with her—which her name was Betsy Wade, was the housemaid's—has preserved the details for kitchen ears.

Cook and Betsy was a-walking in Kensington Gardens; a gentleman unknown picks up Betsy's parasol (parasol indeed!) and follows the two home, unbeknown, to their master's house in Westbourne Grove. Not long after, when Betsy was on her knees in the street, cleaning the steps, one morning, the same gentleman goes by; speaks to her—but then it was early & no one was about; says, Would you like a better place? I think I could get you one in (sic) Lord Montagu's nursery. She, taking him for a butler or other man of eminence, says Yes Sir, I should; he then calls in person on her mistress for Betsy's character: and Betsy becomes a nurse in that noble household.

There, her master's favour grows daily towards the humble maiden; and in few weeks, the astonished servants, all but her, are discharged en masse; and Lord Robert proclaims his terrible resolve. But Betsy Wade, though her hands are still rough with blacking grates when my lord claims her for his bride, comports herself with grave propriety: being indeed far less sensible of her new honour than a girl of the middling ranks would be. She goes to see her old friend & fellow servant. 'Hollo Betsy,' says the Cook, 'what, have ye left already? Ye must be a going to be married or somethink!' 'Why yes,' says the fair Griselda, 'I am going to be married'; and she says no more. Would Miss Sugarplum, or even Miss Bolus, have kept such a secret so? The judicious Betsy then retires for a few days to her mother's cottage in some Suffolk village; receives the blessing of her astonished and unpresentable parent; and on her return is made Lady Robert Montagu at once, without any educating or refining preliminaries whatever.[43]

That is the tenor of the story, but the social results are even more interesting:

> Now I happen to have heard lately the views taken by Society of this fatal deed: I have heard from ladies of the shocking degradation of poor Lord Robert, and of his hopeless exclusion from family and friends by reason of this inexplicable depravity; and have of course expressed my deepest sympathy & horror.
>
> It is therefore amusing to hear what Betsy's friends & equals say. There is envy among housemaids; there is increased yearning for the fortuneteller's promise to us, of being 'a lady'; there is the conviction that we are as good as she is. And among the elders, like Mrs Davis (née Gamp) there is the proud patronising thought that she did well, as a champion of her class. It is scarcely necessary to remark, that Betsy had a sweetheart of her own rank, whom she discarded for her noble lover; and upon this theme, Mrs D. is eloquent & full of praise. 'Sweethearts be blowed!' says that matron: 'why' she adds with scorn, apostrophizing our Hannah, 'if you had a chance to marry a gentleman, would you be such a fool as to let a sweetheart stop you?'[44]

Fred Neville, the hero of *An Eye for an Eye*, does not put himself in the position of Lord Montagu. The object of his interest is not from the working class, though Kate O'Hara is far below the heir to the title of Scroope. Fred finds himself torn between his dying, youthful love for the now impregnated, unmarried, isolated and poor Kate O'Hara, and the duty to his aristocratic family, destiny having decided that the leadership of that family is to be his lot in life. To be or not to be is the marriage question which gives the novel its plot, tension and unity. For a Victorian novel it has remarkable unity of purpose which revolves around Fred's dilemma; it is a conflict between duty and love, a conflict which pits the wants of an ancient aristocratic class against the needs of a fallen woman, Kate O'Hara. Robert Tracy puts this conflict into other words, noticing Trollope's habit of doing this elsewhere in his work. 'The book is a further exposition into that shadowy area between moral reality and social reality which is implicit in his whole concern with the definition of the gentleman.'[45]

Fred Neville, the man who will be destroyed by the conflict between social reality and moral reality, is the son of the younger brother to the incumbent Earl of Scroope. Fred's father dies when he is young. This, when combined with the disgrace and premature death of the Earl's only son, leaves Fred the heir to the title, and the future head of the household. It is the stroke of luck which visits the world of Victorian comedy with regularity, but in Fred's case it will be the catalyst which leads to his tragic death. Despite coming from one of the poorer wings of his family he is brought up learning the skills necessary for one of his age and class—social poise, the ability to hunt, the ability to survive as an officer in the army. All this education, or miseducation as the case may be, leaves him incapable of filling in time and gives him a distinct desire for adventure:

> Fred, to look at [it is typical of Trollope to put the reader on his guard through the use of an insignificant word like look] was a gallant fellow—such a youth as women love to see about the house—well-made, active, quick, self-asserting, fair-haired, blue-eyed, short-lipped, with small whiskers, thinking but little of his own personal advantages, but thinking much of his own way.[46]

He is the likeable restless type after Arthur Donnithorne in Eliot's *Adam Bede* and Bellingham in *Ruth*. They are not black villains, but are sufficiently restless and wilful to cause some trouble when they give vent to their instinctual drives. All three young men have the hopes of their respective families resting on their shoulders. The going, however, is not smooth. Donnithorne and Bellingham have youthful traits they share with Fred Neville, but the intentions of the novelists differ. Both Eliot's and Gaskell's young men are minor characters. Trollope's narrative, for the first time that I know of, looks at the fallen-woman crisis from the male point of view, making him the hero of the novel. We have a fallen woman as the heroine of the novel, but she is not the main character in it. Although Gaskell and Eliot draw their young men very well one cannot help but get the feeling that they exist for purposes of plot manipulation, to precipitate the action which affects the main characters for whom the novels are written. It is not unusual to give the fallen woman and her lover a minor role in Victorian fiction, nor is it unusual to give those male lovers in the novels, whose major concern is the fallen woman herself, a minor role or total anonymity. In either case above the man who causes the fall is seldom given the complex attention a character needs before he enters the group of memorable characters one carries around in one's head after contact in a novel. Fred Neville in Trollope's novel is certainly the exception.

None the less the three young men help their respective guardians to share the following anxiety: 'When young men are anxious to indulge the spirit of adventure, they generally do so by falling in love with young women of whom their fathers and mothers would not approve'. (*Eye*, p. 14) Bellingham's mother, Donnithorne's uncle, Earl and Lady Scroope, and Munby's father all share the distinct fear of imprudent sexual adventures. 'In these days a spirit of adventure hardly goes further than this, unless it takes a young man to a German gambling table.' (*Eye*, p. 14) As much as the guardians above would fear the German gambling table they would be far less perturbed by that fear than by those raised by sexual scandal, for 'when young men will run into such difficulties, it is, alas, so very difficult to interfere with them'. (*Eye*, p. 18) Had Bellingham in *Ruth* not fallen ill his mother would have had far more difficulty wresting her son away from Ruth, for a while—at least until Bellingham tired of the poorly educated young girl. Kate O'Hara's mother is well aware of the sexual needs of young men, but she does not have the ability to rob her daughter of the first potential husband to visit their humble home in the wilds of the west coast of Ireland. Her husband is not there to help her, since he is serving time in a prison galley, a fact which Mrs O'Hara keeps well hidden. When Fred sends Kate a present of a seal skin he shot on one hunt, the mother is in two minds about the discretion of accepting it. One of the points Trollope makes in the novel is the pity that young daughters do not share their mothers' knowledge about the sexual energies of young men. There is something quite naïve about the characters of Ruth, Hetty in *Adam Bede*, and even Kate, though the latter is a little more conscious about the ways to entrap a man, possibly because her education has been far more sophisticated than that of the other two. Mrs O'Hara muses on the potential fall of her daughter. That she is willing to take the risk is a fine point which Trollope does not want us to forget. In a sense there exists within

Mrs O'Hara the same conflict between moral reality and social reality which we will see working within Fred and other characters in the novel. Putting the daughter in danger is one social reality which the mother, normally protective, must submit to. The daughter must be exposed to threat or she will never be sold on the marriage market. Exposure to young men like Fred may destroy her daughter—no exposure will destroy her. The mother opts for the 'may';

> Mrs O'Hara was by no means that most prudent mamma, and made, not only the seal-skin, but the donor also welcome. Must it not be that by some chance advent such as this that the change must be effected in her girl's life, should any change ever be made? And her girl was good. Why should she fear for her? The man had been brought there by her only friend, the priest, and why should she fear him? And yet she did fear: and though she herself liked the man, though she even was gracious to him when he showed himself near the cottage—still there was a deep dread upon her when her eyes rested upon him, when her thoughts flew to him. Men are wolves to women, and utterly merciless when feeding high their lust. Twas thus her own thoughts shaped themselves, though she never uttered a syllable to her daughter in disparagement of the man. This was the girl's chance. Was she to rob her of it? And yet, of all her duties, was not the duty of protecting her girl the highest and the dearest that she owned? If the man meant well by her girl, she would wash his feet with her hair, kiss the hem of his garments, and love the spot on which she had first seen him stand like a young sea-god. But if evil—if he meant evil to her girl, if he should do evil to her Kate—then she knew that there was so much the tiger within her bosom as would serve to rend him limb from limb. (*Eye*, p. 47)

Fred's ultimate conflict is one in which duty to family and love for Kate do battle. Here, in Mrs O'Hara's mind is another battle between duty and love. Her love of her daughter takes priority over her duty as protectress. It is this type of thematic synthesis which makes the novel seem tightly knit and consciously planned. The depths of the conflict are made more obvious by the knowledge she has of male unfaithfulness. Men, she reflects, 'so often are as ravenous wolves, merciless, rapacious, without hearts, full of greed, full of lust, looking on female beauty as prey, regarding the

love of woman and her very life as a toy'. (*Eye*, p. 44) Her hatred of
men is, no doubt, connected to her unfortunate experience with her
husband, an experience which Trollope leaves out of the novel's
frame of reference. The novelists are rarely as hard on their young
men. Gaskell humanises the young Bellingham to save her novel
from the effect of too many stock melodramatic characters. Eliot is
surprisingly sympathetic in her presentation of Hetty's despoiler,
Arthur Donnithorne, and Trollope does not actively condemn his
hero whom he presents as tragically caught between two abstractions, love and duty, the total allegiance to one or the other being
quite impossible. The novelists seem to collectively allow for a
natural male energy that will out. It is ironic that their work which
tries to understand the plight of women never allows them a similar
energy, especially of a sexual nature.

There is something unworldly and reverential in Kate's love for
Fred, something spiritual rather than physical. She sees his coming
as the appearance 'of a god'—'of the man as a lover she had never
seemed to think'. (*Eye*, p. 48) Ruth is also presented as a girl who
has no sexual understanding. 'She had heard of falling in love, but
did not know the signs and symptoms thereof; nor, indeed, had she
troubled her head much about them.'[47] Being 'innocent' and 'snow
pure' does not allow Ruth to have any sexual drive. Hetty Sorrell in
Adam Bede does not think of Arthur Donnithorne as a sexual lover.
She loves things, portable property which will make her more
beautiful, and rich, and powerful. Arthur can make her a lady and
give her far more than the inarticulate country suitors who seek her
hand. The upstanding, good-looking Adam Bede is no match for
the young man who gives Hetty presents, and who can, in her eyes,
give her many more. Hetty has no idea that 'No gentleman, out of a
ballad, could marry a farmer's niece'.[48] The Victorian novelists do
not follow Scott's romantic lead in *The Heart of Midlothian* when he
marries Effy Deans to an aristocrat. She becomes an aristocrat
herself and is passed off at court in the best pygmalion fashion as a
woman of breeding. Rank, dress, demeanour all seem to make the
young men attractive, rather than their attractiveness as sexual
partners. This is how Kate sees Fred:

> Then Lieutenant Neville had appeared upon the scene, dressed
> in sailor's jacket and trousers, with a sailor's cap upon his head,
> with a loose handkerchief round his neck and his hair blowing to
> the wind. In the eyes of Kate O'Hara he was an Apollo. In the

eyes of any girl he must have seemed to be as good-looking a fellow as ever tied a sailor's knot. (*Eye*, p. 44)

Kate forgets to realise that marriage to Greek gods is something which belongs to the mythical past and not the social reality of Victorian England. Yet hope is always part of the human heart, and it is hope for a better future which transforms the carnal man into a god-like character. Kate, Hetty and Ruth in their poverty and isolation all look for something else. Even the down-to-earth Tess does the same thing. Hardy, in Chapter 1 of *Tess of the d'Urbervilles* reminds the reader that 'Our impulses are too strong for our judgement'. The Victorian novelists being studied here give young men sexual impulses but endow their young women with romantic ones. It is this germ of romantic hope which makes them vulnerable when their Apollo appears on the scene. Notice Hardy's point on the first appearance of Angel Clare in his study of Tess. The scene is at the club walking dance:

> And as each and all of them were warmed by the sun, so each had a private little sun in her soul to bask in; some dream, some affection, some hobby, at least some remote and distant hope which, though perhaps starving to nothing, still lived on, as hopes will.[45]

The appearance of an Arthur, an Angel, or a Fred is too much for the poor, lonely or isolated girl to resist. They see the Apollo figure as the hope in human form. I must admit it does worry me that the conventions of the novels included here simply do not allow for the existence of female sexuality. Not only do they not do that but they make it clear that they do not. Neither Kate nor Hetty, neither Tess nor Ruth ever think of physically loving the man prima facie. Trollope tells us that Kate certainly does not think of loving the man. Eliot is as direct, making it clear that other things interest Hetty:

> For the last few weeks a new influence had come over Hetty— vague, atmospheric, shaping itself into no self-confessed hopes or prospects, but producing a pleasant narcotic effect, making her tread the ground and go about her work in a sort of dream, unconscious of weight or effort, and showing her all things through a soft, liquid vale, as if she were living not in this solid

world of brick and stone, but in a beautified world, such as the sun lights up for us in the waters. Hetty had become aware that Mr Arthur Donnithorne would take a good deal of trouble for the chance of seeing her; that he always placed himself at church so as to have the fullest view of her both sitting and standing; that he was constantly finding reasons for calling at the Hall Farm, and always would contrive to say something for the sake of making her speak to him and look at him. The poor child no more conceived at present the idea that the young squire could ever be her lover, than a baker's pretty daughter in the crowd, when a young emperor distinguished by an imperial but admiring smile, conceives that she shall be made empress. But the baker's daughter goes home and dreams of the handsome young emperor, and perhaps weighs the flour amiss while she is thinking what a heavenly lot it must be to have him for a husband: and so poor Hetty had got a face and a presence haunting her waking and sleeping dreams; bright, soft glances had penetrated her, and suffused her life with a strange, happy languor. The eyes that shed those glances were really not half so fine as Adam's, which sometimes looked at her with a sad, beseeching tenderness; but they had found a ready medium in Hetty's little silly imagination, whereas Adam's could get no entrance through that atmosphere. For three weeks, at least, her inward life had consisted of little else than living through in memory the looks and words Arthur had directed towards her—if little else than recalling the sensations with which she heard his voice outside the house, and saw him enter, and became conscious that a tall figure, looking down on her with eyes that seemed to touch her, was coming nearer, in clothes of beautiful texture, with an odour like that of a flower-garden in the evening breeze. Foolish thoughts! you see having nothing to do with the love felt by sweet girls of eighteen in our days; but all this happened, you must remember, nearly sixty years ago, and Hetty was quite uneducated—a simple farmer's girl, to whom a gentleman with a white hand was dazzling as an Olympian god.[50]

In trying to capture the essence of the girl's complex feelings for the hero, Eliot uses the same metaphor as does Trollope—the god figure. This choice is interesting not only because it captures the emotional reaction of the maid but because it emphasises the double advantage which Fred Neville and Arthur Donnithorne possess—male superiority and class superiority. The sense of euphoria being experienced by the young women makes them doubly vulnerable when combined with what they see as their greatest need—Kate's is to escape the isolation and loneliness which has been her lot; Hetty's is to dream of luxuries and power. The god figure is supposed to be the bringer of great gifts, and indeed they do bring something, but the gift of an unwanted child out of wedlock is not the gift expected. As Hetty struggles to come to grips with the reality of her lot, so different to that which she imagined, and as Kate waits for the father of her child to return to marry her, the god figures become horribly human, and the euphoric dreams turn into horrific nightmares. One of the dimensions to *An Eye for an Eye* is its 'stern indictment of romanticism, the romantic hero, and the romantic wish to live a life that is out of the ordinary . . . Foolishly romantic dreams are at the heart of *An Eye for an Eye* . . . '[51] Kate's romantic dream of a god figure turns out to be a misleading tragedy. Hetty's ends up in the death of her child. Fred himself has a romantic dream of an out of the way affair, far from the boundaries of civilised England, where he can play a game that is as wild and romantic as the scenery itself. His dream and Kate's dream clash, ending in their respective deaths. This is the essence of the tragedy in the novel.

The young men in the novels do differ, but the similarities are striking—youthful ardour, boredom and natural instinct react in an expected manner in the face of forthcoming worship from equally youthful innocent young women who dream of something better or a release from the strictures of a world which keeps them down. Most of the young men enjoy hunting. Bellingham hunts and tames the deer in his mother's park. Arthur is an excellent horseman. Fred Neville is an inveterate and seasoned huntsman. The hunt is an ideal symbol for the sexual game they play. 'Why should you shoot the poor gulls?' is the first question Kate asks Fred Neville. His reply is honest—'I believe there is no other reason—except that one must shoot something'. Kate presses him further, asking for reasons why one must shoot. 'To justify one's guns. A man takes to shooting as a matter of course. It's a kind of institution. There ain't any tigers, and so we shoot birds. And in this part of the world there ain't any pheasants, and so we shoot gulls.' (*Eye*, p. 45) Hetty, Kate, and Ruth provide sport for the young men simply because of their beauty, and their isolation from the protection of the herd. Added to Fred's love of the hunt is the romance of a strange land as it interacts with the worship of a beautiful girl. Her individuality, that she belongs to another world, that she is pure and innocent because of it, all combine to make her attractive to the young officer. Her total attention, the lack of any competition, and her relationship to a romantic, natural world sweeten the euphoria Fred feels:

> Neville, as he made his way down to Liscannor, where his gig was waiting for him, did ask himself some serious questions about his adventure. What must be the end of it? And had he not been imprudent? It may be declared on his behalf that no idea of treachery to the girl ever crossed his mind. He loved her too thoroughly for that. He did love her—not perhaps as she loved him. He had many things in the world to occupy his mind, and she had but one. He was almost a god to her. She to him was the sweetest girl that he had ever as yet seen, and one who had that peculiar merit that she was all his own. No other man ever pressed her hand, or drank her sweet breath. Was not such a love a thousand times sweeter than that of some girl who had been hurried from drawing-room to drawing-room, and perhaps from one vow of constancy to another? But how was it to end? His uncle might live those ten years, and he had not the heart—nor yet the courage—to present her to his uncle as his bride. (*Eye*, p. 67)

Despite his euphoric regard for Kate, there is a pragmatic vein in his thought which works on a rational level. It is this pragmatic vein which will grow, eventually to replace the emotion he calls love. He is well aware of the social reality which places expectations upon him. Despite his effort at running away from his rank and society to the edge of the civilised world, he cannot escape his familial duty. It is his duty to make a good marriage—yet his passion, his instinct, his search for romance, his very humanity push him in another direction. It is these phenomena which he recognises by the name of 'love'. Early in the novel, when his relationship with Kate is in its early passionate state, his duty seems like a ghost from another drawing-room world which follows him, but which retreats under the fire of his passion, and his characteristically selfish nature. The conflict is refined and defined in the novel as a battle between passion and duty. The setting of the novel reflects this duality, again helping to relate the aesthetic structure of the novel to the thematic concern to produce what I feel is a remarkably unified and well-controlled work of art. Duty and Scroope Manor have direct affinity—Passion and the wild Atlantic coast have obvious relationships.

The narrator of the novel describes the family seat through the eyes of a lively young man. Like the whole concept of duty to family honour and tradition, it reaches into the past with its own measure of ghost-like gloom. To the young Fred Neville it represents a death in life. The house and familial demands of self-control, self-sacrifice and self-discipline cannot be totally separated. They mean responsibility. The demands they make on the young officer are one and the same. In the early stages of the novel they threaten to smother him, but as his passion dies they become the dynamic force in his life. On the other hand the wild, rocky coast of Western Ireland with its craggy reaches and primitive aspects, is the milieu in which passion can have a free rein—there is something basic and energetic about primitive instinct and wild places. Trollope takes care to relate the two different settings of the novel to his hero's crisis. In that way the very setting of the novel becomes both part of the hero's personality and therefore part of his innermost conflict. He also makes sure that the settings are presented from the point of view and perspective of his hero. Their importance lies in that they represent the two parts of the conflict which will result in Kate's metaphoric fall as a woman, and Fred's actual fall as the despoiler of Mrs O'Hara's daughter, and his metaphoric fall as tragic hero.

The first picture of the Manor presents the concepts of the continuum of the Scroope Family and the relationship of that family to the whole community. But from Fred's point of view it is not a colourful vestige from the past, but a huge stultifying pile tucked away in the wilderness of its own introspection. It is not presented as a grand, old house which tourists are wont to visit. However it is dominant in the village, dull and lifeless. This is Fred's initial opinion of his duty itself. The village is described only to the point that the size of the duty is realised. Fred's responsibility is to the house, its inhabitants and the wider community. He can feel little affinity with this community, and even less with the interior of the house itself, the heart of the family. The interior is gloomy in the extreme, tomb-like, musty—the relic of an age gone by:

The house was large, and the rooms were grand and spacious. There was an enormous hall into one corner of which the front door opened. There was a vast library filled with old books which no one ever touched,—huge volumes of antiquated and now all but useless theology, and folio editions of the least known classics,—such as men now never read. Not a book had been added to it since the commencement of the century, and it may almost be said that no book had been drawn from its shelves for real use during the same period . . . The Earl's own room was at the back . . . of the house, near the door leading into the street, and was, of all rooms in the house, the gloomiest.

No doubt this appeared so to Fred who was rather close to in-habiting the room permanently. It is this potential relationship with that room which makes it the dullest in the house, although the dead remainder of the interior is little better:

> The atmosphere of the whole place was gloomy. There was none of those charms of modern creation which now make the mansions of the wealthy among us bright and joyous. There was not a billiard table in the house. [A detail which a young man like Neville would be sure to notice.] There was no conservatory nearer than the large old fashioned greenhouse, which stood away by the kitchen garden and which seemed to belong ex-clusively to the gardener. The papers on the walls were dark and sombre. The mirrors were small and lustreless. The carpets were old and dingy. The windows did not open on to the terrace. The furniture was hardly ancient, but yet antiquated and uncomfor-table . . .
>
> To a stranger, and perhaps also to the inmates, the idea of gloom about the place was greatly increased by the absence of any garden or lawn near the house. (*Eye*, pp. 2-3)

The terms used to describe the antiquated, gloomy house could well be used by Fred to describe the duty to which he is called. Whenever Fred is at Scroope Manor his instinct is to leave it, just as his instinct calls him to ignore the sense of duty which has been instilled in him by his uncle and aunt. From the day he is welcomed to Scroope as heir he is stifled by the place; using the excuse of duty to his regiment, an ironic excuse to be sure, he returns to Ireland despite protestations that he ought to remain at home to learn his duty. Life with Kate and his regiment is far more attractive by comparison. On all of his forced visits to the Manor he feels the boredom and purposelessness experienced on his first visit. On one of these occasions he thinks of going to bed since life is dull. He has just listened to one of his aunt's lectures on the right things for the family and the community, the first right thing being the rejection of regiment, Ireland and Kate whom she fails to mention till later in the conflict. In the back of her mind Lady Scroope is making one or more good marriages which will ensure a more settled approach to life on the part of the young heir. 'He began to think,' Trollope writes, 'that a man might pay too dearly even for being the heir to Scroope.'(*Eye*, p. 75) He sits in the gloom, thinking of his aunt's lecture, and regarding the dark shadows cast by the candles which are surrounded by dark paper, dark curtains, dark wainscoting, and huge mahogany furniture. The room is lined with paintings of the whole tedious, wooden family painted by an artist whose 'works had, unfortunately, been more enduring than their names'. (*Eye*, pp. 75-6) He sees himself as one of these dead hideous figures. The more he makes an effort to learn the customs, responsibilities, tenants' names, financial systems the more he feels he is dead already, one of the long line of duty-bound Scroopes. He does try to fit into the plan for his education as the future Earl, travelling to the far corners of the estate which is to become his microcosm in the near future. As he rides with the steward, or asks polite questions to the farmers, labourers and cottage dwellers there is the feeling that the whole exercise is futile. He is like a schoolboy who is being forced to learn in a claustrophobic classroom by tedious, soporific schoolmasters. Here he is riding with the steward:

> 'My Lord' had never cared for game. The farmers all shot rabbits on their own land. Rents were paid to the day. There was never any mistake about that. Of course the land would need to be revalued, but 'My Lord' wouldn't hear of such a thing being done in his time. The Manor wood wanted thinning very badly. The wood had been a good deal neglected. 'My Lord' had never liked to hear the axe going. That was Grumby Green and the boundary of the estate in that direction. The next farm was college property, and was rented five shillings an acre dearer than 'My Lord's' land . . .
> He could not escape from the feeling that he was being taught his lesson like a schoolboy, and he did not like it. (*Eye*, pp. 80-1)

So the Manor, and what its gloom symbolises, is everything that an active young man like Fred Neville detests. Yet his duty is part of his nature. It will surface at a later time, especially when he needs an excuse to desert Kate, the woman whom he vehemently claimed he would never desert. For the moment, however, duty and Scroope Manor are inexorably tied together and to be avoided at all cost.

The less ordered aspect of his personality, the desire for adventure and excitement finds its affinity on the Irish coast where Fred might give vent to his natural energies and his passions. The longing for release probably makes him more careless than he may have been without the weight of duty on his shoulders. Whenever he feels the weight of Scroope he 'longed for the freedom of his boat on the Irish Coast, and longed for the devotedness of Kate O'Hara'. (*Eye*, p. 81) 'All his brightest thoughts were away in County Clare, in the cliffs overlooking the Atlantic.' (*Eye*, p. 75) The bright, energetic world in Ireland is his release, giving a loose to his soul, an escape from one part of himself. His romantic hope is, of course, that the gloomy duty will disappear, that his conscience will not step in and spoil the fun. Lady Scroope senses this need in his character. That is why she does her best to keep him at Scroope. She asks her husband, the Earl, to stop his going, but that peer knows the truth of the matter—forcing the young man's hand will not change his future; he will accede to the title, come what may. She is unable to see that forcing him may push him in the wrong direction. She knows that hunting partridge and pheasant on his own domain is the sphere of the respectable country aristocrat, not the wilds of Ireland and the arms of Kate O'Hara.

As expected he will have his way. The cliffs are sensuously described, having a life and personality of their own, which is in tune with Neville's inner life. They are 'beautifully coloured, streaked with yellow veins, and with great masses of dark red rock; and beneath them lies the broad and blue Atlantic'. (*Eye*, p. 34) The primary colours, yellow, red and blue, contrast powerfully with the sombre civilised tones of decay that infiltrate Scroope Manor. The vibrancy and life of one show up the lifelessness and lustreless character of the other. On the edge of this new, bright world nature takes its course. Like other writers, who look at the seduction of the potential fallen woman, the natural setting is where the instinctual desires of the young man seem to have more encouragement and play. Tess is seduced in an ancient forest. Ruth is taken to a mountainous region in Wales. Effy Deans, the prototype of them all, loses her virginity in the wilds of Scotland. Hetty Sorrell meets Arthur in the forest where huge, dominating trees provide a

Freudian background to the seduction. Esther Waters meets her fall in a field which is ripe for harvest. In other novels, those which look at prostitution, the scene is usually in the gloom of city alleys and dark corners, providing the notable exception to the rule.

For the purposes of *An Eye for an Eye* the house of the O'Haras is 'the nearest house to the rocks . . . ' Its geographical placing, its bordering the wild primitive world, places the inhabitants at risk, but as the novel proceeds that risk moves from a geographic emphasis to a moral one. Neither Fred nor Kate is aware of this, both being lost in their romantic fantasy—'Of one thing he was quite sure—that there was much more of real life to be found on the cliffs of Mohar than in the gloomy chambers of Scroope Manor'. (*Eye*, p. 75)

Trollope's use of setting is an effective way to stress the various aspects of his hero's dilemma. He is a mixture of passions, wildness, lack of discipline, and these do not have a comfortable affinity with his social, cultural self. Nor is the dichotomy clear cut. He has a duty to family, society, and its standards of behaviour, but he also has a duty to himself and his emotions, the total repression of which is the destruction of individuality. Fred Neville is too young, too inexperienced to see this complexity, this conflict of command-ments. He is also too close to it to see or accept the issues at stake. His responsibility for others, however, is given more attention on the death of his uncle, when he becomes the Earl of Scroope. Like it or not he is no more the poor, young, fancy-free officer with adventures unlimited at his feet. He is not always to long for his boat in Ireland, and Kate's devotedness. In fact, he is going to regret the cliffs, their power to affect his behaviour, and of especial regret is his former presence there. 'What an ass had he made himself, coming thither in quest of adventure.' (*Eye*, p. 180) In other words when he dispels the romantic haze which he was sure existed in Ireland, he discovers the social reality of his situation. His dilemma is now a moral one. He tries to synthesise disparate elements in his life and fails. What changes Fred Neville's mind? This is one of the questions central to Trollope's intention in the novel. The internal and external forces which work to change the mind of the young earl are both socially and psychologically important, and they are as complex as they are intractable. The social forces which try to work on Fred Neville are more complex and certainly more multifaceted than are the sexual drive and romantic readiness which drive him to his affair with Kate. These social forces and his psychological reaction to them form the main study of the novel.

In many ways Fred inherits and adopts the first dynamic force which changes his self-image, his relationship with Kate, and his whole future. He becomes the heir to Scroope with all its traditions, responsibilities and power. He is not born to the position, being the son of a younger brother. It is his lot, however, to witness the disintegration and degradation of the Scroope family. The Earl loses his first wife. This is his 'first blow'. The second blow comes with the death of his only daughter who is about to give birth. The baby also dies. All his hopes then centre on his only son who, unfortunately, has little to recommend him, being 'a youth indeed thoughtless, lavish and prone to evil pleasures'. (*Eye*, p. 5) This young man, though only mentioned in the early part of the work, is typical of a fairly common type—the miseducated young aristocrat who has little to do but shoot, gamble, fornicate, spend some time at Oxford or Cambridge before being sent down. Filling in time is the most difficult thing for them to do, till they tire and exhaust themselves of the very pleasures they seek. Although Trollope was not an aristocrat he was educated with many in the same way. Later in life he complains bitterly about its ineffectiveness. He reviews his state prior to his entry to the civil service:

> I could read neither French, Latin, nor Greek. I could speak no foreign language,—and I may as well say here as elsewhere that I never acquired the power of really talking French. I have been able to order my dinner and take a railway ticket but never got much beyond that. Of the merest rudiments of the sciences I was completely ignorant. My handwriting was in truth wretched. My spelling was imperfect. There was no subject as to which examination would have been possible on which I could have gone through an examination otherwise than disgracefully. And yet, I think, I knew more than the average of young men of the same rank who began life at nineteen.[52]

Like many young men thrown on the world after experiencing years at school, both middle-class and upper-class individuals, Trollope had great trouble surviving in London. For a while he seemed incapable of elementary budgeting skills and common sense. He did not eat properly or look after his health. His education, like that of the son of the Earl of Scroope, did very little to fit him for the real social world of which he was very much a part. The Earl hopes that reliability, sensitivity, fairness and usefulness will come with age, accompanied by a concomitant reduction in the number of dissipations which filled up time with 'evil pleasures'. It is ironic in Trollope's case that his father never found economic survival possible, he too finding his place in the world impossible to understand or control. Marriage did not change Trollope senior, and did not change everyone, but the Earl of Scroope looks to marriage to settle his son. It is one pathway to respectability and a calm life. Lord Neville does not respond well to the Earl's choice of his bride, a poor but well-related young lady with the 'best blood' in the nation. The Earl finds he is married already in the most Munby-like manner imaginable—in fact he out-Munbies Munby by marrying a French prostitute. This is not acceptable. After the son is shipped to the Continent with his disgraceful wife the Earl is never able to hold up his head again. This is the fatal blow the Earl experiences in a series of disasters, though Fred's indiscretion will cause him future pain. It is his largest cross to bear. The disgrace of his son is more difficult to bear than is his wife's death. The son dies three years later, leaving the seat for his cousin, Fred Neville. In this context it is not surprising to find the Earl and his new wife very much pained to hear rumours from Ireland about the future Earl's developing regard for the unknown Kate. The novel's strength lies in its ability to capture the Scroopes at a moment of crisis, when Fred's respectability is the last chance to return the family to its traditional reputation for uprightness and order. As the Scroopes are seen in a moment of crisis so is Fred himself who is faced with the need to change, and do so rapidly. Till the death of his wayward cousin nothing ties Fred down. His education has also made it impossible for him to pursue a career which does not involve much shooting, riding and play. His new responsibilities change him imperceptibly at first, but in increasingly obvious ways as the novel proceeds. He refuses to avoid Kate at first, claiming that stuffy traditions of a gloomy family ought not to change his emotional wants.

The need to make a good marriage in order to save his family is the single most obvious pressure on Fred Neville from without. Blood is the key. It is not wise to marry someone with no money, but it is even worse to marry someone from a lower class. This is manifest several ways in the plight of different characters in the novel. The Earl's second wife is penniless, as is the Earl's choice for his son, but she is from a good family. The second Lady Neville 'was very proud of her blood, and did in truth believe that noble birth was a greater gift than any wealth. She was thoroughly able to look down on a parvenu millionaire—to look down upon such a one and not pretend to despise him.' (*Eye*, p. 7) When the Earl of Scroope asks for her hand she is dependent on a brother. Her marriage prospects look bleak indeed, but she would rather stay an embittered old maid than be happy with a commoner. Fred himself must not marry below him. Sophia Mellerby, brought to Scroope Manor to meet Fred, is attractive not to Fred but to his brother Jack. His forthcoming proposal to Sophia cannot be accepted by the maid because that proposal comes from a man of inferior social status. Even Kate cannot consider a marriage with any local shopkeeper or farmer—they too lack the necessary qualifications for a good marriage. So many characters in the novel seem to be bound by the strict laws which govern marriage. The fallen woman in the novel is created by these laws. If a young man cannot marry then he must make the object of his love a social outcast, with no legal rights and with the scorn of a whole community.

It is essential that Fred be married as soon as possible after his nomination as heir. The Earl and his wife set about finding a wise match, deciding on one who has blood and money—the perfect find! It is essential to bring Sophia Mellerby to Scroope as soon as possible to lure the young man away from his regiment in Ireland. Sophia's credentials are perfect, or nearly perfect: her grandmother is a duchess; her father is a commoner but a very rich one. The maternal line is sufficiently illustrious to ameliorate the common blood in the Mellerby line. To make Sophia's visit respectable, and the intention of it a little more subtle, Fred's mother and brother are summoned to Scroope Manor at the same time. It is 'imperative that he should marry at least a lady, and at least a Protestant'. (*Eye*, p. 19) When Fred arrives at Scroope to meet Sophia he is deliberately on his guard, being well aware of his aunt's scheming, so he visits his horses first, leaving the young lady to await his pleasure. The following record of their first meeting would be matter-of-fact in a novel of lesser quality, but the visage of the hopeful Kate in the background of the novel's action and in the background of Fred's mind gives the telling an ironic dimension which is never to leave the novel:

> The introduction was made, and Fred did his best to make himself agreeable. He was such a man that no girl could, at the first sight, think herself injured by being asked to love him. She

was a good girl, and would have consented to marry no man without feeling sure of his affections; but Fred Neville was bold and frank as well as handsome, and had plenty to say for himself. It might be that he was vicious, or ill-tempered, or selfish, and it would be necessary that she should know much of him before she would give herself into his keeping; but as far as the first sight went, and the first hearing, Sophia Mellerby's impressions were all in Fred's favour. It is no doubt a fact that with the very best of girls a man is placed in a very good light by being heir to a peerage and a large property. (*Eye*, p. 22)

It is typical of Trollope's narration in the novel to push his own opinions on marriage into the background, and to let conventional opinion have its say. All its habits, weaknesses and absurdities become rather obvious. As the last sentence conveys in the quote above, Trollope is content to let it show itself up, at the same time playing with words like 'doubt', 'best', and 'good'. He continues in this vein. 'Fred Neville,' he later writes, 'who had literally been nobody before his cousin had died, might certainly do much worse than marry her.' (*Eye*, p. 24) At times the narration sounds as if it is quoting the conversation of commentators on the potential marriage. Earlier in the novel the same applies—the dominant social voice, as Trollope hears it,—speaks for itself:

Very little was required of him. He was not expected to marry an heiress. An heiress indeed was prepared for him, and would be there, ready for him at Christmas . . . But he was not to be asked to marry Sophie Mellerby. He might choose for himself. There were other well-born young woman about the world—duchesses' grand daughters in abundance! (*Eye*, p. 19)

Trollope makes his point with no blatant authorial intrusion, and in the century of didactic lectures, which present themselves in the author's voice, this is rather refreshing. The power of the situation itself speaks more than the writer. Its ironic comedy becomes more bitter in retrospect as the tragic conclusion to the novel becomes more imminent.

The tragedy begins in Fred's own personality, his lack of independence, his passionate nature, his ignorance of his own society's ways. He knows that 'he was ignorant of the laws respecting marriage'. But the tragedy also springs from a social source which tries to change Fred's natural inclinations and force them into a conventional mould. Despite Lady Neville's plan, the ideal match, the initial positive response, Fred and Sophia do not respond. Kate is too much with him. He cannot develop a relationship which is supposed to be pragmatic if not passionate. They do become good friends, confidants, but certainly no more. Fred's brother falls in love with her instead, as mentioned above. She cannot think of marrying him for he is very poor and without title, a combined state which makes him a very poor prospect for the 'best' girls. The point is typical of Trollope—Nature's way is not man's. The Earl of Scroope and his wife can plan, scheme, and try to force, but without Nature's agreement the artificiality of the relationship remains all too obvious and potentially dangerous. Likewise, Fred's nature does not fit with his uncle's picture of the perfect heir. The novel then is a study of the schism between what nature would have and what man would not. It is this conflict which is the source of Fred's pain. Society, his relations being the obvious representatives, would have him give up Kate. His natural instincts do not perceive the possibility, yet as society has its way within him, he rejects his instinctual desire to protect Kate and do the right thing by her. The *Spectator*, 15 February 1879, senses this trend in the character as he changes, including the following in one of the most positive reviews the novel received:

> There is something simple and great in the story, and we turn to it with the more pleasure . . . The guilt, the grief, and the crime all have their roots in the natural instincts of man, and these are known to us in such a society as our own; and all appear to be just what they are, without any artificial disguises. Nothing can be more striking than the picture of the manner in which hereditary pride takes hold of the heir to the English Earldom, almost without his own consent, and against his own better nature and feelings, and yet assumes to itself the air of disinterested duty and high necessity, driving him to do what he is ashamed of, and yet only ashamed of as a man; whilst as the head of a house and the heir to a great name, he seems to himself to owe more to society than he owes even to his own conscience and his God.[53]

Loyalty to others versus loyalty to self is one way to look at the universal conflict between internal man and the social position that man holds. He is both individual and part of a complex system. Fred

Neville is not forced to understand this duality abstractedly, he must come to grips with it, poorly educated as he is, at an early age. Failure is imminent. He is faced with the type of dilemma which has plagued man since Adam—he faces two conflicting commandments, the obedience to one making him disobedient to the other. Just as Adam could not multiply and replenish the earth without tasting the fruit of the forbidden tree which he was commanded not to touch, Fred Neville cannot be loyal to his family and to Kate. The frustrations of Munby, Lord Montagu and the like are evidence enough to prove the existence of an intractable but powerful social force which controlled marriage in Victorian England. Mrs O'Hara is also placed in the Adamic-like bind. She cannot find a partner for her daughter because she is not allowed to forego the demands of blood. Like the second Lady Scroope she would rather have Kate live in unsullied spinsterhood than marry beneath her. Good blood in the novel is a curse for Mrs O'Hara, Kate, Fred Neville, Lady Scroope and the young Lord Neville. It seems to do little to make life more bearable, and is the one thing which stops the unification of nature's way and man's. Life on the distant shores of Western Ireland was

> to her daughter life within a tomb. 'Mother, is it always to be like this?'
>
> Had her child not carried the weight of good blood, had some small grocer or country farmer been her father, she might have come down to the neighbouring town of Ennistimon, and found a fitting mate there. Would it not have been better so? From that weight of good blood—or gift, if it please us to call it—what advantage would ever come to her girl? It cannot really be that all those who swarm in the world below the bar of gentlehood are less blessed, or intended to be less blessed, than the few who float in the higher air. As to real blessedness, does it not come from fitness to the outer life and a sense of duty that shall produce such fitness? Does anyone believe that the Countess has a greater share of happiness than the grocer's wife, or is less subject to the miseries which flesh inherits? But such matters cannot be changed by the will. This woman could not bid her daughter go and meet the butcher's son on equal terms, or seek her friends among the milliners of the neighbouring town. The burden had been imposed and must be borne, even though it isolated them from all the world. (*Eye*, p. 43)

But if this is the way of man, Trollope cannot resist including his romantic unification of man and nature in a vision which sees Kate's future as positive and wholesome:

> It was needed that the girl should go out into the world and pair, that she should find some shoulder on which she might lean, some arm that would be strong to surround her, the heart of some man and the work of some man to which she might devote herself . . . Was it not fit that she should go forth and be loved— that she should at any rate go forth and take her chance with others? But how should such a going forth be managed? (*Eye*, pp. 43-4)

The above demonstrates Trollope's limits and his humanity. Many would see this vision of the supportive-but-dependent wife as negative, and rather sexist, and potentially destructive. Here he is the voice of his age, which still saw women as weak and needing the strength of a dominant male. None the less, as conventionally limiting as his vision is, it is preferable to the tomb-like existence which seems to be the lot of Kate O'Hara. She is an archetypal example of what Gissing is to call an 'odd woman'. And odd women are easy prey, especially when a young man, with the power inherent in good blood, comes to call, even when the motto of that young man's house happens to be 'Sans Reproche'. Fred takes his refuge in the power of his good blood, his family name. Again the *Spectator* sees this as one of Trollope's most powerful novels:

> Mr. Trollope has hardly ever painted anything so striking as the mode in which the promise not to disgrace his house and name grows unconsciously and involuntary in the young Lord Scroope's mind, till it takes all the life out of the more binding and far more sacred promise under the faith of which he has gained from Kate O'Hara all she has to give; and this, though far from wishing to desert her, though he is really willing to give all he has to give in the world, except his rank and social position, to make atonement to her for what has been done. Of all the strange perversions of which the moral nature of men is capable, probably none is stranger than the tendency of certain so called 'social obligations' to over-ride entirely the simpler personal obligations in certain men's breasts, and yet to work there with all the force of a high duty, and all the absoluteness of an

admitted destiny.[54]

Trollope is careful in his handling of the aristocratic pressures which change the good-natured but blind young man into the careless, heartless, pompous and arrogant young Lord. He manages to paint the aristocracy in the novel as a close-knit group who join together to fight for the preservation of the unwritten laws which stop the pollution of their ranks by the fallen, the socially disgraced or the common. Trollope manages to give the sense of aristocratic community without destroying the unity of his work. Trollope invents the Quin family who live in the relatively impoverished family seat of Castle Quin. They happen to live in the same part of Ireland as do the O'Haras, and are close enough to hear the rumours which they quickly repeat by letter to Lady Scroope. So Trollope is able to use the Quins in a structural sense, as a device to carry all the activity in Ireland to the gloomy halls of Scroope Manor. At the same time he is able to give the impression of a united front which the upper classes built for self-protection. Mary Quin feels it is her duty to warn Lady Scroope. Her letters are part gossip and part duty, but above all they are from the pen of the representative of a class which is consciously and unconsciously reacting to the potential threat from a continually and rapidly changing world, which does not even leave the distant parts of the Kingdom untouched:

> I have seen this young lady . . . and she is certainly very pretty. But nobody knows anything about them; and I cannot even learn whether they belong to the real O'Haras. I should think not, as they are Roman Catholics. At any rate Miss O'Hara can hardly be a fitting companion for Lord Scroope's heir. I believe they are ladies, but I don't think that anyone knows them here, except the priest of Kilmacrenny . . .
>
> I daresay nothing shall come of it, and I'm sure I hope nothing may. But I thought it best to tell you. (*Eye*, pp. 16-17)

The partnership between Lady Scroope and Mary Quin is unheralded, but certainly understood. The latter offers to be watchdog when she assures Lady Scroope of her best attention—'if I can be of any service to you, pray let me know'. (*Eye*, p. 17) It is difficult to know which aspect of the O'Haras' situation is the most worrying to Mary Quin. She cannot accept their Roman Catholicism, yet their unknown background is almost a worse crime. The close proximity of Castle Quin, its isolation, the poverty of the inmates, all would have combined to encourage some sort of communication with the rather refined O'Hara ladies. But no contact can be risked until their genealogy is well checked along with the history of their lives. The priest, however, is an obvious individual to blame, so Mary Quin latches onto him as the diabolic influence which has the potential power to bring down the House of Scroope. 'I am most unwilling,' she writes, 'to make mischief or to give unnecessary pain to you or Lord Scroope; but I think it is my duty to let you know the general opinion about here is that Mr Neville shall make Miss O'Hara his wife—if he has not done so already. The most dangerous feature in the whole matter is that it is all managed by the priest of this parish . . . ' (*Eye*, p. 68)

No doubt some duties are more enjoyable than others—the rapidity and energy with which Mary Quin writes gives us some indication of her character, even though she does not play more than a mechanical role in the working out of the plot. She certainly enjoys writing of events which could come out of a novel, but which happen a few miles from her doorstep. Her own boredom, caused by the family's poverty which cannot stretch to a London season each year, makes her a more energetic watchdog than she would otherwise have been. News of Kate's pregnancy was sent to Scroope 'with great rapidity', but because Fred is of good blood, the blame must not fall on him. Trollope, like Gaskell and Wilkie Collins, finds this phenomenon one of the most frustrating aspects of the fallen woman in society. Both Mary Quin and Lady Scroope never take the side of Kate:

According to her thinking it could not be the duty of an Earl of Scroope in any circumstances to marry a Kate O'Hara. There are women, who in regard to such troubles as now existed in Ardkill cottage, always think that the woman should be punished as the sinner and the man should be assisted to escape. The hardness of the heart of such women—who in all other views of life are perhaps tender and soft-natured—is one of the marvels of our social system. It is as though a certain line were drawn to include all women—a line, but, alas, little more than a line—by over-stepping which, or rather by being known to have overstepped it, a woman ceases to be a woman in the estimation of her own sex. (*Eye*, p. 157)

Trollope then repeats the argument for expulsion as a means of social control, which he admits and counteracts so well in *The Vicar of Bullhampton*:

That the existence of this feeling has a strong effect in saving women from passing the line, none of us can doubt. That its general tendency may be good rather than evil, is possible. But the hardness necessary to preserve the rule, a hardness which must be exclusively feminine but which is seldom wanting, is a marvellous feature in the female character. Lady Mary Quin probably thought but little on the subject.

Lady Scroope, like Mary Quin, accepts the 'valued custom of the magic line', but she has to battle with her own conscience which almost makes her rethink. The temptation is short lived. The sanctity of the realm of the pure can only be kept so by a united front. Trollope has his two ladies represent this united front against which Fred must do battle, and against which Kate has no hope. In their heart of hearts both upper-class women approve of a 'different code of morals for men and women. That which merited instant . . . [and] perpetual condemnation in a woman might in a man be very easily forgiven.' (*Eye*, p. 158) The reasons for this inequality are, no doubt, rather complex, but the fact that women do not have it in their power to ostracise men is one aspect of the problem which is straightforward.

The central conflict in the novel of passion versus duty is not one which is clear cut. It is often deliberately confused by Trollope himself in his presentation of his characters. Lady Quin, and to a greater extent Lady Scroope herself, have a passion for duty. They expect Fred to have a similar bent, whereas Fred's passion is for adventure and young ladies of particular charm, and especially for a combination of both. His aunt speaks of his duty in spiritual rather than social terms: 'The Lord God has placed you . . . You are here and must obey his decree; and whether it be a privilege to enjoy, you must enjoy it, or a burden to bear, you must endure it.' (*Eye*, p. 162) This self-sacrifice, however, is difficult for a young man's comprehension, especially if his passion is for something other than duty. His longing for Kate is the deciding factor early in the novel, and it seems that duty is to take second place in his life at least. When it is clear to him that he cannot have Kate as his wife, his title and his respectability, he hopes to solve the dilemma by passing the estate and its management to his brother, then wander the globe with a *de facto* wife who would keep him in romantic bliss for the rest of his life. He is quite determined early in the novel not to abandon Kate. Why then does he do so? The several reasons Trollope gives for his change of heart and mind make him one of the most fascinating of Trollope's heroes, and one of the most believable. It is not simply that he responds to external pressures from those around him to give up Kate. That would not be consistent with the presentation of his determined, self-willed nature. The arguments of his aunt do suggest a quasi-moral framework which he can use when he wishes to get out of the adventure, but the decision not to marry Kate comes from within his own character, not because he is a pawn to his aunt's wishes, or even his society's demands.

He makes several conflicting promises early in his adventure. He promises Kate he will marry her, after he promises his uncle that he will not. He promises the priest and Kate's mother that he will not hurt Kate, then promises himself a way out which can do little to save the girl's reputation. These promises germinate to grow into the basic conflict in Fred Neville, that of duty versus passion, and this then becomes the main theme of the novel. He spends little time musing over his dilemma, hoping, subconsciously that it will resolve itself:

> He knew that he had given a pledge to his uncle to contract no marriage that would be derogatory to his position. He knew also that he had given a pledge to the priest that he would do no harm to Kate O'Hara. He felt that he was bound to keep each pledge. As for that sweet, darling girl, would he not sooner lose his life than harm her? But he was aware that an adventurous life was always a life of difficulties, and that for such as live adventurous lives the duty of overcoming difficulties was of all duties the chief. Then he got into his canoe, and, having succeeded in killing two gulls in the Drumdeirg rocks, thought that for that day he had carried out his purpose as a man of adventure very well. (*Eye*, p. 63)

The ultimate plan of marrying but not marrying Kate, and leaving the running of the estate to his brother, is as ill conceived as it is naïve. It is almost a Lear-like abnegation of responsibilities, whilst keeping the benefits of the position. Jack, with good sense, becomes Trollope's moral voice in the novel by refusing to be party to the plan, and by insisting that he must marry Kate and bear the responsibility. Jack sees Fred's loyalty to Kate as being more pressing than his loyalty to his uncle. Fred is annoyed but not taken aback when the priest and Mrs O'Hara refuse to accept the plan, insisting that he must do as he promised and marry the girl legally. No one in the novel will allow him to solve the problem simply. It is when he finally realises this that he looks for a way out.

One of the aspects of his personality which foreshadows doom to their marriage is the tendency he has to look down on the girl he claims he loves. I suspect that this has as much to do with his change of heart, as does the discovery that there is no way out. He is ashamed of Kate's position in terms of class and wealth, yet he is attracted by the fact that she does not belong to the drawing-room society for which he has little time. From the beginning of their relationship his attitude towards her is never unequivocal, but his sexual desire and his love of romance overwhelm any subconscious criticism he might have of the girl's situation and station. While he is obsessed with her physical attractions his overt recognition of her social inferiority is repressed. As the difficulties resulting from the adventure surface so do the criticisms he feels towards her. He is a little ashamed of her education, not because he has evidence to support an argument that she is not well educated, but because he assumes that such a one as Kate would have to be poorly educated since her poverty and lack of status must take some sort of toll. In fact the opposite is true, but his pride refuses to see it, or cannot see it. Kate was educated in France before her father was imprisoned. She is probably far better educated than he, and certainly as gifted as Sophia Mellerby herself. Kate can write and speak French fluently. Her letters reflect her youth, but they are well-controlled and very well written. Fred may have been to an 'excellent' school but Trollope makes it clear that he lacks ability to use his native language with skill and subtlety. Her education, it is clear, has left her better off than Fred himself, yet 'he was a little ashamed of his Kate, and thought that Miss Mellerby might perceive her ignorance if he showed her letter . . . ' which he recently received from Ireland. In one of the few interviews with his uncle his deep-seated pride surfaces for a moment. He is embarrassed by Kate's ordinary standing:

'Are you willing to be known only as one of those who have disgraced their order?'

'I do not mean to disgrace it.'

'But you will disgrace it if you marry such a girl as that. If she were fit to be your wife would not the family of Lord Kilfenora have known her?'

'I don't think much of their not knowing her, uncle.'

'Who does know her? Who can say that she is even what she pretends to be? Did you not promise me that you would make no such marriage?'

He was not strong to defend his Kate. Such defence would have been in opposition to his own ideas, in antagonism with the scheme he made for himself. He understood, almost as well as his uncle, that Kate O'Hara ought not to be made Countess of Scroope. He too thought that were she to be presented to the world as the Countess of Scroope, she would disgrace the title. And yet he would not be a villain! And yet he would not give her up! He could only fall back upon his scheme. 'Miss O'Hara is as good as gold,' he said, 'but I acknowledge that she is not fit to be mistress of this house.' (*Eye*, p. 99)

Without this agreement the thoughts of his uncle and aunt would have remained impotent. Underneath the sexual attraction there exists the innate prejudices of his class, which mould the expectations, the desires and the actions of the thinker. So pride of place, *noblesse oblige*, duty and arguments which use them as evidence, carry weight in Fred's heart because he, in part, already agrees with them. That he is mentally inferior to Kate, and that he is too headstrong and proud to notice it, makes him the potential tragic hero. So-called superiority based on name, not nature, is as artificial a state to live by as is the public moral hypocrisy which accompanies it. The acceptance of pride of place is to provide Fred with the pragmatic argument he needs to leave the girl stranded whom he swore never to desert in the most Micawberian style. Unfortunately he does not have Mrs Micawber's heart. 'Birth does go for something . . ' Fred reminds the priest when that cleric pleads for the acceptance of O'Haras as 'ladies'.

Fred is fortunate in that he has the chance to appear injured when it is publicly known about Captain O'Hara's shady past on his return from the galleys. The young Lord Scroope has sufficient funds to pension the shell of a man, provided that he remains in France. Father Marty sees the return of Captain O'Hara as a disaster, because he senses it will give Fred an 'honourable' way out:

From that moment Father Marty said in his heart that Kate O'Hara had lost her husband. Not that he admitted for a moment that Captain O'Hara's return, if he had returned, would justify the lover in deserting the girl; but that he perceived that Neville had already allowed himself to entertain the plea . . .

But when he heard the words which Neville spoke and marked the tone in which they were uttered he felt that the young man was preparing himself a way of escape.

'I don't see that it should make any difference,' [Father Marty] said shortly.

'If the man be disreputable—'

'The daughter is not therefore disreputable. Her position is not changed.'

'I have to think of my friends.' (*Eye*, pp. 115-16)

When we witness the 'strange perversions' of which Fred's moral nature is capable we are not sorry when Mrs O'Hara plays God of the Old Testament by pushing Fred Neville off the cliff. In a metaphoric sense he was willing to do the same to Kate, not for his friends' sake but for his own. So he writes to his aunt in righteous terms assuring her that 'it is out of the question that he should marry the daughter of a returned galley slave'. He is sufficiently concerned about his aunt to put her mind at rest—no jury in the land, he is pleased to say, would find him guilty of breach of promise under the circumstances. The sad thing is that he is quite correct. 'After all,' he muses, 'he could not pollute himself by marriage with the child of so vile a father.' (*Eye*, p. 123) Very adeptly does he transform his need for an excuse into the most noble of terms. Duty can be, and is in Trollope's novel, a nice mask which hides the corrupt visage. 'Moralists might tell him that let the girl's parentage be what it might, he ought to marry her; but he was stopped from that, not only by his oath, but by the conviction that his highest duty required him to preserve his family from degradation.' (*Eye*, p. 128) The most horrifying aspect of all this is that he is quite convinced he is morally right—Trollope is fascinated by the depth of self-deception of which man is capable. So Fred comforts himself with the 'knowledge' that he would never have promised himself to the girl had he known about the father. He hangs on to this because he has nothing of more substance to buoy his faulty argument. His downfall has really happened before he is pushed off the cliff. As in most tragedies, the death is a confirmation of an earlier fall, as well as being the direct result of it. When he visits Ireland for the last time with the intention of ridding himself of the bothersome girl, he steels himself for the task by reflecting on his own greatness:

> he had to strengthen his courage by realising the magnitude of his own position. He made himself remember that he was among people who were his inferiors in rank, education, wealth, manners and nationality . . . He was still willing to sacrifice himself, but his family honours he would not pollute . . .
>
> And then as he made his way past the burial ground and on towards the cliff, there crept over him a feeling as to the girl very different from that reverential love which he had bestowed upon her when she was still pure. (*Eye*, pp. 178-9)

Trollope has the character unwittingly revealing the truth of the matter, but not noticing the truth for himself beyond an uneasy feeling at the bottom of his heart. There are three spheres of reference which Trollope feels important when considering the human being in the art of self-deception—the way others see it, the way the actor sees it and the way the reader sees it. Only the reader can approach the truth of the matter. This truth, however, is not simple, and requires another look at Fred's psychology.

There is no doubt that his early passion for Kate wanes. He is only willing to give her up once that happens. The moral argument and his sense of duty are adopted to fill the emotional gap left by the departure of his passion, or to counteract his subconscious feelings of guilt. Trollope again measures the change in Fred through his reaction to the wild cliffs and turbulent ocean.

> All the charm of the adventure was gone. He was sick of the canoe and Barney Morony. He did not care a straw for the seals or the wild gulls [he has tired of the hunt!]. The moaning of the ocean beneath the cliff was no longer pleasurable to him—and as to the moaning at their summit, to tell the truth, he was afraid of it. The long drive thither and back was tedious to him. He thought now more of the respectability of his family than of the beauty of Kate O'Hara. (*Eye*, p. 124)

The thrill of the romantic life no longer appeals to him—he accepts it for the dream it has been. As the youth dies, the youth of indiscretion, passion and vulnerability, the civilised man takes over.

He becomes, according to his aunt, well-disciplined; to Trollope, corrupt. But duty only wins by default when passion dies. Fred can only hear 'the melancholy moan of the waves, which he had once thought to be musical and had often sworn that he loved'. (*Eye*, p. 132)

His loss of passion for Kate, so adeptly handled by Trollope who reflects his inner changes by his responses to the wildness of nature, is bitterly ironic and, in one important sense, quite Victorian. Initially Kate is the displaced virgin in the tower; pure, unworldly, untouched, untainted—almost a vestige of the medieval Mary Cult which had its nineteenth-century revival in the figure of the pure, unworldly mother, or the spotless, untouched child-wife. Her attractions lay in her freshness, her unworldliness, her beauty and in her isolation from the London season. She was the ideal woman to be loved from afar by the questing knight. Unfortunately Fred only saw Kate as playing a part in the fantasy—his worship is not from afar; and the mere act of his despoliation changes her in his eyes. From the moment of loss of innocence she is no longer the object of worship:

> Alas, alas; there came a day in which the pricelessness of the girl he loved sank to nothing, vanished away, and was as a thing utterly lost, even in his eyes. The poor unfortunate one—to whom beauty had been given, and grace, and softness—and beyond all these and finer than these, innocence as unsullied as the whiteness of the plumage on the breast of a dove; but to whom, alas, had not been given a protector strong enough to protect her softness, or guardian wise enough to guard her innocence! To her he was godlike, noble, excellent, all but holy. He was the man whom Fortune, more than kind, had sent to her to be the joy of her existence, the fountain of her life, the strong staff for her weakness. Not to believe in him would be the foulest treason! To lose him would be to die! To deny him would be to deny her God! She gave him all—and her pricelessness in his eyes was gone forever. (*Eye*, pp. 108-9)

Fred, then, is Victorian enough in the worst sense to love purity and destroy it by loving it. The preservation of female purity is an essential aspect of the unreal Victorian dream—perhaps it is a subconscious admission of the corrupt nature of the male world. I am not quite sure. Certainly a consideration of the vision of the virgin wife, the pure mother and her antithesis, the fallen woman, is one way to have a glimpse at the depth of one aspect of the Victorian mind. Fred wants to have his cake and eat it—and, no doubt, many comfortable Victorian gentlemen who led double lives felt they managed to do this quite well. The Englishman's home is his castle. It is interesting that the place belongs to the medieval romance where life is often the ultimate quest for purity. Fred is one of the few who is caught by his own net. On first reading the novel I felt the climax on the cliff face to be melodramatic in the most negative sense—too contrived, too unlikely, too sensational. Whilst not entirely changing my mind, when reading the conversation below between Mrs O'Hara and Fred Neville, I am rather pleased that she does push him off the cliff:

> 'You would have her as your mistress then?' As she asked this the tone of her voice was altogether altered, and the threatening lion-look had returned to her eyes. They were now near the seat, confronted to each other, and the fury of her bosom, which for a while had been dominated by the tenderness of the love for her daughter, was again raging within her. Was it possible that he should be able to treat them thus—that he should break his word and go from them scathless, happy, joyous, with all the delights of the world before him, leaving them crushed into dust beneath his feet. She had been called upon from her youth upwards to bear injustice—but of all injustice surely this would be the worst. 'As your mistress,' she repeated—'and I her mother, am to stand by and see it, and know that my girl is dishonoured! Would your mother have borne that for your sister? How would it be if your sister were as that girl is now?'
>   'I have no sister.' (*Eye*, pp. 192-3)

Within that last sentence lies the cruel heart of a large and careless class, the bearers of a powerful male immorality which, to the incredulous modern reader, is the phenomenon which almost vindicates the most militant nineteenth-century suffragette and the most unbending twentieth-century feminist. Trollope, the most conventionally Victorian of writers in this study, for a moment justifies the murder of a careless, self-deceptive young man. More than that — he shifts the emphasis in the fallen-woman novel from the woman herself to the man responsible. His point is not directly stated by the author; his story does it for him—and powerfully: any fall in the female world is evidence of a fall in the male world. As Fred falls to his death, his destruction is even more tragic than Kate's. He has been given the potential to act: Kate's only gift is the potential to suffer.

Notes

1. Helen Heineman, *Mrs. Trollope: The Triumphant Feminine in the Nineteenth Century* (Athens, Ohio: Ohio University Press, 1979), p. 185.
2. Ibid., p. 215.
3. Mrs. Trollope, *Jessie Phillips: a Tale of the Present Day* (London: Colburn, 1843), pp. 252-3.
4. Anthony Trollope, *An Autobiography* (London: Oxford University Press, 1950), p. 33.
5. Ibid., p. 2.
6. Ibid.
7. Ibid., p. 301.
8. Ibid.
9. Michael Sadleir, *Trollope: A Commentary* (London: Constable, 1945), p. 401.
10. Trollope, *An Autobiography*, p. 329.
11. Ibid., p. 330.
12. Ibid., p. 225.
13. Donald Smalley (ed.), *Trollope: The Critical Heritage* (London: Routledge and Kegan Paul, 1969), p. 334.
14. Ibid., p. 335.
15. Unsigned notice, *Saturday Review*, 4 May 1870, xxix, 646-7, rpt in Smalley, *Trollope*, pp. 335-8.
16. Ibid., p. 335.
17. Ibid., p. 336.
18. Anthony Trollope, *The Vicar of Bullhampton* (London: Oxford University Press, 1940), p. 188. Subsequent quotes have their pagination marked in the body of the chapter.
19. Trollope, *An Autobiography*, p. 225.
20. Trollope, 'Preface', *The Vicar of Bullhampton*, p.v.
21. Ibid., p. vi.
22. Ibid.
23. Ibid.
24. Margaret Lane, 'Introduction', *Ruth* (London: J. M. Dent, 1967), p.v.
25. Trollope, 'Preface', *The Vicar of Bullhampton*, p. vi.
26. Beatrice Curtis Brown, *Anthony Trollope* (London: Arthur Barker, 1950), p. 16.
27. Ibid.
28. Ibid., p. 17.
29. Ibid.
30. Ibid.
31. Sir Walter Scott, *The Heart of Midlothian* (London: Collins, 1952), pp. 93-4.
32. Ibid., p. 111.
33. Ibid., p. 109.
34. Trollope, 'Preface', *The Vicar of Bullhampton*, p. vii.
35. Unsigned notice, *The Times*, 3 June 1870, p. 4, rpt in Smalley, *Trollope*, p. 338.
36. Smalley, *Trollope*, p. 445.
37. Ibid.

38. Ibid.

39. Derek Hudson (ed.), *Munby: Man of Two Worlds* (London: Abacus, 1974), p. 318.

40. Ibid., p. 309.

41. Ibid.

42. Ibid., p. 319.

43. Ibid., pp. 145-6.

44. Ibid.

45. Robert Tracy, *Trollope's Later Novels* (Berkeley: California University Press, 1978), p. 129.

46. Anthony Trollope, *An Eye for an Eye* (London: Anthony Blond, 1966), p. 9. Subsequent quotes will have their pagination marked in the body of the chapter.

47. Elizabeth Gaskell, *Ruth* (London: Everyman's Library, J. M. Dent, 1982), pp. 43-4.

48. George Eliot, *Adam Bede* (London: Collins, undated), p. 147.

49. Thomas Hardy, *Tess of the d'Urbervilles* (London: Pan Books in association with Macmillan, 1978), p. 23.

50. Eliot, *Adam Bede*, pp. 106-7.

51. Tracy, *Trollope's Later Novels*, pp. 129-30.

52. Trollope, *An Autobiography*, p. 41.

53. Unsigned notice, *Spectator*, 15 February 1879, lii, 210-11, rpt in Smalley, *Trollope*, p. 446.

54. Ibid., pp. 446-7.

4   MERCY

Like Mrs Gaskell, Wilkie Collins showed some interest in fallen women and their social survival, before he joined the Dickens circle. This interest coincided with his love of the theatre, for the first recorded public performance in which he took part was a fund-raising activity to benefit The Female Emigration Fund.[1] This charity provided the means for the relocation to the colonies of unfortunate women of the streets who desired a second chance. 'A Court Duel', the name of the play, was adapted by Collins from the French, then performed at a now ironic location, the Soho Theatre, on 26 February 1850. Collins's participation in the project may have been prompted more by his love of the theatre than by his concern for the fallen. This could be supported by the fact that fallen women do not play a noticeable part in his early fiction of the 1850s, or in his great fiction of the 1860s. It was to be the mature Collins of the 1870s who was sufficiently interested in fallen women to devote three major novels to their cause. There is every reason to suspect that his private life was, in part, responsible for the change. He created and supported at least two women who would have been seen by a certain section of middle-class society as fallen.

The first woman, known as Caroline Graves, lived with Collins from about 1866 to his death, with the exception of a brief period of one or two years when she was legally married to another man. That marriage did not last. She returned to Collins and was ultimately buried with him. Mrs Kate Perugini, Dickens's younger daughter, intimated on several occasions that Caroline was the original woman in white. This still remains unsubstantiated. Though he was not ashamed to mention his relationship to his closest friends, he was discreetly circumspect, rarely mentioning her in public.[2]

About the time of Caroline's marriage to a Joseph Clow, Collins formed a liaison with Martha Rudd, which was to lead to his illegitimate family; Martha changed her name to Mrs Dawson. They had three children, all acknowledged as such in Collins's will. To his close friends he was open about his 'intimacies', as the *Dictionary of National Biography* so termed his relationships, but never publicly.[3] That Dickens whole-heartedly accepted him as a friend, perhaps his closest friend for many years, would suggest

Dickens's private moral sense was more liberal than his public voice, even though on their first Continental Tour he complained of Collins's 'code of morals, taken from modern French novels, which I instantly, and with becoming gravity, smash'.[4] If Dickens's public and private voices were not quite one and the same, neither were Collins's. He was well aware of the public pressure which could be brought to bear on the women themselves. Liberal relationships could also affect the sale of numbers. Collins's private life would have continually kept the whole woman question to the forefront of his sensibility. In his three novels of the 1870s there exists a noticeable distrust of society, which is far more vehement than it is in Mrs Gaskell's poetic study of Ruth. He was very much closer to the problem. He did not share Mrs Gaskell's equivocal stance towards the heroine, whose overwhelming sense of guilt is vicariously shared by her creator, a minister's wife who could never quite decide whether the book was wicked or not. Although Collins works within the limits of contemporary conventions, he does not share Mrs Gaskell's discomfiture when vindicating his heroines, ultimately uniting them to very respectable husbands: Miss Silvester to the elderly but admirable lawyer, Sir Patrick Lundie, in *Man and Wife* (1870), Mercy Merrick to the liberal and aristocratic priest, Julian Gray, in *The New Magdalen* (1873), and Simple Sally to Amelius Goldenheart, the idealistic, young Christian Socialist from America, in *The Fallen Leaves* (1879).

All three follow *The Moonstone*, so are commonly classed as novels from Collins's elongated period of decline as a novelist. The first revival of critical interest in this century, led by Eliot, allows for this decline. The second revival produced the long-needed biographies of differing reliability and depth, the first and most impressive by Kenneth Robinson (1951), the second, a less comprehensive work by Robert Ashley (1952) and the third, a study by Nuel Parr Davies (1956). All three are unanimous in their general negative approach to Collins's fiction after 1870. A quick reading of the later works, timed to coincide with a rereading of *Woman in White*, makes it very difficult not to concur with the general critical opinion. None the less is it fair to say that critics deal with the later works all too briefly, often concentrating on that which is not there rather than that which is. In the twelve pages he allotted to all the novels after *Man and Wife*, Ashley expresses the opinion that these works 'are best considered collectively rather than individually'.[5] He feels this is justifiable on the grounds that from 1870 on Collins was 'unable to make up his mind just what kind of novelist he wanted to be, sensationalist or social critic, romanticist or realist, with the result that his fiction follows no consistent line of development'.[6] Surely this difficulty with generalisation, caused by the lack of a consistent line of development, is evidence to support the argument for a closer look at individual texts. The works are almost impossible to consider collectively, especially in twelve pages. Studies in the last decade continue the trend set by Ashley. William Marshall in *Wilkie Collins* (1970) tries to give the later works some individual attention, but can only give each novel one or two pages, because, once again, they are covered in one short chapter. The later works find themselves cramped in chapters which follow laudatory criticism of *Woman in White* and *The Moonstone*. The unavoidable comparison can lead to overstatement on the defects of the minor works, because they are just not like the major ones. Ashley concludes his few pages on the former insisting that 'Collins' status as a social critic is negligible for he lacked almost all the qualities needed by a purpose novelist'.[7] Whilst agreeing that his most impressive work comes before 1870, I take exception to this overstatement. It is time the minor works were treated as the subject of a major study, both their merits and their flaws being discussed at some length. In order to avoid a typical cramped discussion of the three fallen-women novels, I will concentrate on *The New Magdalen*. I give a brief discussion of the other two novels below, mainly to put *The New Magdalen* into Collins's perspective.

The Fallen Leaves was published with the title *The Fallen Leaves: First Series*, but the implied second series never eventuated. This is not surprising. The first series was the least popular of all Collins's works. Critical acclaim, or the lack of it, did not seem to worry Collins, being the independent soul he was, but he did on many occasions express his faith in the tastes and needs of his reading public. That public normally responded enthusiastically even when the critics did not. In this case he was wrong. *The Fallen Leaves* was never a success.[8] Part of the reason must lie in Collins's choice of hero. He is a perfectly nice, honourable young man, but he is so good that he is almost insufferable. His character is epitomised by his name, Claude Amelius Goldenheart. A young idealist from America, he rescues a very young prostitute who offers herself to him. Simple Sally is her name. Amelius falls in love with her and is freed from a previous engagement when Regina breaks it on discovering that Sally spent a night in the cottage of her fiancé.

Amelius and Sally marry, demonstrating that although Collins was unconventional and distrusted the norms and habits of the middle classes, he used the spirit of them to tidy the denouement of the novel.

Collins uses Amelius to symbolise reasonable, caring Christianity it its pure form rather than in its dogmatic shape. His upbringing in Illinois isolates him from the habitual social mores taught by the conventional Christian pragmatism of the old world. Collins hopes to expose the unfeeling double standards of his society which closes its eyes to the terrors of individual suffering, and he hopes to expose this through the incredulity of Goldenheart on being confronted with it. The ploy works to a certain extent. It is a pity that Amelius is not a little more human. He is too good to be true, too righteous to be Quixotic, and too naïve to be perspicacious. He is a character-type which the reader would never expect to exist, not even in the imagination. It is the presence of this character, who is supposed to be the mouthpiece of the writer, and the rather contrived plot, which leads Swinburne to point out that in

> *The Fallen Leaves* there is something too ludicrously loathsome for comment or endurance. The extreme clumsiness and infelicity of Wilkie Collins as a dramatic teacher or preacher may be tested by comparison with the exquisite skill and tact displayed by M. Alexandre Dumas in his studies of similar objects. To the revoltingly ridiculous book just mentioned I am loath to refer again: all readers who feel any gratitude or goodwill towards its author must desire to efface its miserable memory from the record of his works.[9]

If Swinburne had really been sincere about the latter I doubt that he would have mentioned the novel at all. His emotive terminology, which includes such phrases as 'revoltingly ridiculous', 'miserable memory', and 'extreme clumsiness', is sufficient to ensure that all who read his review will never fail to remember the novel and his opinion of it. Whilst the work does have flaws, and reasonably large ones, Sally saves it from being 'revoltingly ridiculous' on her own. Her presence makes the novel worth reading. She is a finely-drawn figure who is discovered in the novel as living between the world of her own youthful innocence and the world of prostitution. Necessity makes her a prostitute long before she can understand the ramifications or meanings of the sexual experience. Collins takes pains to ensure that her beauty is sullied by hunger and pain. She is not a very successful prostitute. Amelius meets her for the first time when being propositioned. The hero is surprised, both by the offer and by the enigma he discovers. If Collins is going to induce readers to change their minds about the women of the streets, then he has to paint a character with unexpected traits. The description in the following rather long passage is both the work of an adept artist, and a feeling humanitarian, that part of Collins's personality too often ignored:

> His heart ached as he looked at her, she was so poor and so young. The lost creature had, to all appearance, barely passed the boundary between childhood and girlhood—she could hardly be more than fifteen or sixteen years old. Her eyes, of the purest and loveliest blue, rested on Amelius with a vacantly patient look, like the eyes of a suffering child. The soft oval outline of her face would have been perfect if the face had been filled out; they were wasted and hollow, and sadly pale. Her delicate lips had none of the rosy colour of youth; and her finely modelled chin was disfigured by a piece of plaster covering some injury. She was little and thin; her worn and scanty clothing showed her frail youthful figure still waiting for its perfection of growth. Her pretty little bare hands were reddened by the raw night air. She trembled as Amelius looked at her in silence, with compassionate wonder. But for the words in which she had accosted him, it would have been impossible to associate her with the lamentable life that she led. The appearance of the girl was artlessly virginal and innocent; she looked as if she had passed through the contamination of the streets without being touched by it, without fearing it, or feeling it, or understanding it. Robed in pure white, with her gentle blue eyes raised to heaven, a painter might have shown her on his canvas as a saint or an angel; and the critic would have said, Here is the true ideal—Raphael himself might have painted this![10]

The two images of Sally present a meaningful comparison. The Sally of the London streets and the Sally of a Renaissance painting in turn describe the Sally of the present and the potential Sally. The choice of a painter from the Italian Renaissance is quite deliberate: the perfectibility of man, the beauty and nobility of the individual, the confidence of being the master of one's own fate; these are the most common themes in Renaissance art. Juxtaposing them with Sally's social fate stresses the difference between the social reality of Victorian England and ideal humanism. Despite the realisation of the social crisis, Collins still manages to include, in the passage above, faith in the innate potential of the individual. The ideals of the Renaissance may not lie in the social realities, but they still exist in the heart and soul of man. Sally is the physical expression of that faith, and so plays a symbolic role in the novel in addition to her literal one. She follows Amelius around, not as a lap dog, but as a constant reminder of what might be. The plainness and power of the description above, and the introduction to Sally's role in the novel (which it is) speak for themselves.

It could be argued that the passage quoted above is ludicrously sentimental—that the idealisation of Sally makes it impossible to accept her other than as a rather unearthly 'fallen angel'. There exists a subtle touch of realism, however, which makes the transition from prostitute to saint harder to accept. Her face is 'hollow'. Her hands are 'reddened by the raw night air'. Her chin is disfigured by a 'piece of plaster'. These touches of realism emphasise her humanness—the idealistic figure described is the figure she might have been.

Collins continues to discuss the innate nobility at the heart of man, by introducing two older prostitutes who know Sally. They overhear the short conversation between the two characters and come to Sally's aid when she faints from hunger and exhaustion. They give Amelius a short history of her life and a clarification of her social state, resting briefly, and almost nonchalantly, on the violence of Sally's pimp whom she eulogises as 'father'. One of these prostitutes refuses to take money from Amelius, insisting that Sally has the greater need. Collins uses Sally's attractive innocence and the nosy good-heartedness of her acquaintances to prove that virtue can lie in the unlikeliest of places. If these women are not quite credible, they are certainly admirably appealing. They embody Collins's love of humanity: 'All that is most unselfish, all that is most divinely compassionate and self-sacrificing in a woman's nature, was as beautiful and as undefiled as ever in these women—the outcasts of the hard highway!' (*The Fallen Leaves*, p. 187) In contrast to these outcasts, in which virtue and goodness can reside, the socially respectable like Mr Farnaby can be foul at heart. Mr Farnaby's crime of having his own child thrown out into the world to fend for herself, so that he can better his social position, is a constant reminder throughout the novel that social position and material wealth have little to do with goodness. The fact that Collins feels it necessary to write a didactic novel to make this point, and the fact that the comment was necessary at all, is, in part, a vindication of the work itself. Amelius is determined to help Sally no matter how ridiculous he appears in the eyes of the society around him. Wilkie does the same thing. He takes a stand which seeks to reverse narrow moral thinking on the so-called natural and inevitable corruption of the poor. Amelius is also like Collins when he ultimately prefers the girl he rescued to the conventionally virtuous Regina. The obsession with Sally is ironically described as 'innate depravity'. (*The Fallen Leaves*, p. 236) Rufus, Amelius's clumsy friend, tries to help Sally realise the inflexibility of the society around her, after she runs away from the cold comfort of the Refuge to which she is sent:

> 'But, you see, you have got the world about you to reckon with—and the world has invented a religion of its own. There's no use looking for it in this book of yours. It's a religion with the pride of poverty at the bottom of it, and a veneer of benevolent sentiment at the top. It will be very sorry for you, and very charitable towards you: in short, it will do everything for you except taking you back again.' (*The Fallen Leaves*, p. 327)

This could be considered a restatement of the theme of an earlier novel of Collins, *The New Magdalen*. It could be the similarity of theme which led to the later novel's unpopularity.

But the critics did not seem to object on these grounds. That they also did not object on moral grounds tells us something of the changing, broadening attitude towards treatment of the fallen. The first part of this change is discussed by Rufus in the speech above. The cold, open contempt for the fallen which threw them back on the streets because they deserved it, has been replaced by a cold, charitable smile, which has, none the less, the same stony heart behind the apparent kindness. The growth of the number of women's refuges is reflected in Collins's work. What Collins is angry about is the fact that these so-called charities worked against their professed aims. Membership of a refuge was a social stigma which was almost impossible to efface. A writer in the *Saturday Review*, for 2 August 1879, does not see the irony of this situation, nor does he complain about the lack of delicacy in treating the subject of the fallen woman. He complains about the veins of realism running through Collins's descriptive art:

> It will be noticed that Mr. Collins claims for himself . . . scrupulous delicacy only in certain parts of the story. Is he, we might ask him, scrupulously delicate when he describes the open mouth of the quartermaster of an American steamer 'from which the unspat tobacco-juice trickled in a little brown stream'? Where, in these days of word painting, as it is called, are we to draw the line?[11]

On the other hand the Dissenter-supported publication, *The British Quarterly Review* (October 1879) praises the delicacy of the novel, especially where the topic of prostitution is concerned.[12] *Ruth* was certainly a more discreet publication, but it raised a more terrible storm. The nature of the compliments and the complaints received by *The Fallen Leaves* points at least to a change in the critical voice as it responds to the treatment of the fallen. When introducing The Doughty Library edition of Trollope's *An Eye for an Eye*, Simon Ravel reminds the reader that the theme of the impregnation of a fatherless young girl by a young aristocrat, was only 'faintly daring'.[13] Trollope's novel was published in the same year as *The Fallen Leaves*, 1879. To a certain extent then, the novelists who dealt with the fallen, Dickens, Eliot, Gaskell and Collins, were changing people's minds. That Thomas Hardy found it necessary to write *Tess* nearly twenty years later, however, would suggest that the change in the critical voice did not reflect the internal, habitual workings of society. As it is, Collins's major thrust is to expose the inflexibility behind the façade of so-called Christian concern. 'Christian concern' widened the gulf between the virtuous and the rescued fallen women. In each of the three novels on fallen women, Collins juxtaposes the penitent fallen woman with the conventionally virtuous one. He makes the comparison such that the natural loyalty of the reader moves to the fallen woman. Sally's innocent simplicity, her faith in the hero who rescues her, her unworldly loyalty—all plead for her against the cold, calculating Regina who feels as she is meant to feel rather than because she is responding to her inner self. Sally is more loyal to herself when she follows the dictates of her heart. Collins studies exactly what moves his characters to action, and too often he shows them as members of a larger body, doing as that body would have them do, at the expense of individuality, and faith in the heart. Regina's decision to break off the engagement with Amelius is not really prompted by the dictates of her heart, or even her head. Convention makes the decision for her. What Sally and Amelius actually did or did not do in the cottage has nothing to do with the demands of convention. This seems to make her less a woman in the finer sense, and Sally more so. *Man and Wife* uses a similar pair of women to further the didactic aims of its author.

Man and Wife was the first of the three novels, being published in 1870. Unlike the future fate of the as yet unwritten *Fallen Leaves*, Mrs Oliphant acknowledged the popularity of the work which had been read by 'most readers of fiction'.[14] The rather complex plot revolves around the relationship between Anne Silvester and the athletic brute, Geoffrey Delamayn. On promise of marriage, Anne gives herself to Geoffrey, becomes pregnant, then finds herself deserted when Geoffrey decides that nothing can be gained from a marriage with someone who is little more than a governess. To avoid the responsibility, he tries to prove that Anne is actually married to his straightforward friend, Arnold Brinkworth. Because they spent a night at an hotel in Scotland, Geoffrey did have a case under the strange Scottish laws of marriage by common consent. Using the same marriage laws, Anne sacrifices herself by proving that she is actually married to Geoffrey. She does this to protect the new wife of Arnold, and the young man himself. Geoffrey takes Anne to his home where he imprisons her, then tries to murder her. His hatred is founded on the fact that he could not marry the rich, vain, youthful widow of an industrial magnate, Mrs Glenarm. It is this vain, selfish woman who is the foil to Anne. Whilst Anne is continually presented as the suffering victim who rarely feels sorry for herself, Mrs Glenarm is quite the reverse. She is vain, selfish and hollow. Her sexual attraction to Geoffrey is bravely, but delicately, drawn by Collins. She is the Temptress, the potentially promiscuous lover of physical man:

Mrs. Glenarm put out a little hand, ravishingly clothed, in a blush-coloured glove, and laid it on the Athlete's mighty arm. She pinched the iron muscles (the pride and glory of England) gently. 'What a man you are!' she said. 'I never met anybody like you before.' The whole secret of the power that Geoffrey had acquired over her was in these words.[15]

She is more interested in the sexual Geoffrey than vice versa. Collins obviously does not agree with one prevailing contemporary Victorian myth which held that women do not feel sexual desire. That is why the anonymous critic in the *Saturday Review* (9 July 1870) could not understand how the noble, self-sacrificing, sensitive and modest Miss Silvester could be the type of woman who would have illicit sexual intercourse with an obviously attractive man.[16] The article implies that sexuality is the opposite of sensitivity and innate nobility. Collins does not feel it necessary at any time in the novel to apologise for the sexual relationship between Anne and Geoffrey, which takes place before the action of the novel opens. The review is also rather petty. Geoffrey stands as the candidate for a rather important inter-county foot race. The critic claims that Mr Delamayne weighing 'at least thirteen stone . . . was by no means the man for a four mile race'.[17] What the review does not point out is that Geoffrey nearly dies in the process of trying to run. This accident would seem to vindicate Collins's handling of the character. The portrayal of Geoffrey as a self-confident boor, who does not know his own limitations, seems consistent with his conception in the novel, and his role in the plot. By making this man attractive to both types of women, Collins can openly write on the results of sexuality as power. It is not surprising that Ruth is never presented as a sexual creature at all by Mrs Gaskell, though Bellingham certainly is. Collins is more of the sensualist. One of the powerful episodes in the novel is when the two women who are connected with Geoffrey meet. Sympathy is on one side only;

> Mrs. Glenarm rose from the piano. The two women—one so richly, the other so plainly dressed; one with beauty in its full bloom, the other worn and blighted, one with society at her feet, the other an outcast living under the bleak shadow of reproach— the two women stood face to face, and exchanged . . . cold courtesies . . . (*Man and Wife*, p. 304)

The irony is that their sexuality gives them something in common, although Anne's is in the past, and Mrs Glenarm's is to be fulfilled in the future. The double standards of the Victorian sexual enigma are also close to the heart of Collins's complaint. Anne bears all the negative results of the relationship. She is expelled from society because of it. She has to watch the death of her own child in a shady hotel room while the father courts a rich widow. Anne also has to bear the shame of realising her attraction to Geoffrey was a physical infatuation. After Geoffrey's timely death Anne is rewarded with marriage to Sir Patrick Lundie. The non-sexual nature of the union points to another of the contradictions which underlie the resolution of the conflict in Collins's fallen-women fiction. Although the marriage could well be seen as more ritualistic than actual, it represents the return to a unified society, the true acceptance and integration of a penitent woman. It does feel a little disappointing, none the less. It seems a pity that Collins feels he must resolve the conflict of the novel on society's terms, especially when it is realised that he despised the norms and habits of that very same society. He was to be unconventional, only within selling limits. Often the business head won.

The juxtaposition of the two women is sometimes lost in the web of action which is characteristic of the plot of *Man and Wife*. By endowing *The New Magdalen* with a surprisingly simple plot, the comparison of the truly penitent fallen woman and the conventionally virtuous woman becomes the central concern of the novel. With more craft than in the other two novels, Collins manipulates the reader's reaction to the whole moral question of responding to the supposed existence of only two types of women.

Mercy Merrick, a woman who is beguiled into prostitution in the first place, manages to leave her so-called Refuge in London, and take up a nursing position on the continent, during the Franco-Prussian War. She has made several attempts in the past to re-enter society, but has been rejected once her past becomes common knowledge. Mercy meets the recently bereaved Grace Roseberry at the front. Her father, and only relative, has just died in Italy. She is travelling to England to take up the post of companion to a certain Lady Janet Roy. An unfortunate, but hardly surprising, explosion lodges a small piece of metal in Miss Roseberry's skull. She appears dead, so Mercy adopts her name, returns to England, and presents herself to Lady Janet Roy. She is welcomed by the whole Roy circle, becoming engaged to Horace Holmcroft, a friend of the family's, who actually helps Mercy when she leaves the continent. The reader is informed that Grace is not dead, as soon as Mercy leaves for England. A German doctor operates on her, ultimately leaving her free to return to England to claim her place. The plot is very simple indeed. Only one other character needs introducing.

When Mercy was an inmate of the Refuge, a young Anglican clergyman gave her hope at a time when she was close to despair.

Julian Gray, the priest in question, happens to be Lady Janet's nephew, and Horace's very good friend. Julian falls in love with Mercy, whilst his presence reminds her of her wicked lie. He also looks after Grace when she returns to England, thinking her a poor, deluded creature. As in most didactic fiction one character speaks for the author more than others. In this case the spokesman for Collins is Gray, who articulates Collins's appeal for pure Christian concern, much as did Benson in *Ruth*, and as Amelius was going to do later.

Collins's control of the plot, however, speaks more powerfully for reform than do the overt comments he makes through Gray's character. The initial presentation of Grace and Mercy, and the manner in which they are shown as the novel develops, does a great deal to shape the reaction of the reader. It is only on a second reading of the work that one becomes aware of Collins's manoeuvring which affects the reader's reaction to the women. Ennobling Mercy, and minimising our sympathy for the isolated Grace, is his first task in the novel. It is essential that he forces us to react favourably towards Mercy, and not quite so favourably towards Grace. It is on this foundation that he will ultimately build the case which will support Mercy. The two women enter the novel together:

> The nurse led the way—tall, lithe and graceful—attired in her uniform dress of neat black stuff, with plain linen collar and cuffs, and with the scarlet cross of the Geneva Convention embroidered on her left shoulder. Pale and sad, her expression and her manner both eloquently suggestive of suppressed suffering and sorrow, there was an innate nobility in the carriage of this woman's head, an innate grandeur in the gaze of her large grey eyes, and in the lines of her finely proportioned face, which made her irresistibly striking and beautiful, seen under any circumstance and clad in any dress. Her companion, darker in complexion and smaller in stature, possessed attractions which were quite marked enough to account for the surgeon's polite anxiety to shelter her in the captain's room. The common consent of mankind would have declared her to be an unusually pretty woman . . . The languor of her movements, and the uncertainty of tone in her voice, as she thanked the surgeon, suggested that she was suffering from fatigue.[18]

Mercy is the more interesting of the two. We are fortunate to be able to glimpse inside her personality for a brief moment. The 'pale and sad' eyes are windows to internal suffering, a suffering which does not detract from her innate grandeur and nobility of spirit. On the contrary, it adds to it. She is not only beautiful and graceful, she is 'irresistibly striking', and is so partly because of that brief glimpse of the internal dimension. The mystery about that suffering adds to the intrigue. Even though we discover that she has been a prostitute we have no idea how that came about until the end of the novel.

On the other hand, Grace is a rather flat character, though an attractive one. Her beauty attracts the French surgeon, but we do not know what there is about her which makes it so. The 'common consent of man' which would have declared her attractive, is a rather guarded compliment. Any reader of Collins would realise that the power of 'common consent' is to be neither trusted nor admired. Collins subtly intimates that whilst he understands what makes her attractive, he does not share the enthusiasm. She is a rather indefinite character. Her voice is 'uncertain', her movements 'languid'. She relies on the nurse for protection, weakening her status as a result. Mercy's uncertainty is the secret she holds in her heart. It is that and her suffering which make her fascinating. Grace's uncertainty is at the base of her inability to arrest our attention. She simply comes to our notice. There is little doubt, after reading the passage above, that Mercy has captured the loyalty and heart of her creator.

Collins's reasons for his choice of setting in the early part of the novel become clear when we realise that he is trying to mould our reaction to Mercy's character. The war-front certainly gives him the opportunity to have Grace killed, then brought back to life. It also gives him a chance to show Mercy off at her best. Grace is relieved at her rescue, then frightened when her safety is threatened by the German shelling. This is quite understandable. Mercy, however, does not show any selfish signs at all, and looks to the welfare of others. Grace is quite relieved to have the French surgeon's help to escape. Escape means less to Mercy than the welfare of the wounded men she tends. Mercy remains with the sick, putting her welfare last.

> She was thinking of the helpless men in the inner chamber, and she quietly recalled the surgeon to a sense of his professional duties . . . Monsieur Serville shrugged one shoulder—the shoulder that was free. (Grace was clinging to the other.) (*The*

New Magdalen, p. 24)

The judgement of the wounded French soldier is borne out by Mercy's action. 'Madame', he said, 'you are sublime!' (*The New Magdalen*, p. 24) The fallen woman is capable of sublimity; the virtuous woman is weak and selfish. Even though the latter is understandable in the war-torn circumstances, it is still difficult not to be mildly judgemental when the actions and attitudes of the two women are placed side by side.

Although Mercy's heroic nature is important to Collins's presentation of her character, he deliberately makes her paradoxical by stressing her internal fears and weaknesses. The paradoxical picture of strength and weakness, vulnerability and dynamism, energy and apathy, makes her far more than a character type. Collins highlights the negative, suffering aspects of her personality simply by describing the habit she has of shrinking away from those she feels are socially pure. Before Mercy tells her story to Grace she fears to be close to the traveller. This is not because she does not want to be close to a fellow human being, but because she knows they do not want to be close to her for fear of contamination. Mention of Canada by Grace makes Mercy start. It is the scene of one of her former rejections, so on the reminder, 'she shrank back into her corner'. (*The New Magdalen*, p. 10) The unenlightened Grace wishes to shake hands shortly after this, but 'Mercy shrank back'. (*The New Magdalen*, p. 12) The physical placing of Mercy in the room captures the essence of her habitual alienation from fellow creatures. On making her admission to Grace, the latter is told to move her 'chair a little farther away'. (*The New Magdalen*, p.1 5) When Mercy's tale does proceed, the shocked listener moves her chair and places it at a 'safe and significant distance from the chest' (*The New Magdalen*, p. 17) on which Mercy sits. The movement in the room, the corners and dark places which Mercy feels appropriate at the time, both become symbols which capture, in the simplest manner, Mercy's plight. Her alienation is such that she must continually turn within, shrinking into her own misery and loneliness. The movement of the chairs within the room, a movement which is initiated by Mercy herself, then carried out by Grace, is an ideal situation for exposing the fear Mercy has of the society which rejects her, and the suspicion that society feels towards her. The fire in the room dies as the conversation proceeds, and as the possibility of reciprocal human communication dies as well. The room is left, as is the whole society, in darkness:

> 'I am accustomed to stand in the pillory of my own past life. I sometimes ask myself if it was my fault. I sometimes wonder if Society had no duties toward me when I was a child selling matches in the street—when I was a hard-working girl, fainting at my needle for want of food . . . Society can subscribe to reclaim me—but Society can't take me back.' (*The New Magdalen*, p. 15)

This same line, almost to a word, was to appear in *The Fallen Leaves* several years later. It was obviously the grand irony which angered the writer. He could never forgive the generous hand which was extended from a cold heart. Collins's bitterness, at times not well controlled in the novel, is subtly and effectively conveyed in the early part of the book. He plays with this sense of irony by having Mercy Merrick actually save Grace Roseberry when she is between two armies, with no luggage, horses, or money. Despite the obvious debt Grace has to pay, she is 'simply embarrassed' by the sad story, and shocked by the revelation that Mercy would dare to think of having tender feelings towards a member of the clergy who saved her from despair.

The sermon which saved her is based on the assurance from Luke 15, 7 that 'Joy shall be in Heaven over one sinner who repenteth, more than over ninety and nine just persons which need no repentance.' (*The New Magdalen*, p. 19) Society's ways are not heavenly. This is exactly what Collins is trying to say through his characters and his plot, whilst being rather detached himself. Early in the novel the moral reformer and the story teller have achieved an acceptable synthesis. The contemporary claim, and one echoed by modern critics, is that Collins was not capable of this synthesis.[19] Nor does this early part of the work seem to fit the terse opinion Swinburne expressed on *The New Magdalen* which he thought 'merely feeble, false and silly in its sentimental cleverness'.[20]

Collins's subtle control of our reaction continues throughout the novel. When Mercy carries out her lie we tend not to condemn her because of the suffering she undergoes as a result. I would go so far as to suggest that the workings of her conscience provide the major, and most interesting, conflict within the story. Collins certainly feels Mercy is almost correct when she assumes the new identity. After all, it seems the only way in which a fallen woman may find acceptance in respectable society, and marry within conventional circumstances. Collins's heroine, however, cannot agree with her creator. She cannot rationalise her lie with a pragmatic coldness, despite her efforts to do so. On making the decision to impersonate Grace, Mercy avoids facing her conscience, as she shrinks from other people. 'She had decided, and yet she was not at ease; she was not quite sure of having fairly questioned her conscience yet.' (*The New Magdalen*, p. 39) Despite her immediate and great success at Mablethorpe House, a success we discover as soon as we cross from the war front to Kensington, she cannot enjoy the luxury or the respectability. The real war of the novel starts, her battle within, her 'secret remorse'. She lived 'under the slow torment of self-reproach'. (*The New Magdalen*, p. 60) The irony is typical of Collins: Mercy spends all of her adult years rejected by the world around her. The minute she is accepted by that world which has treated her so badly, she rejects herself. She is the forerunner to the modern outsider. It is the confusion into which her mental agony throws her which makes it impossible to reject Horace's pressing proposal of marriage. Whilst she accepts him she knows in her heart that the union can never be. Her conscious self feels that it would kill her to tell the truth, her subconscious self knows that not telling is doing the same thing. She has every characteristic of the conventional tragic hero latent in her personality and her situation. Instead of wishing for death as a release from the fallen state, as Ruth, Hetty Sorrell, and Little Em'ly all did at one time or another, Mercy hopes for it as an escape from the lie of her respectability. This is yet another reversal Collins presents in dramatic terms.

She continues to shrink from those who care for her, the most obvious trial coming from the man who saved her from despair in the Refuge in days gone by, Julian Gray. It is difficult totally to equate Julian's voice with that of Collins. When Julian is determined that Mercy ought to tell the truth no matter what the consequences may be, one wonders if Collins agrees. He stresses Lady Janet's need to have Mercy in her household, even though she is by then aware of her past, and her lie. None the less it is Mercy who shapes her own fate, especially when she feels a strong moral tie with Julian. She fears that she cannot lie to him, that it is not in her power:

> Could she deceive him as she had deceived others? Could she meanly accept that implicit trust, that devoted belief? Never had she felt the base submission which her own imposture con-

demned her to undergo, with a loathing of them so overwhelming as the loathing that she felt now. In horror of herself, she
turned her head aside in silence, and shrank from meeting his
eye. (*The New Magdalen*, pp. 190-1)

At the very worst, Collins sees his heroine as a good woman who
sins, not a sinful woman who is basically corrupt and bad. Her
imperfection makes her human and miserable.

It is the treatment of the lie which characterises the difference
between Collins's stance and that of Mrs Gaskell. In the chapter on
Ruth it can be seen that the lie was a grave sin in the Bensons' minds,
in Ruth's own conscience it remained so, and in the writer's own
moral sense it was so. With such a consensus it iunnot surprising that
Ruth must suffer. Her rise cannot take place until her lie is expiated.
Mercy is as hard on herself. In a sense, she is more alienated than
Ruth whose guilty secret was shared by three others. Ruth also had
the comfort of Lionel's upbringing. Mrs Gaskell's moral voice,
however, is unequivocal; Collins's is not so unbending. Like Ruth,
Mercy does rise through her ultimate openness. Julian affirms her
nobility; sees morality in absolute terms. There is another vein
which runs through the novel which pleads for the relativity of
morality. I have already mentioned the determination of Lady Janet
to accept Mercy despite her knowledge of the truth. In addition to
this, Grace Roseberry's whole position in the novel helps Collins to
express his sense of the ralativity of truth and mortality.

Our dislike for Grace lies in the threat she poses to the heroine.
She personifies righteous pride and bitter revenge, and, strangely
enough, conventional truth. She is, in conventional terms, morally
justified, and quite correct when she seeks to gain that which is her
right. Her presence is distasteful to all at Mablethorpe House.
Although she is scrupulously honest, Collins takes every opportunity to make her the very essence of unpleasantness. On the
second meeting of the two women in the novel, Mercy faints. Grace
reacts in 'savage triumph'. (*The New Magdalen*, p. 132) Despite the
efforts of those in the house, the evicted Grace manages to return.
Her contact with Mercy is undertaken with 'vindictive pleasure'.
(*The New Magdalen*, p. 179) She waits in 'sinister silence'. (*The
New Magdalen*, p. 214) When Mercy finally looks as if she is about
to tell the truth Grace 'could feel no pity' and 'could spare no
insolence of triumph'. (*The New Magdalen*, p. 217) She is described
as having 'viperish eyes'. (*The New Magdalen*, p. 228) Grace insults

Mercy by telling the truth, but it is only the truth as she sees it. She is only technically correct in Collins's eyes, but she represents everything that is evil and vindictive. When she tells the truth as she sees it, the reader has to accept that she is, in part, wrong. Mercy is not 'one shameful brazen lie from head to foot!' (*The New Magdalen*, p. 218) Grace is theoretically right, but she is devilish. For a while in the novel we are almost suspended in a moral no-man's land which forces the reappraisal of what is moral and what is not. Collins's denouement relies on the confession and the marriage of Mercy, both tenets of middle-class values he dislikes. There exist three different moralities in the novel—the conventional moral voice which claims that Grace is right; there is a morality of the head, and a morality of the heart. Ironically, Grace is the one who captures most effectively the moral confusion which exists through the presentation of the plot: 'The truth itself turns liar, and takes *her* side'. (*The New Magdalen*, p. 138) Lady Janet is forced to reconsider her whole attitude to right and wrong, once she realises what Grace means. She rejects conventional stands and opts for a new morality of the heart: 'Not a living creature in this house shall say she has deceived me. She has not deceived me—she loves me! What do I care whether she has given me her true name or not? She has given me her true heart.' (*The New Magdalen*, p. 294) It is the tainting of traditional absolutes of morality, loyalty and truth which may have led Matthew Arnold to admit that *The New Magdalen* was his favourite sensation novel.[21] Edmund Yates, sensing the equivocal moral stand in the work, did not agree with Arnold. The following extract from Yates's review is a good example of the habit of superimposing conventional moral sensibilities on a situation to which they are not relevant. He feels Julian's physical attraction to Mercy ruins the moral of the story. He implies that the idea is dirty, and that good novels must not reflect feelings which living characters do have:

> we feel that it is Mercy Merrick's beautiful figure and 'grand head' which constitute her saving grace, and influence Julian Gray, and this conviction kills the moral of the story at once. The author's pen was too human for his theme.[22]

If Collins pays lip service to the spirit of the middle-class myth by marrying the heroine to the hero, there is more evidence to suggest that he felt ill at ease with the society which expected such conclusions. He ends his novel with a scathing attack on the habits of that society, in the form of Horace, Grace and their class, making an exception of Lady Janet Roy, whose continual association with Mercy makes her mad in the eyes of the righteous. Grace speaks the truth again when she reminds the company around her that 'Christian charity has its limits'. (*The New Magdalen*, p. 281) These limits have been exposed in the novel in the symbol of the Refuge. The name is horribly ironic. The Refuge is little more than a prison, a stigma which ruins lives; Mercy sees the terms 'refuge' and 'despair' almost as synonymous. Even escape to the colonies is a questionable move—the past follows Mercy to Canada. This was the most fashionable way to help fallen women to re-enter some sort of society. There was little real chance of discovery in the colonies. Many of the type who followed Little Em'ly to Australia did find a new life. The shadowy Martha from the same novel marries. I do not think Collins really wishes to argue that relocation in the colonies is a useless activity. What he stresses in *The New Magdalen* is that it is English society which needs to reform, and if it claims to be Christian, that Christianity ought not to be of the limited type Grace nominates and, indeed, represents. She is the cold, judgemental spirit of the Old Testament. The very names of the homes for fallen women reflect this spirit which Collins detested. He chose the name Refuge for its ironic bite. Others include The London Female Penitentiary, The Home for Penitent Women, and The British Penitent Female Refuge.[23] That no homes exist for fallen men should be an obvious fact to highlight the unfairness which makes Collins so angry in his three novels on fallen women. There is every reason to argue that the distinct need for reform vindicates Collins's lack of tact. The criticisms of Swinburne, though their subjectivity suggests they ought to be termed otherwise, do not seem to allow for the social problems these women had to face if they wished to have anything to do with the middle or upper classes. In the novels at hand Collins declines to forgive society at all. The Epilogue of *The New Magdalen* studies the need for change. On one hand is Janet Roy; on the other is Horace and the rest of the world. The latter have the numbers.

The Epilogue is composed of the correspondence of Grace and Horace, and diary extracts written by Julian Gray. Mercy has returned to the Refuge when the Epilogue opens. She intends to work with homeless children. Lady Janet is re-evaluating her position, especially when Julian pleads with her to intercede on his behalf for Mercy's hand. Grace has returned to her friends in Canada. The letters of Horace and Grace hint at a potential romance. They are united in their inflexibility, their blindness and their mutual hatred of Mercy. They are far away indeed from Collins's true Christian:

> The true Christian virtue is the virtue which never despairs of a fellow-creature. The true Christian faith believes in man as well as God. Frail and fallen as we are, we can rise on the wings of repentance from earth to heaven. Humanity is sacred. Humanity has its immortal destiny. Who shall dare say to man or woman, 'There is no hope in you'? (*The New Magdalen*, pp. 192-3)

Grace and Horace look on in horror at the hope shared by Lady Janet, Julian and Mercy. They can only explain Lady Janet's efforts at reconciliation as at best indiscreet and at worst, madness and senility. Horace's stand is tied up in the self-preservation of his class which he feels is being deserted by Lady Janet, and even more by Julian who wishes to marry a prostitute. Love does not enter his head when he considers the purity of blood of the aristocratic family. He remonstrates with Lady Janet on this basis. She reminds him that an individual's goodness is far more important than his or her history, or his class. This heart-felt religion, new to Lady Janet, is regarded by Horace as a 'decay of principle' or a 'decay of mental powers'. (*The New Magdalen*, pp. 379-80) He even writes that he may have to take steps to ensure that Lady Janet's senility does not interfere with the management of the estate. The threat is fleeting but there. As Julian must remain an outsider for marrying Mercy, Lady Janet comes under threat for supporting them. It is the old story: people who do not agree with convention must be seen as outsiders. It is the only way to preserve the *status quo*. So the marriage is, according to Mrs Holmcroft, 'An Outrage on Society'. Collins would agree, but he would see such outrages as the only way to save society from itself, and from its morality which has self-preservation at heart rather than justice for mankind. Horace's stand is vindicated by his society when members of it come to the reception Lady Janet holds for the engaged couple.

Because Lady Janet has had great social influence society does attend the ball, but no single daughters arrive. The novel opens with Grace's refusal to shake Mercy's hand. The novel closes with many people doing so with their teeth gritted and their smiles fixed. The unspoken fear for the contamination of their daughters speaks in louder terms than their polite smiles, and their healthy appetites. Lady Janet fails to lead society to a more enlightened stance. Julian's diary has the last word. He sees through the thin veneer of civilisation which hides the coarse heart: 'I really had no adequate idea of the coarseness and rudeness which have filtered their way through society . . . The days of prudery and prejudice are days gone by. Excessive amiability and excessive liberality are the two favourite assumptions of the modern generation.' (*The New Magdalen*, p. 401) When Ruth is discovered by the folk of her town she is a total outcast, but for the Bensons who keep her. Mercy, and the Ruths of her day, had a place provided—the Refuge. It was unfortunate that that place of separation and disgrace hid behind the conventional Christian arm of charity. It is this which the novel condemns as 'civilised human nature in its basest conceivable aspect'. (*The New Magdalen*, p. 402)

The New Magdalen, Man and Wife and The Fallen Leaves all show the selfish crimes, the political manoeuvrings, the thoughtless habits, the misuse of the purest forms of worship and the careless self-preservation of the middle and upper classes in England during the last century. In *The New Magdalen*, the Epilogue proves that Collins knew his reform novel would not change society. Society is too nebulous, too unyielding, too morally inbred. He is content to see the change in Julian, Lady Janet Roy and, hopefully, in his reader. The fallen-women novels of Wilkie Collins tell us a great deal about the women who are their subjects. They do, however, tell us more about the society around them. That fact alone makes them well worth reading, and more important than they have been taken to be since their publication.

Notes

1. Kenneth Robinson, *Wilkie Collins: A Biography* (London: The Bodley Head, 1951), p. 53.
2. Ibid., p. 131.
3. Ibid., p. 135.
4. Ibid., p. 82.
5. Robert Ashley, *Wilkie Collins* (London: Arthur Barker, 1952), p. 113.
6. Ibid.
7. Ibid., p. 121.
8. Robinson, *Wilkie Collins*, p. 291.
9. Algernon Charles Swinburne, 'Wilkie Collins', *Fortnightly Review*, 1 November 1889, n.s. cclxxv, 589-99, rpt in Norman Page (ed.), *Wilkie Collins: The Critical*

Heritage (London: Routledge and Kegan Paul, 1974), p. 261.

10. Wilkie Collins, *The Fallen Leaves* (London: Chatto and Windus, 1893), pp. 185-6. Subsequent pagination will be marked in the body of the chapter.

11. Unsigned review, *Saturday Review*, 2 August 1879, xlviii, 148-9, rpt in Page, *Wilkie Collins*, p. 206.

12. Page, Introduction, *Wilkie Collins*, p. 27.

13. Anthony Trollope, *An Eye for an Eye* (London: Anthony Blond, 1966), p. x.

14. Mrs Oliphant, *Blackwood's Magazine*, November 1870, rpt in Page, *Wilkie Collins*, p. 188.

15. Wilkie Collins, *Man and Wife* (London: Chatto and Windus, 1892), p. 235. Subsequent pagination will be marked in the body of the chapter.

16. Unsigned review, *Saturday Review*, 9 July 1870, xxx, 52-3, rpt in Page, *Wilkie Collins*, p. 184.

17. Ibid., p. 185.

18. Wilkie Collins, *The New Magdalen* (London: Chatto and Windus, 1893), p. 7. Subsequent pagination will be marked in the body of the chapter.

19. See unsigned review, *Spectator*, 15 May 1880, liii, 627-8, rpt in Page, *Wilkie Collins*, p. 207.

20. Swinburne, 'Wilkie Collins', p. 261.

21. Robinson, *Wilkie Collins*, p. 261.

22. Edmund Yates, 'The Novels of Wilkie Collins', *Temple Bar*, August 1890, lxxxix, 528-32, rpt in Page, *Wilkie Collins*, p. 277.

23. Phillip Collins, *Dickens and Crime* (Bloomington: Indiana University Press, 1962), p. 105.

5 IDA STARR

In many ways *The Unclassed* has a very special relationship with the life of its creator which makes a combined biographical and textual study of the work quite rewarding. Not only does this critical approach help to explore the novel's complex and elusive meaning, it also provides momentary glimpses into Gissing's personality, glimpses which would not be seen if his life and work were studied in isolation. Not only is Gissing's art enigmatic—his personality certainly was, to the man himself, to his contemporaries and to his small but avid readership which is now one hundred years old. That the concern of the novel centres on the fallen woman is fortunate for the purposes of this study. Gissing is the closest of all Victorian novelists to fallen women, in the sense that he married one who was a prostitute. Collins writes of his fallen women out of moral outrage, late in life when his poor health makes the concern a theoretical one, and certainly not a sexual one. Gissing, on the other hand, writes of his fallen women when he is still young, and at the very time when he is trying to sort out his personal problems, both of a sexual and philosophic nature. In any case a study of the problems faced by nineteenth-century women which did not include Gissing could well be considered delinquent in ignoring his exploration and understanding of the subject.

The Unclassed was written when the young novelist was recovering from his first traumatic marriage. He was then separated from Nell, the woman he had married in 1879 and who was more formally known as Marianne Helen Harrison. His turbulent relationship with Nell was brought about by breaking several taboos: he looked seriously upon the prostitute with whom he was having sexual intercourse instead of treating her flippantly as was the norm; he stole from fellow students at Owens College, Manchester, in an effort to provide the funds to save her from prostitution; he married a prostitute; he married a working-class girl when he was obviously from another class. Enlightened or iconoclastic members of Victorian society may well have been able to come to grips with one or two of Gissing's rebellious acts, but it would take a radical mind indeed to cope with them all. If they could accept the sexual freedom, the interclass marriage and the open liaison with a prostitute, they may have had more trouble coping with the ethical revision necessary before the theft could be seen as an acceptable form of behaviour. Even Gissing himself had a lifetime of doubt and sorrow and guilt, all tied up in what was to become one of his closely guarded secrets, all of which were related to the crime and the punishment which followed in jail. He was trapped by a combined faculty/police plan, which was set up to catch the thief in the students' common room, and was apprehended in the middle of the act itself. Several obvious questions come to mind: why did he have a protracted relationship with someone like Nell?; why did the relationship fail, and fail traumatically for him?; why did he shortly follow the final separation with a novel like *The Unclassed* which idealises a fallen woman in the form of Ida Starr?; what does the text of that novel tell us about the writer, and what information does it provide for someone interested in the lot of the fallen woman? It is the task of this chapter to answer, or to try to answer, these questions.

Jacob Korg argues in his well-known critical biography of George Gissing that the relationship cannot be explained away by suggesting it was the result of youthful folly, or related to the common (and tacitly accepted) middle-class habit of sowing a few wild oats. Korg sees Gissing as someone who was never

> too young to be dutiful and conscientious. The sense of duty instilled by his upbringing in the puritanical environment of a north-of-England manufacturing town had been reinforced by his success in the conservative atmosphere of his schools. He was certainly no hypocrite. He took Victorian propriety seriously, and he earnestly tried to make himself an example for his younger brothers and sisters. Even minor breaches of conduct tortured him with remorse, and he was capable of suffering agonies over imagined faults. Yet his crime did not represent a sudden shattering of his youthful inhibitions. Gissing never became the sort of person who conscientiously acts upon pure desire. He would have examined his motives closely, using all of his fine student's intellect to rationalize the conduct into which he was being forced.[1]

At first sight this seems reasonable enough, but it does not leave the reader without some begging questions. In what ways was he 'forced' into stealing, and into the relationship in the first place? I am not sure that I find the Gissing-as-victim supposition quite convincing, nor does the fact that he was a fine student with a lively mind and a sharpened intellect mean he was incapable of making emotionally charged decisions. And his so-called puritanical up-bringing did not stop him forming the liaison with the prostitute in the first place, a fact which would question the behavioural primacy of such an upbringing. If Gissing was 'forced' it was at his own hands. External pressures such as his economic condition, and the conditions which made prostitution the only way, ought to be considered, but they would certainly be less dynamic than the internal life within the individual young man. His was a timely revaluation of what was really moral and what was not, and this, coupled with his emotional sexual involvement, laid the founda-tions of the paths he followed. I think Korg overemphasises the picture of Gissing as a lonely intellectual, friendless in an alien city whose only recourse is to find human companionship in the slums. There is no doubt that he was socially reticent, but socially reticent people need not be totally isolated. The picture Korg gives is, in part, reinforced by Gissing's comments later in life on the period in question. He liked to give the impression that the crime was based on his unprotected youthful state and his lonely life. Clearly he spent a lifetime trying to justify the crime which weighed upon his mind. Gillian Tindall's book *The Born Exile* was written ten years after Korg's work. She presents a different Gissing, using some additional evidence which points to a more human man than the myth of the lonely student suggests.

More important than the north-of-England puritanical background is the influence of the radical father and the art of low life with which the young man grew up. Dickens was always a favourite of Gissing's. One of the books which most influenced him was the collection of Hogarth's etchings, the realism of which is more obvious than the social comedy typical of Dickens. His approach to low life, then, we would expect to be a mixture of romantic tendencies and a knowledge of social realism. I do believe that Gissing, in his early period, had some trouble deciding which was predominant. Tindall allows for the role played by the sexual drive, claiming for it more dynamism than Korg is willing to suggest, yet she feels that it does not present the complete picture:

> The sexual aspect of the matter is . . . readily explained. (And indeed if the whole affair had stayed on that level there would be

nothing much worth commenting on anyway.) Because of the prudery with which their own women were surrounded and the general de-sexing, in myth, of the 'nice' female ('ladies don't move'), many Victorians undoubtedly found it difficult to regard women of their own class as sex-objects at all. Indeed this observation has become a truism of social and literary history, and no review of Gissing's sexual proclivities is complete without it. It has even been suggested that Gissing (like A.J. Munby and doubtless many other men of the period) was only capable of being sexually attracted to lower-class women. While certain elements in Gissing's life might suggest this (such as making the mistake of marrying beneath him not once but twice), I do not believe that, as an overall explanation of his love-life, it will do. The emotional threads were more complex than that . . . [2]

In addition to Tindall's caution I am not quite convinced that the cultural habit of de-sexing ladies was, indeed, very much stronger than the biological drive itself. The male sexual needs are not so weak as to be restricted by the cultural façade of the modest pose and the demure manner. It was more a question of economical separation which Gissing felt kept him apart from the women of his own class.

Gissing's accounts of the time, Tindall suggests, are inaccurate to the point that she feels he is recreating the past in the novelist's fictional manner. Other considerations than the truth seem to cloud his memory and his judgement. He writes to Clara Cobbet later in life, nominating loneliness as the cause of the disaster: 'I feel it a strange thing when I frequently see and talk with people. The bad beginning of it was when at 16 or so, I was foolishly sent to live in Manchester in miserable lodgings. Hence all subsequent ills and follies.'[3] He does not admit to being a very responsible and mature sixteen year old, which he most certainly was. He does not remember that in Manchester he lived at Alderley Edge, his former boarding school where he was known well enough to warrant the place. And he does not admit that he was more like eighteen than sixteen when he met Nell. In another record, this time by Morley Roberts, Gissing is reported to having lamented the fact that one of his sisters did not go to live with him in Manchester. He seems not to allow for the fact that they were still children. Furthermore he was not quite so isolated as the myth of his tradition might suppose.

He talked quite freely to Morley Roberts whose account of the affair is the only one remaining. He was an old school friend with whom he discussed Nell quite openly, showing him a photograph on one occasion which showed her to be a 'young girl, aged perhaps seventeen with hair down her back. She was not beautiful but had a certain prettiness of youth, and she was undoubtedly not a lady.'[4] Because Gissing seldom mentions his friends, and more often refers to his loneliness, it has become accepted that he was the shy, scholarly recluse whose work and temperament combined to leave him no time for companions. Because she was not totally comfortable with this picture Tindall studied the archive material on Gissing held at the library at Manchester University. This material includes details from the Senate minutes at Owens College which record the reports of the Gissing scandal. Also part of this collection is the number of letters written to the eighteen-year-old Gissing in 1876 by John George Black, another friend at Owens College. The following gives an account of the information which can be gleaned from these records. The picture is not quite the traditional one:

It is partly, no doubt, due to the picture of the hypersensitive solitary intellectual in this situation in *Born in Exile*, that subsequent writers, from Roberts onwards, have tended to gloss over the means by which this supposed pure, high-minded child of sixteen ever became involved with Nell at all. A slightly different picture, however, is given by documents in Manchester University archives which came to light in the 1950s . . .

Judging by his letters, Black was a young man of ebullient, not to say flamboyant character, who had formed a warm friendship with Gissing. (The image of the totally friendless, lonely young man already begins to melt at the edges . . .) The letters make it clear (a) that Nell was known to both of them, (b) that Black himself had slept with Nell, knowing that Gissing had also done so but without realising that Gissing was 'serious' about her, and (c) that Black somewhere caught a venereal infection, about which he asked Gissing's advice, referring to the fact that Gissing himself had a similar or comparable 'inflammation'. One should add that Black seems to have been a good-hearted lad and, when Gissing was taking Nell for a discreet holiday in Southport, he readily supplied the addresses of landladies etc. and added, rather charmingly 'Delicacy forbids me to commend myself to anyone but yourself, I suppose'. By that time he knew Gissing was serious about a preposterous project—which he—Black—

had first dismissed as mere talk: that of marrying Nell. ('I believed everything, except that you had really fallen in love with her.')

By way of an irreverent aside, I have often wondered if the discreet holiday mentioned above was paid for by the unwitting members of the Owens College students' common room. If so, the image of the starving artist stealing to save the starving prostitute needs reshaping. Perhaps the guilt felt by the older Gissing was warranted. Certainly Tindall is more interested in the human Gissing than the myth; I continue where I left off:

Now, young men acquainted—however recently with girls of the town, and capable of swapping the symptoms of venereal disease, the address of a helpful doctor and so forth, are not the absolute innocents that Gissing later presented himself as having been. Frequenting girls of easy virtue was probably, among the students, the dashing thing to do. The impression is less of solitary adolescence than of young men sowing faintly squalid wild oats in the time-honoured Victorian tradition.[5]

This humanising of Gissing is convincing. It does not make him a less intense artist. And if it does not give us the whole truth it provides a more realistic, down-to-earth picture on which to build. None the less it is still fair to say that Gissing will never be seen as a simple individual. Like Widdowson in *The Odd Women*, who also married beneath himself, Gissing shares the following trait: 'I can't take things the simple way that comes natural to other men'. Widdowson is also very frustrated by the marriage he shares with his seamstress wife, though the reasons for his frustration are by no means the same as Gissing's. Yet both marriages are a disaster.

Nell had fits which were often confused with drunkenness and anger. Her low, vulgar friends were a constant source of annoyance and fear, for through them and her own proclivities she might have returned to her old profession (a fact which suggests she was not the 'dollymop' or casual prostitute Tindall prefers to see in Nell). She was disobedient and bad-tempered, dirty and lacked a modicum of self-discipline. Gissing could never ask friends to visit their poor quarters—she was so seldom presentable or sober. Roberts was never allowed to see Nell, despite his closeness to the writer. Roberts recalls the trauma the marriage was for his friend:

They were turned out of one lodging after another, for even the poorest places, it seems, could hardly stand a woman of her character in the house. I fear it was not only that she drank, but at intervals she deserted him and went back, for the sake of more drink, and for the sake of money with which he was unable to supply, to her old melancholy trade. And yet she returned again with tears, and he took her in, doing his best for her.[6]

How unlike Simple Sally is Nell. She bears no resemblance to Nancy, or Ruth. Mercy Merrick and her idealised friends are so often noble figments of the artists' imaginations who feel for humanity to the point that it encourages the creation of better than average fallen women. As I have argued in earlier chapters their reasons for the invention of ideal figures justify their existence. It is just as well however that a Nell appears in this book to balance the view and allow for the unsavoury, victim though she may be.

The frustrations of the type of life experienced by Gissing are well described in his first novel *Workers in the Dawn*. In it the fallen woman is a social victim, therefore deserving not only restitution but eternal patience. The novel is a semi-realistic picture of the world from which she comes. There is an attempt to save her, which, like Gissing's own marriage, is a failure. The plot of the novel is predictable and rather melodramatic in the worst sense of the word. Arthur Golding feels the call to improve life in the slums around which he has grown. He does not dismiss the poor and the downtrodden as a necessary evil, nor as a regrettable fact. He marries the poor, fallen Carrie Mitchell whom he tries to reform. When this does not work and she leaves him, he befriends a more typically virtuous Victorian lady. Helen and he fall in love, but she rejects him on discovering that he is already married. The novel ends melodramatically with his suicide at Niagara Falls; he dies with the name of the virtuous girl on his lips. From his first novel it can be seen that Gissing's regard for prostitutes is aligned to his love of reform rather than being the manifestation of a rebellious spirit which wishes to steep itself in low life. In this sense he is quite conventional—since Dickens and Gaskell Victorian writers have been keen to be indirect agents in the reform of fallen women. After all, his major frustrations with Nell are founded on the fact that he could not change her. In both *Workers in the Dawn* and *The Un-classed* the hero is attracted by the typically repressed Victorian maiden with obvious virtues and a virginal outlook. The two women—the virtuous and the fallen—play a large part in early Gissing fiction, though they are certainly more complex than they are seen to be in the novels of Mrs Wood.

Gissing's literary activity, after he gets rid of Nell permanently, gives a very definite hint on the reason why he was attracted to her in the first place. A year or so after she was admitted to the private sanitarium run by two firm but kindly old ladies, Gissing still writes about the rescue of a fallen woman whom he sees in ideal terms. After living a rather bohemian life for a Victorian, he writes a novel in which the heroine shares more with Mercy Merrick and Ruth than she does with Nell. It was Gissing himself who said that fiction 'puts into literary form hopes which are not likely to be realized'.[7] *The Unclassed* is a permanent record of these hopes, hopes which were as alive in the author of the 1880s as in the student of the 1870s. As a youth the desire to put a romantic ideal into practice through Nell is repeated through art in *The Unclassed*. It is not difficult to imagine the unification of youthful naivety, sexual drive, poverty, alienation from his own class, and the poetic sensibility which had an almost Quixotic desire to find a Dulcinea in a common prostitute. Why then did Gissing not see Nell's crude, unpolished, unsophisticated personality? I think he did, but the strength of his romantic ideal combined with 'falling in love' was sufficient to cloud the issue. On the other hand if reform of her personality was important, then her negative traits needed to be both recognised and recorded. Without these there is no potential saving, no future reform, no confirmation of the youthful dream. Then there existed within Gissing a distinct virtue—his ability to pity the plight of the girl. Compare him to Arthur Golding in *Workers in the Dawn*:

> Arthur, though he could not persuade himself into a belief of reviving passion, yet experienced so intensely the emotion of pity, felt so keenly the full pathos of her broken words, was so profoundly touched by the sense of her helplessness, that the thought of once more being a providence to the poor, suffering outcast melted his heart, and for the moment made him forget to compare her with Helen.[8]

Gissing, when asked by the Senate enquiry at Owens College, replied that he wanted to save her. He did not say that he loved her; I wonder why? I think he was being as straightforward as he could be. To suggest (as Tindall has done)[9] that he was not a good judge of character, so he was unable to see Nell's rather obvious rough edges, is off the mark. His inner life recognised traits that could be there instead. His mistake, if indeed he did make one, was not one of oversight but one of misdirected insight. Tindall agrees here: 'His image of Nell seems from the first to have corresponded more to a romantic ideal of his own mind than to the reality'.[10]

The plot of the novel is not complex, yet its major problem of bringing diverse characters together makes it more than simple. It opens in a schoolroom where Ida Starr is seen holding an injured girl whose forehead bleeds from contact with a thrown slate. Ida is the aggressor, but her violence is excused when we learn that the victim, Harriet Smales, continually insults Ida's mother who is a prostitute. Maud Enderby, a repressed, dreamy, but good-natured girl, regrets Ida's subsequent expulsion. The three main female characters are introduced in this manner. Once this is done Gissing moves the time forward eight years, and introduces the two main male characters. Osmond Waymark, a poor intellectual novelist-cum-teacher, advertises for male companionship. The orphaned Julian Casti (Harriet Smales' cousin who has been brought up by her father) answers the advertisement. They become good friends and the two worlds are brought together. Waymark meets the other two female characters in turn: Maud is a governess for his employer; Ida forms a friendship with him when she sees him help an unfortunate prostitute on her last legs. Ida is also a prostitute. Two events complicate the plot: Osmond Waymark must choose between the two women he admires, Maud or Ida; Julian Casti is forced into a marriage with Harriet Smales when she claims a visit to her room by her cousin has ruined her reputation. The climax of the novel is approached when Ida and Harriet meet again at Waymark's suggestion. Harriet suspects correctly that her husband is in love with Ida, so engineers the crime of theft for which the reformed prostitute is jailed. Waymark becomes engaged to Maud, though is relieved when his fiancée breaks it off. This leaves him free to marry Ida, who has, with surprising Victorian literary luck, been provided for by her long lost wealthy grandfather. Julian Casti's remark, 'how conventional one is, in spite of oneself' can be applied to the conclusion of the novel.[11] The happy ending, by the way, was included at the publisher's request.

Gissing writes the following in his *Commonplace Book:* 'The art of fiction has this great ethical importance, that it enables one to tell the truth about human beings in a way that is impossible in actual life.'[12] In *The Unclassed* Gissing also tells many truths about himself. Not one but two of the main characters in the novel share characteristics with Gissing himself. He is able to explore major aspects of his own nature in his fiction. 'After all,' he communicates with his brother, Algernon, 'one must write what is in one to write . . .'[13] Gissing would not like my approach to his novel—he was sensitive to any comment which drew attention to the autobiographical detail in the work. His sister recognised the similarities and wrote to Gissing about them. He is a little too defensive in his reply:

> You evidently take Waymark's declaration of faith as my own. Now this is by no means the case. Waymark is a study of character, and he alone is responsible for his sentiments . . . If my own ideas are to be found anywhere, it is in the practical course of events in the story; my characters must speak as they would actually, and I cannot be responsible for what they say. You may tell me I need not have chosen such people: ah, but that is a question of the artist's selection.[14]

I must say now that I think Casti and Waymark do stand on their own, and work convincingly in their roles in the novel. However, if they do share a great deal with their creator there is no reason to suggest that this relationship is not meaningful. To discover the complexity of the reasons for the similarities is a far more positive way to react to the phenomenon than to suggest that Gissing was so limited an artist that he was unable to look elsewhere for content or inspiration. Korg sums up one argument: 'So many of the minor details of the novel are drawn from Gissing's own immediate experiences that they cast a doubt on his ability to find other sources of material'.[15] Major details of the novel are also drawn from Gissing's experience, and they are not related to his lack of ability but to the fact that his art helped him to make sense of events in his life as these events related to his visions and his hopes and his disappointments.

Like Gissing, Julian Casti is a bookish boy whose joy is to steep himself in the classics. Their tastes have a great deal in common. Even Julian's good luck on finding a cheap edition of Gibbon is based on a similar event in Gissing's life. Two records of it remain, one in a letter to his brother, and the other in *The Private Papers of Henry Rycroft*. Julian's joy is recorded in a different style, but it probably contains the original enthusiasm felt by Gissing. The love of the classics and related youthful enthusiasm remain:

> That night he solemnly laid open the first volume at the first
> page, propping it on a couple of minor books, and, after glancing
> through the short Preface, began to read with a mind as devoutly
> disposed as that of any pious believer poring upon his Bible. (*The
> Unclassed*, p. 68)

Julian's likeness to Gissing certainly does not end here. He was left
to look after an 'odd woman' in the form of Harriet Smales, his
petulant, difficult cousin. Gissing had to look after his sisters when
they were left without father or husband. Gissing's experience with
his sisters was far more positive than the misery suffered by Julian at
the hands of Harriet. Harriet is, in fact, a personification of part of
Nell. Her drunkenness, her disobedience, her dishonesty and her
wilfulness all bear a resemblance to the most negative aspects of
Nell's behaviour. Not only does Harriet destroy Julian's ability to
write, she destroys Julian himself. His consumption is the outer
manifestation of the spiritual malaise he suffers at the hands of his
wife. Nell's destructive tendencies are well displaced in Harriet but
they are certainly manifest. Her deception and alcoholism loom
largest in the novel. As Gissing liked to see himself caught by
circumstances which led to his marriage, so Julian is trapped into
matrimony. Determined to marry him, and jealous of the time he
spends with Osmond Waymark, she lures him to her room planning
to cry disgrace and knowing that he has no more than fraternal love
for her. Later she appears on Julian's doorstep claiming to have
been dismissed, dramatically retelling her fiction in the worst
penny-dreadful style:

> 'If you only knew what they've been told!' sobbed the girl, still
> clinging to Julian. 'They wouldn't listen to a word you said. As if I
> could have thought of such a thing happening, and that woman to
> say all the bad things of us she can turn her tongue to! I shan't
> never get another place; I'm thrown out on the wide world!' (*The
> Unclassed*, p. 106)

Julian marries Harriet to make her respectable, and though
Gissing's Nell was different, she too became his wife as part of a
saving act. It is their good-natured sensitivity which responds to the
plight of the lonely, unfortunate girls, but it is the same sensitivity
which makes it impossible to live with them. Gissing's vision for

saving the fallen, particularly Nell, is founded on a humanitarian belief in the worth of the human soul. In his portrayal of and approach to Harriet he admits that some souls cannot be saved. It took Gissing some time to admit that it was impossible to live with the unreformed, unrefined working-class prostitute who did not, it seems, have the desire to change. His vision of saving the fallen was one of refinement. Nell could not meet the requirements of his dream. Julian's cry below is so sincerely recorded that one can easily recognise the fact that Gissing's pain, suffered at the hands of Nell, did not die easily:

'Where is the blame?' Julian broke out with a sudden vehemence. 'I cannot think that ever husband was more patient and more indulgent that I have been. I have refused her nothing that my means could possibly obtain. I have given up all the old quiet habits of my life that she mightn't think I slighted her; I scarcely ever open a book at home, knowing that it irritates her to see me reading, I do my best to amuse her at all times. How does she reward me? For ever she grumbles that I can't perform impossibilities,—take her to theatres, buy her new dresses, procure for her friends and acquaintances. My wishes, expressed or understood, weigh with her less than the least of her own caprices. She wantonly does things which she knows will cause me endless misery. Her companions are gross and depraved people, who constantly drag her lower and lower, to their own level. The landlady has told me that, in my absence, women have called to see her who certainly ought not to enter any decent house. When I entreat her to give up such associates, her only answer is to accuse me of selfishness, since I have friends myself, and yet won't permit her to have any. And things have gone from bad to worse. Several nights of late, when I have got home, she has been away, and has not returned till much after midnight. Hour after hour I have sat there in the extremest misery, waiting, waiting, feeling as though my brain would burst with its strain! I have no idea where she goes to. If I ask, she only retorts by asking me where I spend the nights when I am with you, and laughs contemptuously when I tell her the truth. Her suspicions and jealousy are incessant, and torture me past endurance. Once or twice, I confess, I have lost patience, and have spoken angrily, too angrily; then she has accused me of brutal disregard of her sufferings. It would hurt her less if she pierced me with a knife.

Only this morning there was a terrible scene; she maddened me, past endurance by her wretched calumnies—accusing me of I know not what disgraceful secrets—and when the words burst from me involuntarily, she fell into hysterics, and shrieked till all the people in the house ran up in alarm. Can you understand what this means to one of my temperament? To have my private affairs forced upon strangers in this way tortures me with the pains of hell. I am naturally reticent and retiring—too much so, I dare say—and no misery could have been devised for me more dreadful than this. Her accusations are atrocious, such as could only come from a grossly impure mind, or at the suggestion of vile creatures. You she hates with a rabid hatred—God only knows why. She would hate any one who was my friend, and whose society relieved me for a moment from my ghastly torments!'

He ceased for very exhaustion, so terribly did the things he describe work upon him.

'What am I to do, Waymark? Can you give me advice?' (*The Unclassed*, pp. 163-4)

Anyone with the knowledge of that which Gissing had to suffer when Nell was at her worst, would be correct in wondering whether the suffering delineated above would feel so convincing, and true, if Gissing had not had such an experience. The more noble the soul, the deeper the suffering when it is realised that Harriet's or Nell's vileness is permanent. Julian is well aware of the damage this does to the sensitive temperament. That he cannot counteract the impurity of mind inherent in Harriet's personality is one of the major sources of his anxiety. It ought to be remembered, of course, that Harriet is not Nell—Gissing did have sufficient artistic integrity not to let his life dictate to the work in an obvious manner, obvious being the operative word. She does, however, represent the worst aspects of Nell's character. As Julian had to pluck up courage in order to tell his friend the truth about his wife, so did Gissing try to hide, for a while at least, that which was painfully obvious to friends like Morley Roberts. Gissing found talking openly about Nell very difficult indeed, a fact which explains her influence on the formation of Harriet's character in the novel. Perhaps at one stage Gissing felt like Julian above, when he had no choice but to let things out. Certainly after feeling the pathos in the above speech one can easily imagine the rank disappointment suffered by the young idealist who put his romantic vision to the test and failed miserably. It is easy to appreciate Gissing's insistence that one can only write that which is in one to write. Gissing seems to channel his weaknesses, and the disasters which laid them bare into Julian. Julian's death then has obvious ritualistic ramifications for Gissing's whole being. Yet whilst, through art, Gissing can realise his defeat and write it off ritualistically, he can still embody his youthful hope in another character in the novel—this he does through creating Ida Starr, who is in every way the ideal reformed prostitute. It is in this manner that Gissing transforms events in his life into art. He is able to explore his failure, yet still have faith in the dream which had, in part, caused the failure in the first place. Gissing's comment to a friend has especial relevance here: 'One puts into literary form hopes which are not very likely to be realized'.[16]

Gissing's relationship with the hero of the novel, Osmond Waymark, is more difficult to discuss than that with Julian, yet there exist obvious likenesses. Waymark was born into a poor middle-class family, and was left on his own at an early age to fend for himself. They are both young novelists who are thrown into an ugly world with which they do battle for a time till they find they must accept that which they cannot change. Waymark and Gissing both write novels where social realism is central to the thematic concern. These novels fail after they are published at the expense of the writers. Gissing had to tutor to live—Waymark is a poor teacher in a second-rate school. Waymark advertises for a friend, and gets one. The Gissing-Bertz friendship was formed in exactly the same manner. Waymark's philosophic leanings can be found in Gissing's early life. Waymark's father was a radical—so was Gissing's. Both young men give a lecture attacking established religion. Waymark is presented with a set of the same Hogarth prints which were a memorable part of Gissing's boyhood in Wakefield. In fact the similarities are so numerous that Tindall is led to exclaim that Waymark is 'Gissing without most of Gissing's problems'.[17] I think she is only in part correct, for Waymark is left with some Gissing-like enigmas to work out through the action and character of the novel. Understanding the idealisation of Ida Starr is central to a discovery of Waymark's role in the novel.

When *The Unclassed* was written Gissing was living alone in Chelsea in a period of relative calm. He was still enthralled by the sentimental dream of the ideal woman, or the ideal dream of reforming a prostitute, but instead of exposing himself to the threat of another disaster he took the safest way and created one through his art. 'The best part of life,' he writes to Algernon, 'is sentiment, and, for my own part the pain of many sentiments is redeemed by their emotional values.'[18] Gissing had attempted in real life that which novelists of the nineteenth century could never try to do in their work—he tried to reform a really depraved and degraded woman. Ruth, Mercy Merrick and Nancy are all quite noble. In one sense they don't change a great deal throughout their stories; they merely confirm the reader's suspicions that they are worthy of forgiveness and a place in society. The novelists who created them would never have been able to paint a degraded individual and reform her. After Gissing comes a cropper in real life he becomes more like his predecessors in his choice of fallen woman in Ida Starr, whose reform and ultimate acceptance by certain members of society is the confirmation of her innate goodness.

Ida's longing for purity in the novel is, in a very real sense, Gissing's longing for a fallen woman who longs for purity: she is the artistic embodiment of a sentimental hope. Her purification is achieved through manipulation of scene and image. In one of her attempts to stay 'honest' Ida works at a laundry. Here she tells Waymark of her attempts to survive:

> 'By this time I was actually starving. I had one day to tell my landlady I couldn't pay my rent. She was a very decent woman, and she talked to me in a kind way. What was better, she gave me help. She had a sister who kept a laundry, and she thought I might perhaps get something to do there, at all events she would go and see. The result was that I got work. I was in the laundry nearly six months, and became quite clever in getting up linen.'

Gissing does not intend the story to be a simple matter of history. Her sacrifice and her effort purify her spirit in a rather Victorian manner, through work, the symbolic nature of which is obvious when Ida continues:

> 'Now this was the kind of work I liked. You can't think what a pleasure it was to me to see shirts and collars turning out so spotless and sweet.'
>
> Waymark laughed.
>
> 'Oh, but you don't understand. I do so like cleanliness! I have a sort of feeling when I'm washing anything, that I'm really doing

good in the world, and the dazzling white of linen after I'd ironed it seemed to thank me for my work.'

And Waymark's laugh at the light-hearted element in the conversation turns to something else when he realises the importance of that which he hears. 'Spotless', 'sweet', 'dazzling white', 'cleanliness': all change Waymark's thoughtless levity to a serious understanding of Ida's desires:

'Yes, yes, I understand well enough,' said Waymark earnestly. (*The Unclassed*, p. 137)

But Gissing also makes sure he humanises Ida by balancing her desire for purity with failings. Waymark tries to invent complex social excuses for Ida's fall, excuses which stress her weakness and highlight the power of the world around her. Ida makes him face the truth, a truth which he finds discomfiting since it does not fit his image of the pure maid who keeps her purity even though she is a prostitute. Ida tells Waymark the story of her life. Even though she, like all fallen women in the Victorian novel, is left alone at an early age she chooses to be a kept woman because it is the easy way out of a life of drudgery. She is anxious to stress 'how slight occasion had led her from what is called the path of virtue, that he might not delude himself into exaggerated estimates of her character'. (*The Unclassed*, p. 14) It is difficult for Waymark to accept this—he would far rather keep the ideal in his mind and not the reality. Is this Gissing's way of exploring his own self-delusion which he experienced with Nell? Even though this may be so Gissing cannot resist the continuation of the washing motif. He does not allow Waymark to witness Ida's ritualistic baptism—only he and the reader share the experience. The weight of her impurity weighs heavily on her mind. She is at the seaside with Waymark. Their relationship has not developed beyond a frank friendship, though he has a certain passionate feeling for her, and she is deeply in love with him. In the following scene she has returned to her hotel room, where she is stifled by her own sense of guilt. Gissing highlights this by making the night hot and uncomfortable. She sobs in the close bedroom for some time, then determines to put herself through a trial of respectability away from Waymark, so that she can be sure she means to reform. This is borne out by her actions later in the novel. Meanwhile Gissing performs ritualistically that which the future action of the novel does rationally:

> the heat of the room was stifling, for just above was the roof, upon which all day the sun had poured its rays. She threw open the windows and drank in the air. The night was magnificent, flooded with warm moonlight, and fragrant with sea breathings. Ida felt an irresistible desire to leave the house and go down to the shore . . .
>
> She walked towards the place where she had spent the afternoon with Waymark, then onwards still further to the east, till there was but a narrow space between the water and the cliffs. Breakers there were none, not more ripple at the clear tide-edge than on the border of a little lake. So intense was the silence that every now and then could be distinctly heard a call on one of the fishing-boats lying some distance from shore. The town was no longer in sight.

This is one of the few truly romantic moments in all of Gissing's fiction. Civilisation recedes into the dark past as the town disappears. The populated world may reject Ida, or rationalise her plight, approve or disapprove, but nature makes no such decision. Ida and nature seem to share the moment in a Wordsworthian transcendent manner. Here is the existence above conventions and moral concerns, a higher law. All that is left of the social world is the odd call in the distance which, instead of obtruding on the moment of natural sanctification, highlights its calmness. Nature is the mother goddess whose touch is gentle and whose spirit is soothing:

> what little breeze there was brushed the face like the warm wing of a passing bird. Ida dipped her hands in the water and sprinkled it upon her forehead. Then she took off her boots and stockings, and walked with her feet in the ripples. A moment after she stopped, and looked all around, as if hesitating at some thought, and wishing to see that her solitude was secure. Just then the sound of a clock came very faintly across the still air, striking the hour of one. She stepped from the water a few paces, and began hastily to put off her clothing; in a moment her feet were again in the ripples, and she was walking out from the beach, till her gleaming body was hidden. Then she bathed, breasting the full flow with delight, making the sundered and broken water flash myriad reflections of the moon and stars. (*The Unclassed*, pp. 144-5)

This scene of purification could so easily have been overdone. As it is it provides one of the finest moments in the novel, moving from images of the oppressive heat to those of gentle relief. The universal approval reflected in the water is the ultimate confirmation of Ida's real worth. For her own part she leaves with the strength to give up her old ways out of love for Waymark. As expected she returns to the laundry, to the white, crisp, clean linen. Each day at the laundry she works and provides for herself in a more modest manner than was her wont in earlier days. Each day is 'an accession of the strength of purity', and is also a further step away from 'the dark time'. It is quite clear that the most memorable scenes in the novel are those which come from the memory and shock of his first traumatic failure with Nell—the frustration of Julian was the first example studied here: the purification of Ida is another one of these moments. It is the wish-fulfilment dream in print. Ida's longing for purity belongs as much to Gissing as it does to the character herself. He admits this covertly in his Preface to the 1895 edition of *The Unclassed* when he admits that the book 'will be recognized as the work of a very young man, who dealt in a romantic spirit with the gloomier facts of life'.[19] The reviewer, writing for *The Daily Chronicle* of this second edition, takes exception to what he considers Gissing's unduly modest stance, arguing that because the work is sincere it need not be true in the realistic sense. He also claims that it is the novel's sincerity which makes it a moral work:

> We are . . . sometimes compelled to assert that there is such a thing as an 'immoral' novel, the novel no one should write and no one should publish—and we hold this to be the novel which gives an untrue, a partial, or an insincere view of life. The thing which is true or sincerely written—though it be not agreeable reading— must not be counted immoral, though it is of course not necessary, as Aristotle reminds us, to tell everything that is true.[20]

This review accepts that whilst idealised figures like Ida do not walk the streets with the Nells and the Harriets, their legitimacy is confirmed by the fact that they do represent in physical form the hopes and undetected dreams of a young man who has 'no need to turn in shame from a romantic dream or vision of his youth. True to life they may not have been; but they were lovely dreams and pure.'[21]

The whole theme of the ideal woman is, however, more complex than it first appears. The theme is manifest in several different ways, usually through one of the major characters as he or she reacts to the self and a member of the opposite sex. There always seems to be a tension between accepting the reality of human limitation and hoping for something more permanent and enduring. Maud, for instance, struggles to make herself the ideal woman through the adoption of an ascetic life-style which will purify her animal drives. Julian Casti has a poetic vision of the ideal woman in his mind and heart, yet he accepts in Harriet the antithesis of his dream, then must live with the result. Waymark is even more problematic than Julian—the former does not really know which type of ideal woman he most admires. The novel ultimately revolves around the decision he must make—does he see his ideal in the ascetic non-sexual Maud, or the experienced prostitute who still manages to stay pure despite her life and work? It is quite possible that the types after Ida and Maud personify polarities in Gissing's own mind. Is Maud the conventional Victorian ideal the very existence of which proves that her creator was very much influenced by the norms of his own culture? Does Ida spring from his more rational desire, and his radical tendencies? The answer must remain what it is—conjectural and fascinating. In the novel Waymark is initially attracted to Maud, then to Ida, then back to Maud again, finally marrying Ida at the conclusion of the novel. The attraction differs greatly, a fact which goes without saying.

The idealisation of women, it is well to remember, has always been a part of Western civilisation, though the intensity of the concern for her has certainly varied with the age. She was in vogue in the Middle Ages, when the Mary Cult became a central tenet of Christian ideology. She figures in the secular sense in the Medieval Romance. Over the centuries she managed to survive, but her renaissance was to be most obvious in the nineteenth century. One of the things Gissing explores in *The Unclassed* is the concern Waymark has for the type. As has been suggested above, Maud and Ida are attractive to Waymark because they each find a sympathetic chord in part of Waymark's personality. Maud belongs to his Victorian cultural self. Ida belongs to his sexual need and his rational radicalism.

Waymark meets Maud at the school run by the Tootles. She is very much abused by the Tootle children. At the school his worship of her is from afar, in the true medieval tradition. Even though they meet in the nursery when he goes there to give his drawing lessons, they are not allowed to communicate. He watches the Tootle children abuse her time after time to the point that he can watch no longer. The eldest Tootle throws something at Maud's head which reaches its intended target. Waymark moves to her aid, giving the lad a well deserved thrashing which leads to his leaving the school. Though not quite admitting it, he walks to the street in which Maud lives with her ascetic aunt, hoping they might meet. They do meet, Maud informing Waymark that she too is leaving the school, and will be going to Essex to be governess to a family there. Waymark suggests writing, a suggestion which she accepts timidly. The worship from afar continues in this manner.

Although she is a very definite beauty, Maud never arouses his passion, which suggests the conventional Victorian response to the de-sexed, pure woman. Waymark is surprised that a poor man such as he is could be exposed to the tenets of a middle-class myth. For a while the myth becomes what he sees as a reality:

> How the aspect of the world had changed for him in these few minutes: what an incredible revolution had come to pass in his own desires and purposes! The intellectual atmosphere he breathed was of his own creation; the society of cultured people he had never had the opportunity of enjoying. [Gissing himself often complained of the limitations facing Waymark here.] A refined and virtuous woman had hitherto existed for him merely in the sanctuary of his imagination; he had known not one such. If he passed one in the street, the effect of the momentary proximity was only to embitter his thoughts, by reminding him of the hopeless gulf fixed between his world and that in which such creatures had their being. (*The Unclassed*, p. 82)

Even when Gissing found a middle-class lady who would have him she was as poor as he. Gabriel Fleury did have distant aristocratic connection in her native France, but one suspects that her mother discussed them at length to offset her poverty. After Nell died Gissing was free to marry again. He wrote to Bertz in 1890 about his need for another wife, or, more exactly, his need for someone who might substitute for one. His argument is that he must look for a 'decent working girl' because he had no chance of marrying a middle-class woman. He writes in his diary, also in 1890, that work is not possible till he finds a wife.[22] The irony is that his work became

increasingly difficult after he married his second wife, Edith Under-
wood. There is every reason to believe that his reasons for marrying
Nell are related to those given for his marriage to Edith. When
Waymark meets Maud, who is the personification of a type previously thought to be well out of his reach, it is as much the
realisation that the previously unachievable may be possible which
encourages him to pursue the relationship as it is Maud's physical
attractiveness. Waymark and Gissing share some related traits with
the hero in another story—'A Lodger in Maze Pond'. The hero in
that story who has promised to marry a servant girl makes it clear
that he needs female companionship, even when passion is not the
dynamic force behind that need:

> I am a fool about women. I don't know what it is—certainly not a
> sensual or passionate nature . . . there's that need in me—the
> incessant hunger for a woman's sympathy and affection . . .Day
> after day we grew more familiar . . . When she laid a meal for
> me, we talked . . . I made a friend of the girl . . . We were alone
> in the house one evening . . . I was lonely and dispirited—
> wanted to talk—to talk about myself to someone who would give
> a kind ear. So I went down, and made some excuses for begin-
> ning a conversation in the parlor . . . I didn't persuade myself
> that I cared for Emma, even then. Her vulgarisms of speech and
> feeling jarred upon me. But she was feminine; she spoke and
> looked gently, with sympathy. I enjoyed that evening—and you
> must bear in mind what I have told you before, that I stand in awe
> of refined women . . . Perhaps I come to regard myself as
> doomed to live on a lower level. I find it impossible to imagine
> myself offering marriage—making love—to a girl such as those I
> meet in the big houses.[23]

'All the evidence indicates that Gissing himself was speaking
through these words, trying to explain his inexplicable
relations. . . '[24] Waymark's similarities suggest that he too is
related to Gissing himself. Waymark certainly shares the young
man's lack of passion for Maud, though he is certainly attracted to
her by the need for sympathetic female companionship. Certainly
conversation with Maud would never jar. That she has a sensitive,
middle-class personality makes her a more attractive proposition
than the servant girl above.

Because of the ideals he has Waymark is 'moved' by Maud but is without 'serious emotion'. After one or two meetings with Maud he is well aware that he is not 'in love'. In fact he admits that her beauty is of a 'feeble, characterless type'. She is, however, the closest thing to the figure in a previously repressed dream: 'She was indeed the being from a higher world that he would have liked to believe her from the first . . . ' (*The Unclassed*, p. 83) Their relationship is born on a poetic level—the theoretic worship of a fallible man for an equally theoretically infallible woman. Even when they are engaged to be married the relationship has a coldness born out of the spiritual nature of the union:

> There was little that was lover-like in these hours spent together. They kissed each other at meeting and parting, but, with this exception the manner of both was very slightly different from what it had been before their engagement. They sat apart, and talked of art, literature, religion, seldom each other. It had come to this by degrees; at first there had been more warmth, but passion never. Waymark's self consciousness weighed upon his tongue, and made his conversation but a string of commonplaces; Maud was often silent for long intervals. Their eyes never met in a steady gaze.
>
> Waymark often asked himself whether Maud's was a passionless nature, or whether it was possible that her reserve had the same origin as his own. (*The Unclassed*, pp. 263-4)

Ironically it is Waymark who feels no passion for Maud, not the other way around. Maud, with something resembling heroic effort, represses her natural passion for Waymark, feeling that she must not succumb to it. On one of the few occasions she gives him a glimpse of her true feeling with a look and a touch, Waymark thrills, not with passion, but with pity. Waymark is Victorian despite himself. His relationship with women must be a dual one—passion for the prostitute, admiration for the angel. Waymark knows that 'passion would grow upon him with each' of his meetings with Ida. Despite this marriage cannot be a consideration. This must be with the sublime Maud. Waymark claims to have 'contempt for conventional ties', yet still won't marry Ida, and will marry Maud. He is engaged before he realises that he is about to marry an unreal dream when he should be marrying the woman closest to his animal nature. He seems, surprisingly enough, pleased that his relationship with Maud is not a passionate one: 'let what might happen, his loyalty to

Maud would be unshaken. It was independent of passion and passion could not shake it.' (*The Unclassed*, p. 172) Maud has been de-sexed, and as such is the ideal Victorian wife:

> Never was his blood so calm as in her presence. She was to him a spirit, and in the spirit he loved her. With Maud he might look forward to union at some distant day, a union outwardly of the conventional kind. It would be so, not an account of any inferiority to his ideal in Maud, for he felt that there was no height of his own thought whither she would not in time follow him; but simply because no point of principle would demand a refusal of the yoke of respectability, with its attendant social advantages. And the thought of this binding himself to Maud had nothing repulsive, for the links between them were not of the kind which easily yield, and loyalty to a higher and nobler nature may well be deemed a duty. (*The Unclassed*, p. 171)

But from Maud's point of view the relationship is not possible because she enjoys it too much, she feels the passion for Waymark too acutely. Any pleasure is a sin, any joy a mistake, because joy and pleasure based on any earthly state of necessity draw one away from heaven. Maud's tragedy is manifest in her self-sacrifice—she will not marry Waymark because she doesn't love him; she feels she loves him too much, so breaks the engagement. Her attempts to triumph over the possible ascendancy of her animal nature may be misplaced, painful, or even impossible, but they are sincere. Her 'touching spirituality' is her destruction. Maud's most memorable scene takes place when she fully realises the depth of passion she feels for her fiancé. In one of the most frank sections of the novel Maud writes a letter to Waymark which fully demonstrates the emotions she feels. Gissing is searching through the heavy trappings of self-discipline and the well-structured façade which hide the reality of the suffering, repressed female soul. Waymark does not see this suffering because it is outside the frame of reference which structures his perception of the ideal woman:

> Her nerves were excited. The night was close, and there were mutterings of thunder at times; the cloud whence they came seemed to her to spread its doleful blackness over this one roof. An impulse seized her; she took paper and sat down at her desk to write. It was a letter to Waymark, a letter such as she had

never addressed to him, and which, even in writing it, she was conscious she could not send. Her hand trembled as she filled the pages with burning words. She panted for more than he had given her; this calm, half-brotherly love of his was just now like a single drop of water to one dying of thirst; she cried to him for a deeper draught of the joy of life. The words came to her without need of thought; tears fell hot from her eyes and blotted what she wrote. (*The Unclassed*, pp. 265-6)

After destroying the letter she creeps downstairs to discover her mother kissing her latest male friend. She sees for herself her own potential promiscuity in the form of her insane mother—or rather, she thinks she does. The passion felt when writing the letter and her mother's infidelity are seen by Maud as two aspects of the same 'contagion which had seized upon her own nature'. Instead of accepting her sexual desire as part of her nature, she regards it as the result of an external unnatural, diabolic invasion. She will not or cannot accept the newly discovered self, so reverts to the asceticism of her upbringing. The concept of the ideal woman, pure to the point of being sexless, is a deeply-ingrained, well-rehearsed pretence, a fact which neither Maud nor Waymark are prepared to recognise. Victorians like Gissing have the ability and the courage to lay bare the affectations of their age, at the same time feeling empathy for those destroyed as a result of this affection. Waymark is relieved when the engagement is broken, because he comes to realise that something is missing from their relationship. That it takes him so long to recognise the obvious is not surprising—we are all too close to our culturally ingrained prejudices to recognise them for what they are. Maud is left to enter a religious community with her aunt—it is her final attempt to recover her lost purity. She writes to Waymark: 'Do not fear for me; I feel already better. I am always with you in spirit, and in the spirit I love you; God help me to keep my love pure!' (*The Unclassed*, p. 269) In an effort to stop themselves from falling too many Victorian women destroyed themselves in the process. The ideal helps to destroy as many respectable women, who like Maud lead an unmitigated life in death, as the wantonness of thoughtless men does through the fall.

Waymark also likes to think of Ida in ideal terms. Julian Casti certainly dies worshipping Ida—it is the obsession the presence of which makes his death more pleasant. He is too ill to make an effort which will push his view of her onto a more mundane plane. Besides he knows of her love for Waymark. Through Ida Waymark has the chance to put into practice his ideas on the relativity of morality, which cannot accept that purity has anything to do with the presence of virginity. If this seems to contradict his ideal in Maud, then it reveals a basic conflict in his own inner mental life. He makes an effort to live up to his rationalisation of morality. In one scene Ida muses on her unworthiness as a companion for purer girls (whilst Ida is accepted by Waymark for what she is, Ida has an irrepressible longing to be like Maud). Waymark argues that Ida's experience makes her a more capable human being: 'Your knowledge is better in my eyes than their ignorance. My ideal woman is the one who, knowing every darkest secret of life, keeps yet a pure mind—as you do, Ida . . . ' This highlights the contradiction in his character—he is attracted to Ida because she is experienced; he is attracted to Maud because she is not! He needs Maud to be pure and passionless. He recognises his passion for Ida, though she will not allow him to move their relationship onto a sexual plane. At one stage he is convinced that it would be an insult to Ida to marry her in the conventional sense. But he is not sure if Ida would accept him in a *de facto* relationship. Underneath it all he is a little afraid of the changeable nature of passion:

> 'Yes I do love you: but at the same time I know too well the uncertainty of love to go through the pretence of binding myself to you for ever. Will you accept my love in its present sincerity, neither hoping or fearing, knowing that whatever happens is beyond our own control, feeling with me that only an ignoble nature can descend to the affectation of union when the real links are broken?' Could Waymark have felt sure of her answer to such an appeal, it would have gone to make his love for Ida all engrossing. She would then be his ideal woman, and his devotion to her would have no bounds. (*The Unclassed*, pp. 170-1)

One can look at this in a simpler manner, a manner which will clarify Waymark's central dilemma. Ida cannot reach the status of ideal woman because she is trying too hard to be something like Waymark's other ideal woman. Is Waymark's combined ideal an unwitting attempt to have his cake and eat it? Why else do we have two contradictory ideals—one largely Victorian, another largely radical? Is Waymark's suspension between two worlds characteristic of Gissing's own dilemma? He was loyal to his needs, sexual and radical, in marrying Nell, but could not forget his desire to have a more sensitive, cultured wife. Is this the artist making 'material of his own sufferings'? Is this what he means when he suggests that fiction can enable one to tell the truth about a human being in a way that is impossible in real life? I think it is:

> The interview with Maud Enderby seemed so unnaturally long ago; that with Ida Starr, so impossibly fresh and recent. Yet both had undoubtedly taken place. He, who but yesterday morning had felt so bitterly his loneliness in the world, and, above all the impossibility of what he most longed for—woman's companion-ship—found himself all at once on terms of at least friendly intimacy with two women, both young, both beautiful, yet so wholly different. Each answered to an ideal which he cherished, and the two ideals were so diverse, so mutually exclusive. (*The Unclassed*, p. 92)

How then is this resolved in the novel? One of the central situ-ations in the novel is based on the Prometheus myth. Waymark is the Prometheus figure, bound by his very humanity. The myth has a certain humanistic fascination for the hero of the novel. At one stage he discusses it with Maud as an alternate way of thinking to Christianity. He feels that Hercules' rescue of the tied human represents the ultimate faith in human capability. Hercules, the ultimate symbol for the perfectibility of man, rescues Prometheus simply by asserting his right to triumph. Waymark is bound by the conflicting visions of the ideal—he cannot make up his mind. When he is tied up by the strange Caliban-like symbol in the novel for the beast in man, Slimy, this is the physical manifestation and confir-mation of a problem already known to the reader. He is bound on the rock of his own limitations, and his society's making. After all, it is not his fault that the slums are so bad, or that Slimy's life has been so negative. When he is robbed and bound it is the only time in the novel when he really suffers—at a time like that, vague spiritual dreams such as the one represented by Maud have little value. They become cultural fragments from a world of intellectual visions. Whilst suffering and bound up in the dark apartment he

> tried not to think of Ida in any way but this was beyond his power. Again and again she came before his mind. When he endeavoured to supplant her by the image of Maud Enderby, the

latter's face only irritated him. Till now, it had been just the reverse; the thought of Maud had always brought quietness: Ida he recognised as the disturbing element of his life, and had learned to associate her with his least noble instincts. Thinking of this now, he began to marvel how it could have been so.

He discovers that the most commonplace so-called ignoble instincts in man are those which need constant satisfaction. Their primacy is one of need. Thus bound Waymark discovers the difference between intellectual musing, poetic sensibility and human need. Instead of being rescued from his bind by an ideal angel-like woman he is rescued by Ida. The reformed fallen woman takes the place of Hercules, asserting her right to power and serious consideration:

> Was it true that Maud was his good angel, that in her he had found his ideal? He had forced himself to believe this, now that he was in honour bound to her; yet she had never made his pulse quicken, as it had often done when he approached Ida. (*The Unclassed*, p. 235)

Ida's humanity rescues Waymark, the woman who formerly appealed to his less noble instincts. Is this Gissing's ultimate apology for his marriage to Nell? Certainly the Waymark-Starr marriage is the dramatic resolution of the ideological schizophrenia which follows Waymark through the novel. Through Casti, Ida can be seen as the 'imaginative transformation prostitute-into-untouchable goddess'.[25] Through Waymark she is the passionate wife. Ida then can be both wife and goddess to Gissing, because Waymark and Casti are both alter-egos. In the author's own words, this is the way the literary form includes 'hopes which are not very likely to be realized'[26] in real life. I think this is Gissing's way of ritualistically coping with the difficulties of what Arnold calls 'a naked, eternally restless mind'.[27]

Notes

1. Jacob Korg, *George Gissing: A Critical Biography* (London: Methuen, 1965), p. 13.
2. Gillian Tindall, *The Born Exile: George Gissing* (London: Temple Smith, 1974), pp. 71-2.
3. Ibid.
4.1 Ibid., p. 75.

5. Ibid., pp. 74-5.
6. Korg, *George Gissing*, p. 26.
7. Tindall, *The Born Exile*, p. 7.
8. Ibid., p. 83.
9. Ibid., p. 78.
10. Ibid.
11. George Gissing, *The Unclassed* (Hassocks, Sussex: The Harvester Press, 1976), p. 166. Hereafter quotes from the text will be marked with page numbers in the body of the chapter.
12. Tindall, *The Born Exile*, p. 7.
13. Korg, *George Gissing*, p. 265.
14. Michael Collie, *The Alien Art* (Kent: Archon Books, 1979), p. 49.
15. Korg, *George Gissing*, p. 65.
16. Tindall, *The Born Exile*, p. 7.
17. Ibid., p. 83.
18. Ibid., p. 86.
19. George Gissing, 'Preface', 1895 edn *The Unclassed*.
20. Unsigned review, *Daily Chronicle*, 2 December 1895, 3, rpt in Pierre Coustillas and Colin Partridge (eds.), *Gissing: The Critical Heritage* (London: Routledge and Kegan Paul, 1972), pp. 75-7.
21. Ibid., p. 77.
22. Korg, *George Gissing*, p. 170.
23. Ibid., p. 152.
24. Ibid.
25. Tindall, *The Born Exile*, p. 86.
26. Ibid., p. 7.
27. Matthew Arnold, 'Epedocles on Etna', rpt in *The Poems of Matthew Arnold 1840-1867* (Oxford: Oxford University Press, 1913), pp. 94-125.

6   TESS

Three Men in a Boat was published in 1889, two years prior to the *Graphic* serialisation of *Tess of the d'Urbervilles*. These works could not be farther from each other in spirit or intent. One incident, however, in Jerome's fanciful travelogue, brings the divergent works together for a short time. Ten miles above Reading the three men in the boat notice 'something black floating in the water'.[1] The 'something' is the dead body of an unfortunate woman, of the type which is the subject of this book. The men are largely sympathetic; her sin is 'vulgar' not because of inherent wilfulness in her nature, but because of the close-mindedness of the society around her. Her sin, if it be one at all, is no different from the sins of men:

> Of course it was the old, old, vulgar tragedy. She has loved and been deceived—or had deceived herself. Anyhow, she had sinned—some of us do now and then—and her family and friends, naturally shocked and indignant, had closed their doors against her.[2]

She had drowned herself as Hetty Sorrell had thought of doing, as Ruth had attempted to do, and as the heroine of Miss Braddon's *Gerard, or The World, The Flesh and The Devil* had started to do, before helpful but meddling onlookers fished her out. The melodrama of her story is similar to that on which the basic plot of *Tess of the d'Urbervilles* is built. The lines of this plot vary little from the novel's precursors. The pure girl is betrayed by her family and circumstance; she is subjected to the natural sexual energy of a young man; she is rejected once her secret becomes known; left alone she is forced to face an hostile society on its unsympathetic terms; sinking lower and lower she meets a tragic end, the pain of which holds less terror and misery than her daily life. Jerome's victim was rescued by the old river, an aquatic angel of death which had 'taken her into its gentle arms and had laid her weary head upon its bosom, and had hushed away the pain'.[3] Tess's death will also be her only release from the pain of the life she was destined to lead.

This unlikely unification of Jerome's trifling incident and the introduction of one of Hardy's masterpieces exists in this chapter for two reasons. I want to stress this—although Hardy's novel can be studied as a conventional fallen-woman novel it ought not to be treated so. We could list chapters of likenesses shared by Hardy's novel and those which precede it, but would miss the major thrust and personality of the novel. Even the desire to expose the late-Victorian double sexual standard and its concomitant, the inequality of men and women, is secondary to the poetic aura which surrounds and moves within the work. Carlyle's discussion of the musicality of poetry is helpful here. 'A musical thought', he writes in 'The Hero as Poet', 'is one spoken by a mind that has penetrated to the inmost heart of things, detected the inmost mystery of it . . .It is a kind of inarticulate unfathomable speech, which leads us to the edge of the Infinite, and lets us for moments gaze into that!'[4] This is exactly what Hardy does in *Tess of the d'Urbervilles*, and what gives his work a movement into a larger more universal dimension, the social concerns being only a part of the world he creates. Whilst earnestly asserting their importance, Hardy moves beyond them. Hardy's choice of conventional plot is, perhaps, his subtle way of begging comparison. Such a comparison, in light of Carlyle's perspective, would do everything to show the depth of originality in Hardy's prose. This originality will be the major concern later in the chapter.

My second reason for choosing to include Jerome's account is to map the change of heart which sensitive men felt towards the fallen woman late in the century. Like Hardy, Jerome was more than a little fed up with the society which based so much on social, economic and ethical perpetuation of the cult of chastity. The very existence of the incident demonstrates two things—that men like J., George and Harris have moved to a more enlightened stance; that families such as the one which deserted the black figure in the river still exist, and still destroy lives. The world of the late nineteenth century is the same and yet not the same as the mid-century decades before it. It is an interesting exercise to compare the stance of the three men in the boat as they come across their fallen woman, with the reaction of the contemporary reviewers of Hardy's creation who were, on the whole, shocked and depressed for all the wrong reasons. At least the storms caused by novels like *Ruth*, *Esther Waters*, and *Tess of the d'Urbervilles* ensured them more than reasonable sales. When the survival of original novels is considered, Oscar Wilde may well be correct when he palliates the negative effects of dispraise by reminding us that the one thing worse than being talked about is not being talked about, or as his more modern counterpart purports, there is no such thing as bad publicity. None the less, despite the wisdom of these maxims, Hardy has trouble distancing himself from the worst of the reviews his novel had to suffer, perhaps because they become apt symbols for the so-called moral stance of a century which had demanded so many human sacrifices, and which was appalled at the immorality of Tess forty years after it was appalled at the immorality of Ruth.

Many of the moral and literary paradigms used as criteria by the critics judging Hardy's novel can be seen today as comic, were it not for the realisation that the symbolic nature of the reviews, together with the influence they carried, is no laughing matter. Even the best reviews are wanting. *The Speaker* provides an enthusiastic review which recognises the great artist Hardy is, but concludes by wishing for a work which would be 'infinitely more bright'.[5] The writer in *The Daily Chronicle* agrees with *The Speaker* in expressing the desire for 'a more pleasant subject'.[6] The novel was seen as a 'grim Christmas gift'.[7] That these critics should not want to look at anything but happy endings is not surprising, but it would have been disturbing to the novelist who wanted to tell the truth. At best then the reviews are disturbing; at worst they are dreadful.

The Saturday Review was convinced that the characters are 'stagey' and 'farcical',[8] and that the novel tells 'an unpleasant story in a very unpleasant way'.[9] I suspect, however, that the reviewer expressing his view in this article did not read the novel with care. When he feels it is out of character for Tess to return to Alec after she was ruined by him the first time, he forgets that she has the weight of an ineffective mother to consider, along with vulnerable siblings and potential starvation. The century-old misconception moves within the text of the review—it is impossible for virtue to be found in a fallen woman. *The Independent* continues in this vein, seeing Tess's story only as one of depravity because 'pure women do not, save in novels, drop into the arms of men that they do not love'.[10] *The Quarterly Review* employs even more invective over what it sees as 'a clumsy sordid tale of boorish brutality and lust'.[11] On the whole the critical world cannot differentiate between the content of a tale and the nature of the tale itself. It seems even more surprising that a sizeable section of supposedly intellectual circles could not comprehend the grandeur that underlies the sorriest things. When one reads comments like those quoted above, one feels that there must be two different novels in question. None the less, the fact remains to enforce one idea—that cultural milieu plays havoc with the critical art, and that it works silently and subconsciously within the critic. Hardy knew that. The concept is one of the themes of the novel. It can be seen in the presentation of Angel Clare who is not simply a character who plays a part in the working out of the plot as it moves towards Tess's destruction. Without knowing it, early in the novel Angel suffers from a sort of cultural and intellectual schizophrenia. In his rejection of Tess he is not a type after Bradshaw, in the sense that he expels what he sees as a polluting figure who threatens the very being of the Christian moral world he knows. Bradshaw might be very wrong, but he knows what he is doing. Angel is not like Grace Roseberry who sees chastity as constituting a right to be rewarded no matter how bitter the inner self might be. Angel lives in a no-man's land, with one foot in one part of his culture, and one foot in another. He has rejected the outward conventions of his father's church, though like Hardy himself, and others like Matthew Arnold, he can never fully reject the nostalgia which he feels for the cultural/historical aspects of the institution. He does agree with Arnold when that essayist claimed that the men of his day could not do with the church as it was, but could not do without it. Angel feels for the church, as he does towards the old families which he has rejected philosophically; 'lyrically, dramatically, and even historically, I am tenderly attached to them'.[12] It is difficult to characterise Angel's philosophy or to refine it to an exact definition. In his newness of mind he is ultimately passive rather than active, especially when he discovers the secret of Tess's past. To be fair to him he is willing to change some of his thought into action. He does work with the country folk, and is willing to marry beneath himself, although our knowledge of Tess helps us to realise that to marry her is no fall. At the heart of his own belief is a romantic readiness which hopes for a new world:

> It was probable that, in the lapse of the ages, improved systems of moral and intellectual training would appreciably, perhaps considerably, elevate the involuntary and even unconscious instincts of human nature; but up to the present day culture, as far as he could see, might be said to have affected only the mental epiderm of those lives which had been brought under its influence. This belief was confirmed by his experience of women, which, latterly having been extended from the cultivated middle-class into the rural community, had taught him how much less

was the intrinsic difference between the good and wise woman of
one social stratum and the good and wise woman of another
social stratum. (*Tess*, p. 188)

This democratic thought is typical of the nineteenth-century
romantic, but it is more than that. It represents an idea which comes
out of real experience. Tess is somewhat wary of Angel's
romanticism. When he calls her Artemis or Demeter she prefers to
be Tess. And she might well worry, seemingly able to sense that
Angel does not only see her as an attractive prospective wife, he
sees her as an embodiment of the pure figure from the romantic
pastoral myth. She represents his pagan romantic hope in the flesh.
This is where Angel is confused. He has equated his experiences in
the field with one of his ideals, that of a levelling of all human
beings. He sees that it works. The pure and good in the middle class
are the same as the pure and good in the labouring class. He seems
to feel that one embodiment of an ideal is the same as another. The
shock comes when he realises he has been at fault, especially when
he prided himself on the fact that he had the good sense to recognise
such inconsistencies.

Tess's revealed past is the death of his romantic dreams. I suggested that he is not like Bradshaw in *Ruth*, but there is one area
where they meet. Bradshaw rejects Ruth because he believes in the
absolutes of purity and degradation, and that any given woman
must belong in one category or the other. There is no such thing as a
moral shade of grey. Angel believes in Tess also in absolute terms.
She is his goddess, his Artemis, his Demeter. She becomes his
replacement for the faith he has lost, or rather which he feels he has
lost. Although he supposedly has 'considerable indifference to
social forms and observances' he is unaware that his romantic
paganism, as it values Tess, is founded on one of the common norms
of the socio-Christian world he rejects. His philosophy is a search, a
search to find a replacement for the faith he had lost. Again he is
like Hardy himself, a man who never stopped searching. The irony
is that Hardy almost feels Angel should have been a bit more like
Alec d'Urberville:

Some might risk the odd paradox that with a little more
animalism he would have been the nobler man. We do not say it.
Yet Clare's love was doubtless ethereal to a fault, imaginative to
impracticality. With these natures corporeal presence is some-

times less appealing than corporeal absence; the latter creating an ideal presence that conveniently drops the defects of the real. She found that her personality did not plead her cause so forcibly as she had anticipated. The figurative phrase was true: she was another woman than the one who had excited his desire. (*Tess*, p. 269)

It seems subconsciously convenient to Angel that he could combine the biological drive he feels towards Tess with his fine, but untried, poetic philosophy. His need for worship becomes the driving force which leads him to his misery, and to Tess's death. But we would miss Hardy's point if we merely saw Angel as priggish or inconsistent or even hard to credit. He tries not only to see the world through different eyes, but to frame a new way for the future. Unfortunately he cannot wholly reject his cultural self which is a mixture of conscious and subconscious prejudices, hopes, beliefs and needs which are 'lyrically, dramatically, and even historically' part of his past, and therefore part of his whole personality. So when he is shocked by Tess's revelation he subconsciously reverts to his Pauline Christian past, becoming judge. Hardy calls these his 'latent prejudices', attitudes which Angel sees working in his parents, but which he cannot see working within himself. It is interesting to notice the conventionality of his argument when he tries to justify his desire to leave Tess. He claims he cannot have a normal physical relationship with his wife because he would despise himself and her. Alec, he insists, is her husband 'by nature'. (*Tess*, p. 268) He is horribly worried about the matter 'getting known' and the ramifications for future progeny. The free thinker is very much bound by the social power of his own culture, as well as being an unconscious part of it. He tries to be part of a new present but is continually drawn into the past. He is ironically correct when he sees himself as more like his father than his two outwardly conventional brethren — 'he was nearer to his father on the human side than was either of his brethren'. (*Tess*, p. 190) In this way 'old laws operate yet' within Angel's being. He can never really assert himself, which Tess can despite the problems she has to overcome in the process, and despite the fact that her ultimate self-assertion in the murder of Alec leads to her death. Angel's lack of self-assertion, rooted as it is in his untried but nascent philosophies, causes a dilemma which is as much the result of time and place as it is of his own choosing.

I am a little surprised that many who read the novel, and are very satisfied with it on the whole, do find Angel, together with the manner in which he is portrayed, a little discomfiting. In his fine book on the developing manuscript of *Tess of the d'Urbervilles*, J. T. Laird is one such critic. Angel, he asserts, 'is not a fully successful character study'.[13] He feels the presentation of Angel's character is not convincing to the modern reader because, with Henry Knight in *A Pair of Blue Eyes* and Giles Winterbourne in *The Woodlanders*, they reveal 'the tendency to idealise the women they love and to avoid, through timidity or scrupulosity, taking these courses of action which alone could lead to the physical consummation of their love'.[14] I suggest that Hardy's very inclusion of this trait in Angel Clare is what gives him life and makes him believable. That a set of ideas and ideals should interfere with his ability to love in a physical sense is a rather pre-Laurentian idea which makes him a fascinating character for the modern reader. Somewhat like Angel, Will in *The Rainbow* wants to submerge his identity in an external absolute, in the form of Anna or the Church.

Laird goes on to try to prove through the study of the development of the manuscript that Hardy had difficulty with the creation and exposition of the young man. Hardy may well have found it demanding, but it is dangerous to equate the extent of the difficulty an artist experiences with the degree of success which ought to be expected. A struggle may well produce a character of some stature and complexity, as it has done with Angel. He is a young man who is trying to find his way in a new world, trying to put some sort of philosophy into practice, trying to cope with an esoteric, poetic nature (never the easiest at the best of times), who then has to cope with being in love at the same time. Lawrence found this combination fascinating. He manages to see through Angel's cultural, religious schizophrenia, and compares him to the far less complicated Alec who

seeks with all his power for the source of stimulus in women. He takes the deep impulse from the female . . . he could reach some of the real sources of the female in a woman, and draw from them . . . But Angel, as the result of generations of ultra-Christian training, has an inherent aversion to the female . . . [15]

Hardy is not the only novelist of the last two decades to draw heroes whose intellectual freedom clashes ultimately with their real, inbred cultural selves, the unwitting product of the society which shapes them. In the twentieth century we are not surprised to see Hardy's thesis proposed—only a part of our present and future can be affected by our own personal motivation and our decision-making. Tess did not want to make the journey to The Chase. Alec desperately wanted to have a permanent relationship with Tess, not knowing it would lead to his death. That type of thinking which allows for the irony of Fate's beck and call is not at all common in the nineteenth century when men saw themselves as masters of their own fate, or the products of a planned universe led by a benign master-planner. Angel's character can be better understood by looking at two men in Gissing's fiction who suffer from, if not the same problem, certainly a related one. Widdowson in *The Odd Women* 'picks up' his future wife, Monica, in a park. He breaks several social conventions in doing so, appearing to be a rather free-thinking man. The irony is that it is not his free thought which makes him unconventional, as is our first thought, but his inability to find a wife in the normal manner; none the less for a while we think he is a free thinker. We also tend to admire his initial lack of reverence for the normally inviolate class system which he disregards. His future wife spends her daily life in a respectable sweat shop, learning the same trade as did Ruth. Monica marries Widdowson because he 'has a few hundred a year'. He is very respectable. She is quite correct when she appreciates the rarity of his proposal. It is interesting that Gissing also felt that he himself could not marry in his own class. 'I must', writes Gissing to his German friend Bertz, 'resume my old search for some decent working-girl who will come and live with me'.[16] Gissing found his Monica in Edith. Ironically like Angel and Widdowson, things did not turn out as planned. Instead of living in the working-class style he implied was necessary or to be preferred, he opted for a middle-class mode with large house and several servants, complaining rather bitterly that the latter could not be managed by his new wife.[17] Whatever the reasons, he wanted to have his cake and eat it. So did Widdowson. That husband could not tolerate the image of his wife as the type who could be approached as he had approached her. He breaks out of traditional confines, then cannot live with the results. His neurotic, possessive approach to marriage makes him extremely authoritarian, to the extent that he almost forces his wife to become that which he fears she is. The other man, who Monica feels is attractive, does not have the courage to run away with her, letting her down at the last minute. Monica carries Widdowson's child, but he refuses to believe it is his, helping to cause his wife's death at childbirth. Angel and Widdowson certainly do not have a lot in common, but they do have a set of beliefs which fall very short when the practical demands of the world around them have to be met. Both are jealous, a fact which neither admit, and both are very possessive. They carry an idealised picture of womanhood which their own private lives and habits belie. Both manage to move their relationships with women outside the limits of their class. In a sense they are outsiders, but they are only prepared to be minimally displaced.

Angel has even greater affinity with Osbert Waymark, the struggling but determined poet, teacher, and free-thinker in *The Unclassed*. Waymark befriends a girl of the streets, a rather idealised prostitute in the Collins' vein, though she is not quite so young and innocent as is Simple Sally. Waymark educates and cares for this girl who has chosen to adopt her mother's professional name, Ida Starr. There is no doubt that Waymark feels a strong sexual affection for her. He rejoices in the relationship; it is the confirmation he needs to prove to himself that he is really the free thinker. The novel presents him as he sees himself in this light. Ida Starr falls very much in love with him, but he looks in more conventional corners for his future wife. He chooses a rather sexless fanatic whose religion prevents her from being warm or even really human. Despite his open unconventional stance, he deserts Ida in an emotional sense. His actions speak louder than his words. Ida finds her long-lost father who has let his tenements go to ruin, despite great wealth, so she turns into a reforming angel, helping the poor, infirm and the needy. Despite Gissing's exposition of Waymark's real double standards, he is rather kind to his hero. Both Hardy and Gissing seem to sense how difficult it is to move against the social current, and to reconcile theory and practice. New thought is so very hard to turn into action. Not only does society have difficulty accepting the Angels and the Osberts, the latter have trouble accepting themselves. These characters reminds us that beyond the realm of what we say we feel, lies a realm of what we really feel. Hardy makes us see these two realms in his presentation of Angel, stressing the idealism of the youth as it does battle with his inherited cultural self. Hardy is therefore able to show in his novel the reasons why societies change so slowly. When Tess grieves for Angel's 'conventional standards of judgement' it is only she and Hardy who know the inmost heart of her husband. He does not notice the immoral textures of what he really feels, his realisation coming too late. His admitted parochialism towards the close of his South American stay 'made him ashamed', and although illness took its toll, it is the discovery of his inner self which mentally ages him 'a dozen years'. (*Tess*, pp. 370-1) He has allowed himself to be influenced by 'general principles to the disregard of the particular instance'. (*Tess*, p. 372) Ironically that is precisely the crime of the reviewers mentioned early in the chapter, who are so busy discussing general principles about art, morality and depression, that they forget Tess herself, and the particular concern the novel and the novelist have for her.

It is always difficult to come to grips with the central concern of the novel. It ought to be remembered that Hardy was displeased when any of his work was distilled to a major idea or refined into a complete philosophy or essential stance. Bailey felt this reminder was appropriate when he opened the 1973 Summer School organised by the Thomas Hardy Society:

> Hardy rejected fixed dogmas on any subject. When asked to state his beliefs he said over and over that he had no consistent philosophy. So far as I know, the last prose statement that he wrote for publication was the final sentence of the preface to his last volume of poetry, *Winter Words*. He wrote, 'I also repeat what I have often stated on such occasions, that no harmonious philosophy is attempted in these pages—or in any bygone pages of mine, for that matter'.[18]

Nor is it possible to come to the heart of this work through analogy by nominating an individual of some stature who played an important part in influencing Hardy's thinking or his work (as can be done, for instance, when analysing *Esther Waters*—the influence of Zola and Naturalism on Moore are relatively obvious). Hardy's mental life was so vibrant, eclectic and individual that it is easy to discover many influences in his work, but rather difficult to order them in rank of importance. Again Bailey's point seems important: it is possible to prove that Schopenhauer had an influence on Hardy, but so did

the Bible, Wordsworth, Darwin, J.S. Mill, Leslie Stephen, Newman, Whitman, Shelley, Keats, Shakespeare, Sophocles,

Plato, folklore and balladry, music, paintings—and just about everything else available to a widely-ranging reader during . . . his lifetime.[19]

The scope of Hardy's intellectual life combined with the finely-tuned response to his world make it possible for the critic to focus on one artistic tradition or philosophic vein which can be seen to be part of the novel. Jean Brooks, for instance, can write on the pre-existential character of the work.[20] Likewise the critic can concentrate on the Romantic and Naturalistic aspects of the novel's style. Zola would have been as interested in the objective description of Flintcomb-Ash as would Coleridge in the fruitful, sensual landscape of Talbothays.

The novel is certainly not ultimately Existential, Naturalistic, or Romantic—it includes them all, but moves beyond them. It is easy to see what Hardy means when he denies the existence of an harmonious philosophy in his work, and what makes it formidable to a critic. It is simply not possible to view the novel from a conventional perspective. None the less I think it is still possible to come to grips with what is important in it. It is possible to discover the central concern of the novel, and that concern has to do with Hardy's relationship with his heroine, and his presentation of her. Howe, when trying to discover the central concern of the novel, insists that theories which view Tess as the agricultural predicament in metaphor lose the heart of the novel in the process.[21] What is really important is Tess and vibrant individuality. This is what marks the novel; she is as much part of those who read her as are Quixote, Othello or Oedipus:

> What matters in *Tess of the d'Urbervilles*, what pulses most strongly and gains our deepest imaginative complicity is the figure of Tess herself. Tess as she is, a woman made real through the craft of art, and not Tess as she represents an idea. Marvellously high spirited and resilient Tess embodies a moral poise beyond the reach of most morality . . . She is human life stretched and racked, yet forever springing back to renewal . . . For Hardy she embodies the qualities of affection and trust, the powers of survival and suffering which a woman can bring to human enterprise.[22]

Despite my enjoyment of the novels studied in this book, and my argument that the heroines of them are morally and aesthetically important, placed next to Tess the fallen women of earlier nineteenth-century fiction are not real. When they work within the frames of reference of their own plots they have a certain life, and hold a great deal of interest, but Nancy, Ruth, Hetty, Martha, Anne, Mercy and Simple Sally provide no such convincing illusion of real, energetic life as we see in the presentation of Tess. The plot structures of the books in which the earlier heroines figure are not dissimilar to the one in *Tess*. The difference lies in stance of the novelist. The main thrust of Gaskell's novel is didactic. Novelists like Collins continue in this tradition, and it is exactly the existence of this tradition which makes Tess different. Even Gissing's tendency to expose social problems, and Moore's fine social sensitivity, tend to place these writers in the didactic school, with a social exposé taking the place of the re-evaluation of Christian morality characteristic of the earlier writers. There is something refreshingly non-didactic about Tess. The reviewer who asks, 'What does the novelist intend to teach us by this creation?'[23] is on the wrong track. He could have asked the same question about any one of the many novels based on the adventures of a fallen woman, and could be given a reasonably accurate reply. Hardy's novel follows the tradition but it is certainly not one of a type. His work stands alone.

There is one very good reason for this. The source of Mrs Gaskell's sympathy is her Christian faith, and her Christian heart, which combine with her admirable sense of humanity, to promote the resolution of discordant elements in her society. Collins follows Mrs Gaskell's lead in that he is exposing the hypocrisy at the heart of the nation's religion. Hardy, on the other hand, does not take his standpoint from the Christian faith. His sympathy and force come from his very lack of faith, and from his perception of universal forces which combine to destroy innocence and goodness. His love of these abstractions replaces the love of God, and he builds on this new force, leaving the old paradigms behind. The novel is almost a journey Tess and Hardy make together to try to find a new paradigm on which an understanding of the alien universe can be based. They do not quite manage to do this, but they do discover that personal destiny cannot be understood in moral terms. Tragedy, after all, transcends moral principle when it reveals the individuality of motive, cause and result—the well-drawn tragic hero or heroine can, and does, move outside the conventions of normal society. The heroine in *Tess of the d'Urbervilles* has to face the cruelty of Fate on her own, and the vast powers which control the workings of the universe. The scope is too great for petty discussions on morality. Tess has to combat national and universal trends which she can never understand. The novel exposes the heroine to the mystical working of self, religion, society, sex, hereditary gifts and scourges, and universal indifference. The canvas of the novel is broad, however each of the different aspects of the novel exists within its framework only as it relates to Tess's fate — they converge, each sphere of influence out- side Tess moving within her as a dynamic force. It is this convergence which gives the novel its unique life. And it is Hardy's imagery which captures these forces in concrete form, and forces the reader inside the heroine. In no other Hardy novel are the objective correlatives so important. The broad seasonal and geographic landscapes of Marlott, Talbothays and Flintcomb-Ash are not simply settings which provide a background for the actions of the characters. They are part of Tess herself. The fertility and glory of one reflects the internal timeliness of her nascent sexuality and her blooming personality; the sterility and deadness of the winter farm is the winter of her life. Primitive man saw the winter as being the time when the gods had left the earth. Tess has lost her god in Angel. A study of Hardy's search for a name for his heroine reveals a man who struggles to find a name for his child as does any caring father. From his early conception of her as a character, Hardy intended to present her as a child of the soil, not only in the romantic sense as a worker in an Arden or an Eden, but as the embodiment of the type whose very soul is part of all that she has met. His early choice of the name Rose-Mary appears most often in the early Ur-text.[24] The latter part of the name is her human self, perhaps connecting her to the original Magdalen; her nomination as Rose, the symbol for purity, links her to nature. Her personal and impersonal characteristics unite through the name. Earlier pre- cursors to Rose-Mary considered by Hardy included Love Woodrow, Sue Troublewell, and Sue Troublefield.[25] Rose-Mary Troublefield may well have captured the complex nature of Tess's personality, but it is far too much of a mouthful. None the less what Hardy wants to do is very clear—unite the mystic influence of the very soil on which the human being grows with the working, living, developing character. Hardy describes Tess as 'an integral part of the scene . . . ' (*Tess*, p. 102), but he is also adamant that the scene becomes part of her. 'Part of her body and life it ever seemed to be.'

(*Tess*, p. 376) I am glad that he did not finally choose Rose-Mary Troublefield as the name for his heroine, but am very interested in the fact that he saw the name of his character as an image, the embodiment of forces which are very hard to name but which shape lives. It becomes impossible for the personal part of the human soul to act in the face of the larger more impersonal part of it—our 'impulses are too strong for our judgement'. (*Tess*, p. 17) This quote almost opens the novel. It is especially ironic that it should come from the mouth of a man of the church. Nowhere do we see this power of impulse more graphically displayed than at Talbothays. Notice how Hardy has united the fertility of the land with the developing attraction between Tess and Angel:

> Amid the oozing fatness and warm ferments of the Froom Vale, at a season when the rush of juices could almost be heard below the hiss of fertilisation, it was impossible that the most fanciful love should not grow passionate. The ready bosoms existing there were impregnated by their surroundings.
>
> July passed over their heads, and the Thermidorean weather which comes in its wake seemed an effort on the part of nature to match the state of hearts at Talbothays dairy. The air of the place, so fresh in the spring and early summer, was stagnant and enervating now. Its heavy scents weighed upon them, and at mid-day the landscape seemed lying in a swoon. Ethiopic scorchings browned the upper slopes of the pasture, but there was still bright green herbage here where the watercourses purled. And as Clare was oppressed by the outward heats, so was he burdened inwardly by waxing fervour of passion for the soft and silent Tess.
> (*Tess*, p. 171)

Morality is founded on judgement. Against this weight of fruitful timeliness when Nature herself swoons within and without her lovers, judgement is indeed too weak, for impulse is the order of the season. Judgement is not part of the momentary universal passion which is seen through milieu and its mirrored state of minds. So Hardy writes a chapter on the age-old discussion of the heart/head conflict, where the heart is an universal one, against which the attributes of the head, rationality and judgement, are numbed. It is not hard to see why a society raised on the idea of a divine plan based on a benign God's wishes, would see this summer fertility ritual as pagan and wicked, and would reject the novel out of hand which tried to present it graphically. Hardy's picture of an amoral dynamic force which decides dispassionately on matters of love and hate, and life and death, does not fit the conventional scheme of things. Over and over Hardy stresses the impossibility of avoiding the developing passion between Tess and Angel. The 'exultation which she described as being producable at will . . . came now without any determination of hers; . . . ' (*Tess*, p. 144) The couple were 'converging under an irresistible law, as surely as two streams in one vale'. (*Tess*, p. 150) They 'could not help it'. (*Tess*, p. 151) Tess yields to Angel's embrace with 'unreflecting inevitableness'. (*Tess*, p. 173) 'Flesh and blood could not resist it.' (*Tess*, p. 177) And when the knowledge of her past sin plagues Tess she tries to decide against the 'oozing fatness and the warm ferments' of the milieu by writing the letter to Angel. Fate determines she should not have the freedom to decide. She knows that she 'must break down'; her 'religious sense' of the 'moral validity [of] the previous union' is powerless when juxtaposed with the invocative and evocative strength of Nature in her most sensuous guise. (*Tess*, p. 143) Though Tess's conventional conscience stops her from being totally happy at Talbothays, she is certainly rejuvenated there. She is so because it is the closest synthesis she experiences between the personal and impersonal forces which rule her life. Her will and the pantheistic summer world unite for a time. The landscape is not just an objective representation of Tess's state of being, it is part of it.

Hardy continues his complex presentation of Tess's character by studying the role of hereditary traits and powers. These are also transformed into motifs. I have already discussed in this chapter the unconscious part of Angel's sensibility, which he inherits from his father and his cultural tradition. This aspect of Angel is presented by Hardy in direct terms. Tess is seen in the novel as having a more complex inherited personality. For convenience it can be studied in three generic areas—her family, her Christian past, and her pagan past. Her position in her immediate family is seen through the image of Tess as a passenger on a ship the control of which is out of her hands. With her brothers and sisters Tess is a passenger on 'the Durbeyfield ship . . . ' which is 'entirely dependent on the judgement of the Durbeyfield adults . . . If the heads of the Durbeyfield household choose to sail into difficulty, disaster, starvation, disease, degradation, death, thither were these half dozen little captives under hatches compelled to sail with them—six helpless creatures . . . ' (*Tess*, p. 33) As in the Talbothays segment the image reinforces the fact that Tess's own will must be subservient to a larger one. It is ironic that the father who is the leader of the vessel himself seems to have little will, and the mother's stoic acceptance of the will of God inhibits any potential she might have. The second image of importance is also one that relates to transport. It represents the distant familial traits inherited by Tess—the d'Urberville coach. The influence of the distant past is more of a mystery than the influence of the Durbeyfield parents, so the image has to be in itself more mysterious. The legend of the coach is ideal for Hardy's purpose as it suggests a mysterious curse that is inherited by the whole family. As soon as Durbeyfield hears the good news of his noble ancestry he calls a pony and trap to convey him home. Walking is just not good enough. Throughout the novel from that point on horse-drawn vehicles seem to symbolise the involuntary aspect of hereditary traits. Tess never drives. She is always driven. The elder Durbeyfield has an additional inbuilt weakness, the reason, perhaps, for his tendency to drunkenness, laziness and wastefulness; his heart is, his wife suggests, 'clogged like a dripping pan'. (*Tess*, p. 98) His ill health is the springboard from which Tess's ill fortune springs. She is forced to take the horse to market with the honey. It is the first such journey undertaken by Tess in the novel. The disastrous result is an omen for the rest of the novel, and the rest of her life. She is soon carried away in Alec's trap, a passionate induction into the realm of male domination and sexuality. D'Urberville may have bought the name, but he also seems to have bought the family curse as well. The ride in the trap which is going to lead ultimately to Tess's tragic death, will also lead to his. The legend of the d'Urberville coach is also based on the abduction of a beautiful woman and her resulting death.

The wedding carriage which Angel hires is an anachronism which evokes the curse of the white cock. This omen is confirmation of an older curse which plagues the marriages of the whole d'Urberville family. The last dilapidated cart in the novel is the one which moves the fatherless family to the town of their forefathers, and Tess closer to Alec. Hardy is bent on displaying the degenerative force which follows the family wherever they go, but he also is quite fascinated with the aristocratic influence which manifests itself in the heroine. This is one of the things which endows Tess with her grandeur, her nobility and her independence, characteristics which Marian and Izz Huet could never hope to share. They see the nobility in Tess when they freely admit that they are no competition for the hand of the young man they love. Angel himself sees the difference inheritance makes to Tess. He could see a 'bit of distinction in poor Tess's blood' and a 'flash of dignity which must have graced her granddames . . . ' (*Tess*, p. 372) This spirit which he senses enlarges Tess several times in the novel—on baptising her dead child she undergoes a change which overawes her younger brothers and sisters. They have to come to terms with a being who was 'large, towering and awful—a divine personage with whom they have nothing in common'. (*Tess*, p. 113) Ironically Tess is the only member of her family to retain aristocratic traits, but they do not only make her greater, they make her vulnerable. She has the inherent will to be noble, yet carries the seed of destruction which wars against it.

There is another inner conflict which Tess is forced to face—the tension between her Christian self and her pagan past. She is first seen participating in a partially forgotten pagan fertility rite called the May or Club Walking. She is last seen on a pagan altar or martyr stone at Stonehenge. She grew in the area of forests of Marlott which had long since disappeared, but inhabitants were still influenced by them because the old 'customs of their shades remain'. This is Hardy's way of coming to grips with the distant past which lives on in spiritual ways in the hearts and souls of those born and brought up in a specific place. In this way Hardy can explain the totally different personality of two or more different geographic areas which could be very close or far away.

Druidical mistletoe grows on the oak trees at The Chase. There is a sprig in the bedroom of the honeymoon house to which Tess is taken. The Druids' monument becomes her final destruction and her final rescue. Against this pagan past, which is also manifest in legends, songs and ballads which Tess learns from her mother, there exists the force of Christian ritual—the baptism of the child which precedes its death; the marriage with Angel which leads directly to Tess's metaphoric death at Flintcomb-Ash. In an effort to solve the pagan-Christian conflict Tess tries to reject the Christian as she sees it, only in its conventional or dogmatic sense. She claims to want nothing to do with a church which will not baptise the innocent. She seems to sense that the workings of the Christian society she must take account of are not in harmony with Nature: 'She was ashamed of herself for her gloom in the night, based on nothing more tangible than a sense of condemnation under an arbitrary law of society which had no foundation in Nature.' (*Tess*, p. 306) In her desire to sleep on the altar at Stonehenge there is a ritualistic acceptance of a deeper, more ancient law which has its roots in the mysteries of the primitive world, the natural world. The Christian world has more affinity with the sophisticated creeds of civilised man. It has rejected Tess and all those like her. It has taught Tess to reject herself: 'Most of . . . her misery had been generated by her conventional aspect, and not by her innate sensation'. (*Tess*, p. 109) It seems that in the framework of the novel the deeper, more mystical, references to the pagan past have affinity with the impulse which the parson of Marlott saw as subservient to judgement. Towards the close of the novel, another of the Christian characters, Mrs Clare, knows that she would 'throw her theology to the wind' if it weighed against the happiness of her child. The suggestion gives pride of place to impulse and emotional need. Hardy seems to be determined to show how institutionalised Christianity so often does not regard the emotional being of man. The final resolution of the conflict between the Christian desire for self-control and the pagan freeing of passion comes when Tess rejects the former, indulges the latter, and murders Alec, consequently giving herself to the altar at Stonehenge. The murder of Alec is the final proof that she has the strength to assert herself in the midst of 'unspeakable despair'. (*Tess*, p. 414) The death of Alec can be seen as the vindication of impulse in the work:

> By degrees he was inclined to believe that she had faintly attempted, at least, what she said she had done; and his horror at her impulse was mixed with amazement at the strength of her affection for himself, and at the strangeness of its quality, which had apparently extinguished her moral sense altogether. Unable to realise the bravity of her conduct she seemed at last content . . . (*Tess*, p. 419)

At this point in the tragedy Tess's Christian moral sense is not relevant. Tess does not die a Christian. When she and her husband inhabit the deserted mansion they are 'enveloped in the shades of the night'. (*Tess*, p. 422) On their journey through Melchester, the huge cathedral, the ultimate symbol for the power of the Church on earth, its cultural dominance over the landscape of the town and the landscape of the mind, means very little to Tess at the end of her struggle: 'The graceful pile of cathedral architecture rose dimly on their left hand, but it was lost upon them now'. (*Tess*, pp. 425-6) The young couple do not seem to look for or find Stonehenge—it finds them. The structure is roofless, seeming to belong to the larger universe of which it is a part. The stone is not cold. It is warm and comforting. Tess senses that she has come home—'You used to say that I was a heathen. So now I am home.' (*Tess*, p. 427) Tess's sacrifice is not Christian—it is 'Older than the centuries; older than the d'Urbervilles'; older than Christianity. Tess's stature as a tragic heroine depends very much on the fact that she has to fight her way through conventional comforts, hopes and dogmas. She lays bare the philosophic and religious trappings of her age and meets the powers that are really there. Hardy never finally knows what to call the powers that run things, the ultimate will. Bailey reminds us that for what the Christians call God, Schopenhauer the Will, Kant Ding-an-Sich, Shaw the Life Force, Hardy has fifty different names.[26] The President of the Immortals is only one of these names. He remains but a shadow named, known more through what he does or does not do with his creatures on earth, than what he is. The shadows which help to destroy Tess are familial, social and national, but there is an universal power which is larger than these. It is this larger shadow which moves over Tess, and it is this spirit which takes the novel out of the tradition of all the other fallen-woman fiction, and puts the work into the twentieth century. Yet the novel also reaches into the past. Tess is like the literary representative of the hundreds of scapegoat rituals which pervade the imagination of countless cultures, primitive and modern. She has affinity with the straw figure made by the gypsies of southeastern Europe, which is tied to a beam, beaten with sticks and is then dismembered or sawn in two. The dismembered parts are burned, then thrown into the stream. The offering is to appease the vague, frightening figure the gypsies call The Shadow Queen. The whole ceremony is accompanied by singing and dancing. The living are elated that the Shadow Queen has passed them, leaving them unmolested.[27] This is how Tragedy works. Hardy has written a novel about Tess and the Shadow Queen. The novel creates its own mythology which transcends the Christian myth, and which is more important than distillation of theme, philosophy and meaning. In his notebooks Hardy makes an entry which was to have specific importance for Tess. He echoes Schlegel's concern that the 'deepest want and deficiency of modern art lies in the fact that the artists have no Mythology'.[28] *Tess* is the means whereby Hardy transforms his mythology into fiction or, more correctly, into the relationship his heroine has with the universe. It is the presentation of Tess in her world of manifested but inexplicable forces which makes the novel 'not merely an emotional . . . one; it is one of the greatest distillations of emotion into art that English literature can show'.[29]

Her creation makes Tess the ultimate fallen woman. With her, the type dies as we know it. Hardy, by choosing a plot which followed a tradition, was quite happy to beg comparison. Few have dared to do the same thing after *Tess of the d'Urbervilles*. In the twentieth century the fallen woman has become a relatively minor figure in gangster novels, or is seen in displaced form as a Jean Harlow, a Mae West or a Marilyn Monroe. These figures may well be part of the public consciousness, but they are not like Tess who, in the words of Virginia Woolf, is an individual who stands up like a lightning conductor 'to attract the force of the elements'.[30]

Notes

1. Jerome K. Jerome, *Three Men in a Boat* (London: J. M. Dent, 1957), p. 152.

2. Ibid.

3. Ibid., p. 153.

4. Thomas Carlyle, 'The Hero as Poet. Dante; Shakespeare'. *From Heroes and Hero-Worship*, 1840, rpt in Edmund D. Jones (ed.), *English Critical Essays*, (London: Oxford University Press, 1971), p. 221.

5. Unsigned review, *The Speaker*, 26 December 1891, rpt Laurence Lerner and John Holmstrom (eds.), *Thomas Hardy and his Readers* (London: The Bodley Head, 1968), p. 61.

6. Unsigned review, *The Daily Chronicle*, 28 December 1891. rpt Lerner and Holmstrom, *Thomas Hardy and his Readers*, p. 63.

7. Unsigned review, *Pall Mall Gazette*, 31 December 1891, rpt Lerner and Holmstrom, *Thomas Hardy and his Readers*, p. 64.

8. Unsigned review, *The Saturday Review*, 16 January 1892, rpt Lerner and Holmstrom, *Thomas Hardy and his Readers*, p. 67.

9. Ibid., p. 68.

10. Unsigned review, *The Independent*, 25 February 1892, rpt Lerner and Holmstrom, *Thomas Hardy and his Readers*, p. 81.

11. Mowbray Morris, *The Quarterly Review*, April 1892, rpt Lerner and Holmstrom, *Thomas Hardy and his Readers*, p. 86.

12. Thomas Hardy, *Tess of the d'Urbervilles* (London: Pan Books in association with Macmillan, 1978), p. 189. Subsequent pagination will be marked in the body of the chapter.

13. J. T. Laird, *The Shaping of Tess of the D'Urbervilles* (Oxford: The Clarendon Press, 1975), p. 131.

14. Ibid.

15. D. H. Lawrence quoted in Irving Howe, *Thomas Hardy* (New York: Collier, 1967), p. 123.

16. Gillian Tindall, *The Born Exile: George Gissing* (London: Temple Smith, 1974), p. 175.

17. Ibid., p. 176.

18. J. O. Bailey, 'Hardy and the Modern World', rpt F. B. Pinion (ed.), *Thomas Hardy and the Modern World* (Dorset: The Thomas Hardy Society, 1974), p. 5.

19. Ibid., p. 4.

20. See Jean Brooks, '*Tess of the d'Urbervilles*; The Move Towards Existentialism', rpt Pinion, *Thomas Hardy and the Modern World*, pp. 48-59.

21. For a summary see Howe, *Thomas Hardy*, p. 128.

33. Ibid., p. 130.

23. Unsigned review, *The Daily Chronicle*, p. 62.

24. Laird, *The Shaping of Tess*, p. 123.

25. Ibid., p. 25.

26. Bailey, 'Hardy and the Modern World', p. 6.

27. Sir James George Frazer, *The Dying God*, Part III, *The Golden Bough* (London: Macmillan, 1920), p. 241.

28. Richard H. Taylor (ed.), *The Personal Notebooks of Thomas Hardy* (London: Macmillan, 1978), pp. 18-19.

29. J. I. M. Stewart, *Thomas Hardy* (London: Longman, 1971) p. 180.

30. Virginia Woolf quoted in Jean R. Brooks, *Thomas Hardy: The Poetic Structure* (London: Elk Books, 1971), p. 12.

7 ESTHER WATERS

From the Nouvelle Athènes to the Battle with Mudie

Like it or not, the importance of Naturalism to the history of the nineteenth-century novel and the development of the twentieth-century novel is well known and undisputed. When Zola, the main proponent of what was as much a philosophic thesis as a literary style, published that landmark in Naturalistic fiction in 1877, *L'Assommoir*, the great Victorian age of fiction in England had largely died a natural death. The Brontës were dead. Mrs Gaskell followed in 1865, five years prior to Dickens and two years after Thackeray. George Eliot was close to the end of her career with the publication of *Daniel Deronda* in 1876. The rise of English prose fiction in the nineteenth century was so sudden, so spectacular and so varied, that in the history of world literature it will remain one of the most remarkable periods. The hiatus left by the close of the period was not easy to fill in the sense that mere repetition and copying of style and convention would stultify the development of the novel. On the other hand, it was not easy to write new fiction which would equal that of the great Victorians, or to change the tastes of a large reading public. Perhaps for this reason Naturalism was never welcomed in England. Meredith, Hardy and Gissing were certainly influenced by it but none of them followed Zola in his efforts to find new directions for the English novel. Naturalism can be seen working in sections of Hardy's *Tess of the d'Urbervilles*, and more so in *Jude the Obscure*, but this writer was too poetic and, ultimately, far too teleological in spirit to accept Zola's thesis wholesale. His literary independence was such that he did not follow any single novelist or philospher. Perhaps, in any case, he was simply too English to adopt a continental fashion. The introduction of Naturalism *per se* to the realm of English fiction was left to a young, restless, iconoclastic, absentee Irish landlord who was trying to find his artistic feet in Paris—George Moore.

His first two works of fiction, *A Modern Lover* (1883) and *A Mummer's Wife* (1884), were youthful, energetic attempts to copy the works of Zola. After these early works Moore was to continue his search for the literary style which best suited him, and leave Zola's naturalistic stance, but he was to return to it with some modification in 1894 with the publication of his only truly commercial success, *Esther Waters*. It is in this way that Naturalism is going to have a very direct effect on the way the fallen woman is understood and presented in the novel. *Esther Waters* remains the only work of Moore to be continuously published throughout the twentieth century, when the remainder of his large and varied work has had a very chequered career.

Esther Waters is one of the most fascinating of all novels on the fallen woman, fascinating because, like *Tess of the d'Urbervilles*, it is quite unique. It presents the fallen woman in a completely new light—she is a pragmatic servant girl in a metropolitan setting, and she is also a heroine. In *Tess of the d'Urbervilles* the strength of the heroine lies in her poetic sensibilities, as does the presentation of her character. Esther's strength, by way of contrast, lies in her down-to-earth manner, her flexibility and her instinct. She is almost prosaic, but her honesty, warmth and struggle keep her from appearing dull. Whilst Tess's poetic originality can easily be discovered through Hardy's own poetic regard for her, one in the same thing, Esther's originality lies in the unique background, education and personality of Moore. Before Esther is examined in detail a few pages will be well spent looking at Moore's early experiences which prepared him to write in a manner never attempted by an English novelist in the nineteenth century.

George Augustus Moore was born in 1852, at Moore Hall, the family seat in County Mayo, Ireland. His schooling at St Mary's, Oscott in England proved an unqualified failure in all eyes—his own, his father's and his masters'. He hated being there, read Shelley in secret, pretended to have a liaison with one of the young maids, and deliberately failed. His headmaster wrote lengthy letters to his father, one complaining that Moore's indifference could not be counteracted by the masters 'whose labours have produced such infinitesimally small results'.[1] In the same letter the headmaster expresses his dismay about the wayward student's spelling—Jesus was Jeasus; proclaimed, proclamed, etc. Needless to say, George Moore left school before his course of study was completed, to join the select, but none too small, number of men of letters and science who failed at school, then proved to be men of genius. The family moved to London in 1869, the father newly elected to Parliament; in London Moore made a poor showing as an art student at the South Kensington Museum. The death of his father left him independent since he was the older of two sons. He acted the part of the young dandy in London, then moved to Paris in 1873 where he reopened his art studies at the Beaux Arts and the Salon Julian. His real education took place at the Café Nouvelle Athènes, which was the centre of French Impressionist circles. His iconoclastic tendencies were about to be reinforced in this informal setting, where he rubbed shoulders with a remarkable coterie of artists and poets which included Adam, Mallarmé, Pissaro, Sisley, Renoir, Degas, and Manet who introduced Moore to the circle. Quite rightly he regarded this company as providing a far more impressive education than the dusty libraries of Oxford, Cambridge and Trinity. He even met Monet several times—the conversations together remaining in his mind as precious. Freeman, in *A Portrait of George Moore*, shows the young Moore being divested of his last remnants of Victorianism. He quotes Moore: 'One thing I learned, and that was from Monet, who taught me to be ashamed of nothing except being ashamed; yet who knows?' and adds, 'perhaps that was not learned but lay in me all the time'.[2] It was precisely this lack of shame, which seemed to Moore to make the Frenchman more open and honest, that made Manet attractive to him:

> Of Manet's art, and of his alone, Moore speaks with unrestrained praise and fondness; and was it not partly because Manet urged revolt against the old that this younger rebel declared and maintained such a loyalty of admiration? because 'Adam standing in Eden looking at the sunset was not more naked and unashamed than Manet'.[3]

During the years that Manet knew Moore he was never to sell a picture; the price 'that one pays for shamelessness, for truth, sincerity, personality, is public neglect'.[4]

This unusual education was undertaken fifteen to twenty years before *Esther Waters* was written. If there was one thing that the fallen woman needed to divest more than anything else, it was her sense of shame. Nancy, Ruth, Mercy and Little Em'ly are obsessed by shame—it is shame which makes the latter travel to Australia, and shame which makes her feel life as a single woman is her only fate. She is not worthy of a good man. Even Tess is not free from it. Esther's lack of shame, as we will see, is very much part of her own justification. It is almost as if Moore's admiration for the Impressionist painters' lack of shame and their openness is transplanted in an English fictional type, the fallen woman. His personality was not to copy the respectable façade of the Victorian aristocrat—Esther is not to adopt the cowed façade of the fallen woman demanded by a certain section of the mainstream Victorian social or literary culture. The influence of these young Frenchmen was to lead him to a more honest look at the working-class fallen woman, making him determined to show 'people behaving as they do behave'[5] rather than having them behave as his readers would want them to behave. Moore is not to share Mrs Gaskell's fears that the fallen woman is, perhaps, not the right topic for fiction. Ruth's overwhelming conscience is, in part, a reflection of Mrs Gaskell's own worry about the dubious presence of her heroine. It is also, one must remember, her way of showing her readers that Ruth is not a totally corrupt individual, incapable of virtue, truth and honour. Mrs Gaskell may be making an effort to get her readers on her side, by having Ruth behave as a Victorian middle-class woman would expect her to behave. Ruth's shame is certainly no *mauvaise honte*. She is, to be fair, fifty years older than Esther. Had she never existed it would have been very difficult for the other fallen women to follow. As can be expected, Moore's heroine has very little shame at all, once she realises the forces that gather against her. When she discusses her past with a particularly religious suitor he asks if she has repented. Her reply is characteristically brief, to the point and, above all, indubitably honest—'I should think I have, and been punished too, enough for a dozen children'. No other fallen woman in the nineteenth century has been so sure of herself, so direct, and so definite about justifying the repudiation of her sin, a sin which is very much like Ruth's. To imagine the latter or Simple Sally in Collins's *The Fallen Leaves* responding thus is unimaginable: 'If I'm not good enough for you,' she points out to her suitor, 'you can go elsewhere and get better; I've had enough of reproaches'.[6]

The life and personality of his heroine owe their existence to the attitudes he had within himself, but which contact with the Impressionists drew out, encouraged and reinforced. He was also to learn from them that he was no visual artist. The hiatus left by this realisation was, for a time, filled by the writing of poetry, which resulted in the publication of two collections—*Flowers of Passion* (1877) and *Pagan Poems* (1881). It was, I suspect, an innate common sense which told him he was not to be a poet rather than the poor reviews the works received. By 1882, two years after his return to London, still a young man at thirty-one, he was, according to Shaw 'an ex-painter and ex-poet' who was 'incapable of writing a presentable advertisement for a lost dog'.[7] Time was to prove Shaw wrong. In France, literary forces had been, in addition to the Impressionist influence on his attitudes, shaping an approach to prose fiction.

Moore wrote a play, *Martin Luther*, in conjunction with Bernard Lopez, a playwright who had already worked with figures who almost make up a list of who's who in nineteenth-century French literature. Through Lopez, Moore was to have vicarious contact with Dumas Père, Scribe, Rochefort Père, and a host of others. There was also the influence of Dujardin, Balzac and, above all, for a time at least, Zola, whose Naturalist doctrine Moore adopted with youthful enthusiasm. He left London a self-centred dilettante, impatient with the stuffy, hypocritical society in which he moved, though perhaps quietly being grateful for the existence of the stuffy traditions. It is only against the grey of their conventions that his colour would shine. He was always a showman, always enjoying the part he played. None the less there was also something corporeal about his rebellion, and his time in France certainly must bear some responsibility for that. An incident remembered from his first visit to Zola's home (they had met very briefly one or two times in society) shows how very different the French literary milieu was from the world of Dickens, Gaskell, and Thackeray:

> On the wall of the last little flight [of stairs] there were Japanese prints depicting furious fornication; a rather blatant announcement, I thought, of Naturalism—but they were forgotten quickly for in a few seconds I should be in the master's presence.[8]

The frankness which decorates Zola's walls inculcates Zola's fiction. It is related to the same shameless openness encouraged by Monet and Manet. The image of the prints on the wall captures the spirit of the French world which was to make Moore its disciple on his return—in one way or another Moore was to try to unite English fiction with the literary habits of Flaubert, Balzac, Gautier, Dujardin and Zola. It is little wonder that Moore found it difficult to settle on one characteristic style. He was never to express permanent allegiance for one writer. Perhaps he was even too much a rebel for that, and too impulsive a man.

Zola was, in a way, fortunate that Moore followed him in three works. His first two novels, *A Modern Lover* (1883) and *A Mummer's Wife* (1884), were largely Naturalistic. They caused the expected storm. Naturalism was not even welcomed by English

writers, let alone the English public. It was never to be as ener-
getically received in England by writers as it was in America where
Crane, London, and above all, Drieser, were to make Naturalism
an American school, a national institution. Even Moore's closest
literary associates did not give his naturalistic novels unqualified
support. Yeats, demonstrating a vestige of Victorian prudery and
sexism, forbade his sisters to read *A Mummer's Wife*, a novel which
traces the decline of Kate Ede from upstanding late-Victorian
moralist to bohemian drunkard. Susan Mitchell, when living with
the Yeats family, was attracted to the book when Yeats limited its
readership. No doubt many literary works of merit owe their continued existence and popularity to the scandalous nature of their
reputation. Fallen women in fiction may well owe their life to their
so-called poor reputations. Susan Mitchell records her own
reactions to the new fiction:

> I read *The Mummer's Wife* [an interesting mistake in the title's
> article] when I lived with the Yeats in Bedford Park, and chiefly,
> with feminine perversity, because W. B. Yeats had forbidden his
> sisters to read it. I gulped guilty pages of it as I went to bed of
> nights. Its merciless probing into life intimidated me. I shrank
> from it as the periwinkle from the pin . . . I understand that the
> book is regarded as immoral; to me it appeared one of the most
> gloomy moralities in literature . . .
>
> On Mr Moore's return to his native land, when I met him for
> the first time of speech, remembering those tortured readings of
> *The Mummer's Wife*, as nobody was within hearing at the
> moment, I asked him, with the ignorant courage of my Puri-
> tanism, why he wrote such horrible books. He answered by
> asking me had I read any of them. [Moore was obviously used to
> adverse criticism from non-readers.] I faltered 'No'—for I was
> ashamed to confess to *The Mummer's Wife*. He said with that
> instant surrender to attack so characteristic of him: 'I wrote one
> good book, *Esther Waters*. I will get you a copy of it.'[9]

When *A Mummer's Wife* was published it was not only the
Zolaesque content which made it revolutionary; it was published by
Henry Vizetelly in one cheap volume which sold for six shillings.
This was almost more revolutionary than the content. It also owes
its existence to Zola's suggestion, made after Mudie's all-powerful
circulating library refused to include the expensive three-volume *A*

Modern Lover on its lists. The battle fought with the circulating libraries was ultimately won by Moore with *Esther Waters*. Vizetelly, incidentally, was later jailed for publishing Zola's works in England. He died, either in jail, or shortly after being released. Moore was always to feel a little responsible for this as he encouraged the publisher's enthusiasm for the French School.[10]

After his first two novels Moore searched in other directions, and opened his writing to other influences. Between these first two novels and *Esther Waters* (1894) he published in about 200 periodicals, and wrote two plays, four novels, *Modern Painting*, *Parnell and His Island*, and the first of his autobiographical writings, *Confessions of a Young Man. Esther Waters* is, for an inexplicable reason, a return to Naturalism, though in it the Naturalism is modified and more positive than that found in *A Mummer's Wife*, which is very much a fledgling of the Zolaesque family. The storm which accompanied the publication of *Esther Waters* could hardly have surprised Moore. In 1891, three years prior to its publication, Hardy had to face the most vehement criticism when *Tess of the d'Urbervilles* was serialised. The financial ramifications for Hardy are obvious when the novel was banned by the circulating libraries.[11] In 1883 Moore felt similar strains when his first novel was not accepted by the same libraries. Its cost of 31s 6d made it too expensive for the average reader. Moore, who knew *Esther Waters'* frank discussion of the fallen woman's biological and emotional needs was even more realistic than Hardy's novel, must have prepared himself for battle. He would probably have been very disappointed had a storm not ensued. He must also have had the memory of Vizetelly's imprisonment and death still freshly implanted in his mind, because it was only six years since those events. Publishing Naturalistic fiction in England was a dangerous matter. The irony that Vizetelly's editions of Zola were expurgated would not have escaped Moore in any case.[12] A large section of the reading public and the protectors of public morals could not even stomach watered-down Zola. In view of all this the publication of *Esther Waters* is certainly more heroic than one would normally consider the publication of a novel to be. But Moore was not to be so deeply hurt as was Hardy, whose prose writing was brought to an untimely end in the face of adverse reactions to his work. He almost revelled in the battle, enjoyed the notoriety, and fought back successfully. The conflict with Mudie's and Smith's circulating libraries is a literary adventure which was to have long-lasting ramifications for the development of the novel at the end of the nineteenth and the beginning of the twentieth centuries. The battle which he had with Mudie and Smith is almost a literary adventure—that it culminated with the publication of *Esther Waters* gives it special importance here. Moore virtually had to tackle, almost single-handed, one of the mid-Victorian bastions of literary taste—the circulating library. His isolation in this struggle seemed to give him untiring energy, rather than having the opposite effect.

In her book on Mudie's library and its relationship to fashions in the Victorian novel, Guinevere L. Griest takes care to point out that the library was both a creator of public tastes, and a careful response to them. Mudie, being the leader in the lending business, had power to create a set of attitudes in his subscribers, but he was not devoid of sufficient business acumen to ignore the power of demand:

> As the Select Library continued to expand after 1850, readers became less and less disposed to buy, and more inclined to feel that if it was worthwhile, Mudie's would have it . . .
>
> Thus three elements—literary worth, the three-volume form, and subscriptions to Mudie's became intermingled, and the Mudie patron became habituated to borrowing novels. It was natural enough for authors to lose sight of him, behind the massive façade of the library, and to forget that while publishers watched the librarian, Mudie's own fingers were on the pulse of his subscriber. The library had been created to satisfy a demand for 'select' books, and Mudie conscientiously strove to uphold the standards both he and his readers approved. As he did this, however, he solidified tastes and attitudes in some patrons, and actually created them in others. Alexander Macmillan saw the situation more objectively and more clearly than many of his contemporaries; he wrote of Mudie: 'I think his power . . . has been exaggerated, and his willingness to use that power too. He must be a servant of the public in the main, and only in a very general sense its master'.[13]

While Moore may have recognised Macmillan's point, he preferred, no doubt for propagandistic purposes, to paint Mudie and Smith in archetypal terms as monsters—he made villains out of them, and whilst this dramatic habit could be questioned because it was misleading, the ends justified the means. He captured any apparent contradiction, ridiculous moment, or evidence of hypocrisy and used it to the full. It was effective ammunition. Writing in a none too positive temper, he recorded his protest in the *Pall Mall Gazette*, vehemently condemning what he called the 'illiterate censorship of a librarian',[14] arguing that real and important literary battles had little to do with the prevailing conflict between supporters of romantic literature and those who felt realism was the only way to go. Mudie actually bought fifty copies of *A Modern Lover*, but refused to circulate them, according to Moore's account, because the librarian felt it to be immoral. In addition he had received complaints about the content therein: Mudie told Moore that 'Two ladies from the country wrote to me objecting to that scene where the girl sat to the artist as a model for Venus. After that I naturally refused to circulate your book.'[15] These explanations, intended to ameliorate the anger of the young writer, were, in fact, fuel to the fire. They made him more determined to challenge the system. One suspects, however, that the whole thing was relished by the writer whose own accounts of the conflict smack of some of the poetic licence which is often the habit of the literary artist. His background comes to the fore when he railed at the fact that the system created and controlled which writer was to be read and popular, and which writer was not to be read: especially rancorous to Moore is the fact that this censorship was under 'the intolerable jurisdiction of a tradesman'.[16]

As can be imagined, press responses to Moore's vigorous campaign were mixed. Many of the 200 periodical articles written by Moore between *A Mummer's Wife* and *Esther Waters* were directly concerned with the semi-monopoly held by the few powerful circulating libraries; many of the remainder, not directly concerned with this conflict, do not resist the opportunity to mention it at every conceivable moment. The basis of Moore's argument is that the novelist ought to be awarded the right to freedom of speech which he felt more traditionally allowed to the press, the historian, and the biographer. His argument often demonstrated more 'warm language than cool logic'.[17] It attracted, none the less, attention in some powerful circles. Griest nominates the *Saturday Review* as being particularly supportive—she cites one article, 'A Circulating Censorship', which argued that one or two narrow-minded readers ought not to determine the success or failure of new fiction. The article also condemned the influence the libraries had in causing the watering-down of content to move a particular work into the sphere of dreary conventionality. The solution to the problem lies, suggests the writer, in producing cheaper books. The *Saturday Review* points out that Michael Levy's cheap publications in France had saved the French reading public from English limitations, but left the question begging: 'Who will save England?'[18] This article was published in the *Saturday Review* of December 1884. Approximately two months prior to this Moore and Vizetelly had published the cheap six-shilling edition of the young writer's second novel. It seems that the writer in the *Saturday Review* did not know of Moore's revolutionary step. He was still relatively unknown beyond his immediate circle. This was not always to be so. Moore claims that he was the one to save England from the censorious clutches of the library monopoly, by introducing the cheap single-volume work.

Ironically, when *Esther Waters* was published in its six-shilling form (it is interesting that the cost did not change between 1884 and 1894) his attention was turned away from Mudie's to Smith's circulating library. His main antagonist was William Faux, the head of Smith's library department. It banned *Esther Waters* because of 'twenty lines of pre-Raphaelite nastiness'. I have been unable, in several readings of the novel, to find the pre-Raphaelite lines mentioned. There is much in the novel which one would expect to be shocking, but those sections certainly exceed twenty lines. Griest quotes a lively extract from *A Communication to My Friends* (1933) wherein the writer gives a typical example of his lack of patience experienced on one of his customary visits to the enemy camp. He wanted to know, in detail, why Faux had treated Esther so badly:

> [I] mounted a long concrete staircase to arrive . . . at lacklustre rooms in which I discovered a long, lean man, one of those men who have grown old without knowledge of life or literature in the dim shadows of their bookshelves. Mr. Faux was particularly attractive as a specimen. A tangle of dyed hair covered a bald skull, and as he . . . giggled, his false teeth threatened to jump out at me. His withered face betrayed amusement when he heard that I had called . . . to ask his reasons for excluding *Esther Waters* . . . 'You see,' he answered, 'we are a circulating library and our subscribers are not used to detailed descriptions of a lying in hospital.'[19]

The melodrama of the moment is, no doubt, part fiction—looking at his victory in hindsight was apt to make him a little pompous. The fact that Mudie's gave in by accepting *Esther Waters* for circulation did not alter Mr Faux's stand—and made him, in Moore's eyes, all the more ridiculous for his stubbornness. Hence the being of the merciless caricature above. To be fair, Moore did have some help by the time *Esther Waters* was published—no other than the help of Mr Gladstone himself. He had written a postcard to Moore prasing the novel, especially for its anti-betting content. Although he did not take a stand in writing on the fallen woman theme of the novel, a theme which is far more pervasive in the novel than the racing element, it is well known that he enjoyed saving fallen women, especially attractive ones, and very often was aligned to famous ones. 'Old Glad-Eye', often immortalised in the nineteenth century, never appeared to worry about the obscene jingles which were sung in the streets, even when his humanitarian activities with fallen women were misconstrued:

> Eight little whores, with no hope of heaven,
> Gladstone may save one, then there'll be seven.[20]

Many thought that Gladstone's motives for walking the streets at night were not quite moral. He was a 'highly controversial figure' in Victorian society

> on account of his predilection, which amounted almost to an obsession, for saving fallen women. It had developed in his undergraduate days, and had become an important factor in his life. The cause of it was to be found in some of the curiously conflicting emotions which inspired him. On the one side there was his deeply religious outlook, and his strongly-held moral views. On the other there was his highly emotional nature, his romanticism, his deep sense of pity and—admittedly—the strong attraction which pretty women had for him.[21]

Like the Victorian novelists who save fallen women, Gladstone was mostly interested in the attractive ones. There is never a mention in the fallen women novels, as far as the writer knows, which concerns itself with older, uglier, middle-aged or unattractive fallen women. This points to the Victorian love of placing women on pedestals, investing them with classical beauty and medieval purity reminiscent of the Mary Cult. The saving of a girl still with the appearance and beauty of youth makes the metamorphosis from the fallen state more poetically possible. This may well be a trait shared by Gladstone, Dickens, Gaskell, Collins, Trollope and Hardy, though the first acting in social modes rather than in literary style. In any case Moore's Esther is far too busy trying to survive to be placed on a pedestal of the kind reserved for Ruth as she dies a sacrificial death, the ultimate confirmation of her angelic purity. Perhaps Esther's humanity was not sufficiently transcendent for the romantic Gladstone. Despite his failing to mention Esther in the correspondence, Moore made great use of his support. Determined to make as much mileage as possible from Smith's refusal to circulate the book despite Mudie's begrudging approval or a Prime Minister's support, Moore hired an accountant to calculate Smith's losses suffered through their stubborn stand. The figure Moore insists on is in the region of £1,500:

> It was after the publication of these figures that I had the satisfaction of hearing that the partners of the firm sent word to their librarian that it would be well in the future to avoid heavy losses by banning books, especially books that Mr. Gladstone was likely to read and to express his approval in the *Westminster Gazette.*[22]

Moore was triumphant, a fate not to be shared with any of the other novelists who write on the fallen woman studied in this book, with the exception of Dickens. Not only was his novel a commercial success but it was the watershed which marked the new publishing and circulation world from the old. He did have, in the end, Gladstone's help, but he certainly was not given support by any other novelist. He had endeavoured to enlist the help of Henry James but without success. Wilkie Collins had always been irked by the circulating libraries but in the 1880s he was far too ill to help. He died in 1889 when Moore's success was still a long way off. Gissing was happy to agree with Moore in spirit, but did not pledge active support. Shaw did not admire Moore. He fought alone and believed quite firmly to his dying day that he alone broke the censorship of the libraries, and at the same time managing to bring about the timely demise of the expensive three-volume edition which from 1850 had been the Victorian novel. 1894, the year in which *Esther Waters* was published, saw the new circulation of 184 three-volume novels; 1895 witnessed the issue of 52; in 1897 only four were published.[23] Perhaps, in any case, the three-volume novel was dying a natural death. Moore was never sufficiently modest to allow for the timely nature of his victory. None the less it is very difficult to lay credit elsewhere than at the respective doors of Vizetelly and Moore. 'The censorship of the libraries,' writes Moore triumphantly, 'has come to an end . . . and I boasted that I had served the cause of humanity.'[24] The beginning of the end of the power of the circulating libraries can almost be traced to 1894. It is ironic and appropriate that one of the bastions of Victorian middle-class culture was partially destroyed by a fictitious fallen woman and her energetic inventor.

Throughout the century the fallen woman and the sexually promiscuous male were at the centre of the continual censorship battle. Many would have wished the disappearance of *Ruth*, *The New Magdalen*, *An Eye for an Eye* and every novel like them, which looked at extra-marital sexual relationships. Any obvious sexual reference was bad enough, but sex outside of marriage was the ultimate literary sin. Like all centuries it was an age for repressing and banning books. Shelley was sent down from Oxford in 1811 for his writing. His printer, Maxon, was jailed.[25] Thackeray would not publish Elizabeth Barrett Browning's 'Lord Walter's Wife' because of the 'immoral situation'. It is not surprising that when the work was eventually published the circulating libraries did their worst and banned it.[26] Eliot's *Adam Bede* was also treated in a similar manner because it was seen as 'the vile outpouring of a lewd woman's mind . . . '[27] Even the new version of *The Book of Common Prayer* was repressed in 1852. It was almost Unitarian in spirit, when it did not make the point clear that Christ was God. And the compilers of this new work? Queen Victoria and Prince Albert aided by the Chevalier Bunsen.[28] No one was exempt. At times the censor seemed all powerful. At least *The Book of Common Prayer* had nothing to do with extra-marital sex or fallen women.

In *Conversations with George Moore*, Geraint Goodwin remembers the manner in which the ageing but celebrated pan-jandrum of Chelsea reduced this century-old conflict to its lowest common denominator:

> when I first came to England there was a select body of men who were concerned with the purity of our literature. It was I . . .who caused these select worthies much anxiety; they also caused me much anxiety but that is beside the point . . .
> It was not an easy matter, you know, to decide what part of life

should not have any part in life, and what part, on the other hand, was perfectly exemplary. But if this scruple arose, which I very much doubt, they were not going to let it detain them in their noble work. And so they adopted a code or a formula. It was to be perfectly simple—that anyone who found himself the victim of a very ordinary impulse, and who had not gone through the sacred ceremony of marriage was not to be allowed. Here then was the solution, that humanity was to be divided . . . into two great groups, the married and the unmarried. The one was to be the legitimate ground of the artist, and the other—well, the other was illegitimate and that was enough . . . Eventually I called upon Mr.——, who was the moving spirit in this select assembly and who had caused me so much financial loss, and perhaps some moral questionings, by his decision to suppress my books. He was very kind and appreciated many, if not all my qualms. 'But supposing,' I said to him, 'supposing a book is beautifully written . . . what then?'

'Beautiful writing,' he replied with emphasis, 'has nothing to do with it—the book is bad.'

We parted after a while, not before Mr.—— had, in compensation no doubt, regaled me with some of the dirtiest stories I have heard in my life.[29]

The sanctity of Victorian marriage demanded silencing of all content which threatened the innocence of the female sex, and threatened the tenets of its being. For many men, and to a lesser extent some women, the sanctity of marriage was a game, a front, a falsehood, no doubt not quite so licentious and lascivious as Walter's secret life, but secret enough. The game, the pretence, the tradition was, perhaps, perpetuated as much by the old maids who complained to Mudie's about the content of Moore's fiction, as by the men who were forced to believe in it in public but ignore it in private. The dirty stories, told by the gentleman in the extract above, must have been bad to evince critical comment from a very broad-minded late Victorian. The stories, and their seedy content were sufficiently private not to warrant censorship. The situation is an apt symbol for the censorship trends of the nineteenth century. This was the public which, according to Humbert Wolfe, 'fought with beasts in public but bought them elaborate dog collars in private'.[30] To the Anglo-Irish disciple of 'Manet, Monet, Degas and Renoir, a mock puritanism must have seemed as startling and disgusting as leprosy'.[31] Which brings me to my last point before discussing the actual content and meaning of *Esther Waters* in some detail. It is a tendency in the twentieth century, perhaps as a legacy from the anti-Victorian reaction in the first thirty years of it, to feel that the Victorian hypocrisy and double standards maintained by the dog collar buyers is a modern discovery, that they were somehow so deeply involved in it that they could not see the wood for the trees. That is just not true. The century is characterised by the upholders of the *status quo* and those who would expose its weaknesses, flaws and misdemeanours. It was the age of reform because of one tradition—the habit of questioning, and the concomitant action which follows it. Moore is only one in thousands; he is a Victorian who refused to accept things as they were. It is this habit, shared by many, which holds the key to the real greatness of the Victorian age.

Esther Waters was written in this spirit. Moore wanted to tell the truth about working-class attitudes, childbirth, the economics of survival, the animal in man—telling this type of truth required that the novelist study and faithfully record what natural and sociological forces can do when they interact in the life of a down-to-earth girl. The naturalistic novel sees scientific determination as central to the actions and fate of the character. The interplay between heredity, milieu and circumstance is not a spiritual mystery but something which can be observed and understood. Naturalism is one of the novelist's responses to the revolution that modern science produced. Man is to be studied as a being with an individual spirit, but he is first and foremost an animal whose human instincts are animal instincts. The debt to Darwin is obvious. It is ironic, however, that Moore would have to live in France so that the scientific observation of an Englishman could influence his work.

Esther Waters

The idea which would ultimately lead to a novel on the life of a servant girl was first germinated when reading a rather commonplace but fair notion in the newspaper. 'We're always complaining of the annoyance that servants occasion us, but do we ever think of the annoyance we occasion servants?'[32] Moore was quite struck with the idea—it immediately changed from a reaction into fiction:

Pondering upon that as he stepped out, he rejected the notion of a young lady in love with her footman (a mere incident in the story as we read it now), and imagined a girl, a kitchen maid, anxious to get a living. He thought that on fourteen pounds a year she could not rear her illegitimate child, but needed sixteen pounds. The life of a human being being valued at two pounds a year was the subject, and before he had passed from the Temple to the Law Courts the story was decided upon.[33]

Hardy had been the only other nineteenth-century novelist before him to be noted for his treatment of a servant girl, so there were no conventions to follow, no predetermined types to consider. The writer would have to be capable of 'holding the mirror steadily up to a particular phase of "nature" '.[34] The result is unique—like all naturalists Moore tried to give Esther 'the literal fidelity of a photograph', but in addition he was too much of an artist not to give his heroine 'the warm animation of a painting'.[35] Moore claims that the work was, to that date, 'the only English novel that treated a servant girl seriously as the chief person of the drama'.[36] It is, unfortunately, characteristic of Moore to either insult Hardy's work or, as he does in this case, ignore it altogether. His claim would be more accurate if he were to acknowledge the pastoral servant studied through Tess, and claim originality for his metropolitan heroine.

The novel allows for a frank study of the animal in man and woman. It is certainly not the first time an English novelist tries to allow for the nature of man as a conglomeration of instinctual impulses, innate passions, fears and needs, then to point out that these traits clash with the prevailing religious ethics. The nineteenth century will be remembered as the century of self-control. So it may not be the first English novel to study the animal in man, but it certainly is the first to study the animal in woman. Male sexual transgression was the result of natural energy, but female sexuality, especially outside of marriage, was sexually deviant. One of the most explicit novels to include an allowance for the animal in man is Charles Kingsley's *Yeast* (1851), now largely a forgotten, fallen-woman novel. A quick look at the content of the hero's dialogue will reveal a surprising frankness, especially surprising when the date of publication is remembered. It is interesting to wonder how it would be received had the speaker been a woman. The hero of the novel writes to his clerical tractarian cousin, in a surprisingly un-Victorian manner, dwelling on the frustrations inherent in self-control, the purging of the flesh, and the sanctification of the spirit, which in comparison seems naturally weak:

> I am, you know, utterly deficient in that sixth sense of the angelic or supralunar beautiful, which fills your soul with ecstasy. You, I know, expect and long to become an angel after death: I am under the strange hallucination that my body is part of me, and in spite of old Plotinus, look with horror at a disembodiment till the giving of that new body, the perfection of which, in your eyes, and those of everyone else, seems to be that it will be less, not more of a body, than our present one . . . [37]

Earlier in the letter the hero, Lancelot Smith, is even more unorthodox, claiming the right, hedonistically, to regard appetite as god-given: 'I find within myself certain appetites; and I suppose that the God whom you say made me, made those appetites as part of me'.[38] For this to be spoken by a woman as justification for her fall would be unthinkable. The jibe Lancelot has at the expense of religious dogma would, no doubt, have been close to Moore's paganism. The recognition of the sexual drive was implicit, say, in Eliot's presentation of Arthur Donnithorne, or Gaskell's painting of Bellingham, but was not allowed in the presentation of the heroine. Hetty was in love with Arthur and looking to be a lady. Ruth was innocent, only recognising Bellingham's advances in a vague manner. Lancelot, like Arthur and Bellingham, recognises the presence of his innate drives but does not quite know what to make of them. It is the conflict of 'mad noisy flesh' with the 'silent immortal spirit'.[39] His inability to resolve this conflict is, of course, part of the problems of youth itself, but it is also due to the fact that in school and at home the subject of sexuality has been taboo, therefore not to be any official part of his education. Again the point is to be made: if men had more freedom and they were hampered by lack of education in the subject, then how much more did the lack of preparation frustrate the maturation of the woman:

> All conversation in the subject of love had been prudishly avoided, as usual, by his parents and his teacher. The parts of the Bible which spoke of it had been always kept out of his sight. Love had been to him practically ground tabooed and 'carnal'.[40]

This could well have been Moore's protest, except that Moore is to look from Esther's female perspective. Citing Kingsley's attitude to his hero's dilemma proves that the stand Moore takes is not particularly innovative—that he changes the sex certainly is. But if Kingsley can be proved advanced in his thinking by citing one or two passages, in others he gives himself away stylistically. The following exhortation could only be given in a mid-Victorian novel, or a work which imitated the style of that period. None the less if the manner of presentation can be overlooked, the sentiment remains relatively enlightened:

> O fathers! fathers! and you clergymen, who monopolise education! either tell the boys the truth about love, or do not put into their hands, without note or comment, the foul devil's lies about it . . . [41]

In *Esther Waters* Moore intends to tell the truth about love, partly by looking at it from a hitherto unwritten stance. He learnt from Gautier, reminds Wolfe, 'that if you will but occupy yourself with the fact of love, and not its fiction, a thousand thousand stories await the happy novelist'.[42] The truth about love then is that it is an innate animal drive. Examples like *Yeast* and *Mademoiselle de Maupin* were before him. The challenge was to make them part of the truth about women in an English novel.

Esther is the simple Christian girl, brought up by stern but loving parents in the tradition of the Plymouth Brethren. Her father dies, the event being the springboard from which her fate moves. The kind but now powerless mother marries again; this time she is not so fortunate in her choice. Mr Saunders is an aggressive, non-religious, hard-drinking, selfish man. Esther is made to go into service. After two poor postings, Esther is sent to Woodview Lodge, the home of the Barfields, and the centre of horseracing in the district. As a result of her early upbringing Esther avidly believes in 'love of God, and love of God in the home' but the forces she encounters at Woodview continually challenge the purity and simplicity of this belief. As the milieu changes, so does her personality. She reacts to environment, and her nascent sexuality. Opposed to her early Christian training is her own biological nature and the power of all around her. 'But above this Protestantism was human nature . . . ' (*EW*, p. 33) She is well fed at Woodview, not overworked, and surrounded by the beauty that the natural world has to offer. She rejoices in these beauties which, as fortune would have it, are extended to include the human species in the form of fellow servant, William Latch. Despite her Protestant upbringing, and despite the reinforcement received from the lady of the house, also a member of the Plymouth Brethren, the temptations of the flesh so frustrating to Lancelot Smith are felt by Esther herself. In Gautier's words 'the body is an anchor that holds the soul to earth'.[43]

In *Esther Waters* it is the physical world in which the heroine rejoices, but the world described by Moore is not the objective correlative we see so important to the presentation of Hardy's Tess; it is a tempter, a force which challenges the spiritual upbringing by surrounding the subject with purely physical joys. The following scene is one of several precursors to Esther's seduction by William—the scenes like it help to build up the sense of the inevitable consummation to come:

> The pony and the donkey came towards the paddock gate, and she rubbed their muzzles in turn. It was a pleasure to touch anything, especially anything alive. She even noticed that the elm trees were strangely tall and still against the calm sky, and the rich colour of some carnations, which came through the bushes from the pleasureground, excited her; the scent of the earth and leaves tingled in her, the cawing of the rooks coming home took her soul away skyward in an exquisite longing; and she was, at the same time, full of a romantic love for the earth, and of a desire to mix herself with the innermost essence of things. The beauty of the evening and the sea breeze instilled a sensation of immortal health, setting her thinking that if a young man came to her as young men came to the great ladies in Sarah's books, it would be pleasant to talk in the dusk, seeing the bats flitting about the barns and byres vanishing into nothingness. (*EW*, p. 41)

The power of nature works within and without her—by comparison logical, rational self-control seems artificial when considered next to the 'exquisite longing' caused by the physical joys of contact. At no time does Moore shy away from that which he regards as the result of 'a very ordinary impulse . . . '[44] He never regards the consummation of Esther's and William's passion as a fall. Gaskell feels Ruth fell. Dickens feels Little Em'ly in *David Copperfield* fell. At least the fallen woman from Moore on does not have to rise in the eyes of her creator, even though conservative societal forces within the novel refuse to budge. But Moore's stance would not be convincing without his emotive painting of the landscape, which not only records the breathlessness of Esther's desires, but provides part of the force her religious consciousness must try to defeat. His writing in *Esther Waters* is never to be as explicit as in Gautier or Zola, because he knew just how far he could go. He is provocative, but not stupid. Anything more directly describing Esther's growing passion would have been repressed, and would have had to join the underground circulation of dirty books like *Fanny Hill.*

The contact with her fellow servants encourages Esther to think on men and romance. Sarah continually reads romantic fiction to the other girls. Margaret has a boyfriend; the extent of their relationship remains unclear, but its effect on Esther not so. Margaret retells every word spoken on her outings when she and Esther lie awake in the quiet of the night before sleep. Esther is quite correct when she feels that this continual discussion of romance is not good for a Christian girl, especially when the context of Sarah's fiction includes the elopement of a lady and an opera singer. Although Esther recognises the dangers of these narratives she cannot help but weary for a companion. The need for a companion is filled:

> Margaret had gone down to the Gardens with her young man, and one of these days a young man would come to take her out. Now what would he be like? She laughed and thought away, for it did not seem likely that any young man would bother about her. But at that moment, she saw a man coming through the hunting gate. His height and shoulders told her that he was William. (*EW*, pp. 41-2)

Moore goes to great lengths to stress the timeliness of the meeting, not simply to further the plot, but to highlight what he regards as accidents of fate which combine with emotional need, to produce the partnership of the young lovers. It almost seems out of their hands. The naturalist sees circumstance and milieu as being potentially more powerful than human will. This is certainly germane where the sexual transgression is concerned, but especially so later in the novel when Esther's life of providing for her illegitimate son is controlled by the socio-economic world in which she moves.

And so Moore emphasises the subtle powers of the environment in the love scenes. The couple is 'tempted by the warmth of the grass'. The physical contact she loves to have with anything alive is quickened by William's amorous advances, and human contact becomes the ultimate temptation. The fears related to this temptation are powerless in 'the sensation of his arm about her waist, and the music that the striking of a match had put to flight began in her heart, and it rose to its height when his face bent over hers'. (*EW*, p. 42) Moore is hardly subtle when he prepares for the event. Esther's memory centres on William and her close contact with him. He fills her conscious mind with thoughts of him, but more than that, her subconscious mind has a life of its own. On her lonely walk to the sea she is so obsessed by her thoughts of William, so deeply embedded in her being, that she can only return to consciousness 'with difficulty'. The seduction is imminent. Esther's body is, in Gautier's term, the anchor to her soul. This alone speaks of Moore's ability to recreate the physical life, the animal drive as it lives and works within a human being. It is the first time a fallen woman is allowed, in the novel, a physical life.

The scene at the grand ball takes us one step further. The master's horse has just won a major race—the grand ball is the celebration allowed to the servants. Esther does not have a formal gown so does not intend to go, but the Barfields recognise her plight by providing one. The energy of the dance, the dulling effects of liquor and the atmosphere of the revel all serve as distinct symbols of the world milieu in which Esther finds herself placed. Add William to it and the result is predictable—we are moving one step further to Esther's capitulation. Attendance at the ball would have been unthinkable to a strict member of the Plymouth Brethren. In an earlier chapter Moore prepares us for the event, quite adamant that a change in influence and setting will bring about changes to the personality: Mrs Barfield

> loved to hear Esther tell of her father and the little shop in Barnstaple, of the prayer meetings and the simple earnestness and narrowness of the faith of these good Brethren. Circumstances had effaced, though they had not obliterated, the once sharply marked confines of her religious habits. Her religion was like a Garden—a little less sedulously tended than of yore, but no whit less fondly loved; and while listening to Esther's story she dreamed her own early life over again, and paused, laying down her watering-can, overcome with the listlessness of happy

memories. And so Esther's life grew and was fashioned amid the ceaseless round of simple daily occupations, mistress and maid learning to know and to love one another . . . (*EW*, p. 35)

Moore's choice of the religion above is his way of setting two conflicting influences in juxtaposition—sharing the ultimate primacy of the immediate is important to his account of the myriad of small and large things which do change personality. The implied comparison of Esther and Mrs Barfield is also a subtle way of stressing the power of the sexual attraction. It was Mr Barfield, owner of a large horse racing stable, who was to take her away from her faith, despite her father's insistence that he join the brother-hood, which he only managed to do for a short time before his former life took over from the adopted religious façade. The parallels between Esther and Mrs Barfield are obvious early in the novel—they reappear at the end of the book when the two widows return to the simple faith whilst living in the decaying Woodview. In the meantime Esther is an uneducated girl who is facing influences she only half understands, and who is being shaped and fashioned by forces without and within. The physical is about to have more power than the dulled ethical self. She experiences at the ball the animal drive, the instinctual self, which Lancelot Smith terms 'mad noisy flesh'. To be fair, Esther does have very specific qualms of conscience at the ball—she knows the dance is wicked, especially when accompanied by plentiful drink, but this righteous musing is lost when she sees William's physique in action as he breaks a fight in progress. The event is seen through Esther's eyes, as indeed is the whole novel; in this way Moore can record that which is most noticeable to his heroine—and that is the physical power of William:

So her heart filled with love for her big William. What a fine fellow he was! and how handsome were his shoulders beside that round-shouldered little man whom he so easily pulled aside! and having crushed out the quarrel he helped her on with her jacket . . . (*EW*, p. 69)

Love and physical attraction are one in the same thing. Esther's love is not the neo-Medieval worship of the spirit: William's eye is not moved by a love for his pure lady, and a determination to ensure her purity remain untouched. Their attraction is physical—Esther compares the bodies of the two men, a comparison that is to be repeated several times in the novel. Instinctual attraction, and the study of its power, marks Moore's study of the relationship of two young working-class individuals. Not only does he make his sexual references relatively explicit, but he breaks with the literary tradition of only including the middle and aristocratic classes as the proper study of fiction. In retrospect it is this combined aspect of Moore's work which Susan Mitchell sees as evoking so much opposition:

> all Mr. Moore's novels are very distasteful to one who never feels quite comfortable or happy when obliged to voyage in fiction outside the safe harbourage of 'The Wide Wide World', or 'Mansfield Park'. I have an ingrained propriety of mind that makes me most at home in a novel where the young lady marries the Rector, who should, if possible, be next heir to a baronetcy; and where all the characters walk daintily in the guarded paths of life.[45]

Not only does Esther have no guardian angel, but Moore, from his naturalist stand, does not have the wish to even suggest that she should. He is simply there to provide an accurate account of what happens—his novel is not to be a middle-class wish-fulfilment dream.

Love and physical attraction are equated. She loves him because he looks strong, attractive and aggressive. In turn he is attracted by 'the white curve of her neck which showed beneath the unbuttoned jacket . . . ' (*EW*, p. 69) When that which is seen as her loss of virtue does come, though the novelist is never to share that opinion, there is no drama, no high romance, but there is a very matter-of-fact description of the breathlessness of the moment. Moore is, none the less, despite his continual adoption of the iconoclastic role, very careful to word the event discreetly and carefully. He is never to be quite so explicit as Gautier in *Mademoiselle de Maupin*, but he does manage to make the physical point:

> In the evenings when their work was done Esther and her lover lingered about the farm buildings, listening to the rooks, seeing the lights die in the west; and in the summer darkness about nine she tripped by his side when he took the letters to post. The wheat stacks were thatching, and in the rickyard, in the car-

penter's shop, and in the warm valleys, listening to the sheep bells tinkling, they often lay together talking of love and marriage, till one evening, putting his pipe aside, William threw his arm around her, whispering that she was his wife. The words were delicious in her fainting ears. She could not put him away, nor could she struggle with him, though she knew that her fate depended upon her resistance, and swooning away, she awakened, in pain, powerless to free herself . . . (*EW*, p. 70)

That which has remained unsaid for almost a whole century is finally included in a serious study of the fallen woman. Even Hardy dared not be so clear in his presentation of Tess's moment of capitulation. What is interesting is that it is the woman who is allowed to have a moment of sexual passion. Moore emphasises this by presenting the effects of the seduction from within his heroine's emotional self. William's actions are narrated. He put his pipe down, whispered and put his arm round her—all external physical movements. Esther's experience is internalised: 'swooning', 'pain', 'delicious', and 'fainting' all point to her internal emotional experience, and to the powerlessness of the rational. Even under the spell of the moment, she knows she is doing the wrong thing in the ethical puritanical sense, she is also aware that her fate is in the balance, and that in many ways it would be wise to resist. Wisdom, rationality, prudence, discretion—all are powerless in the face of William's attractive aggression. This is the truth about love that George Moore feels is so lacking in the English novel prior to *Esther Waters*. The truth is neither complex, surprising nor disarming. It is not a revelation. Its simplicity, however, is what makes its exclusion culpable according to Moore.

Hardy approaches the moment of Tess's fall with poetic suggestion rather than with physical passion, which we know Alec experiences but not the heroine. The physical needs of women do not play an important role in the fallen woman novels prior to *Esther Waters*. Tess follows, more or less, the line of Victorian fallen women whose innocence puts most of the blame on the youthful foibles of their seducers. This stance is, in fact, necessary to counteract one common social attitude which found it necessary to lay the blame on the female. She was the corruptor in many eyes because she was always expelled from polite society. Pregnancy makes her a public figure—it is her badge of shame. The fact that men look exactly the same after impregnation was a great advantage in the nineteenth century. Moore feels, however, that this conventional painting of the fallen woman as innocent is a way of hiding the truth about their sexuality, so he does not give his heroine naivety as an excuse. Esther knows men and exactly what they want. For all her anger after the event, she is capable of admitting that she 'knew he was like other men'. Her instinctual physical drives are more powerful than her ethical self. Moore feels this, on its own, is justification—Esther herself agrees with her creator, repenting to the extent that she feels reasonable and no more. Her religious scruples come back into play when she marries William legally and has to support his illegal betting. She has far more trouble accepting this than in accepting her fall.

Moore is so determined to stress natural physical attraction, so much part of sexual relationships, and so important to the naturalistic stance, that he repeats the role of the physical as a drawing force between William and Esther when she is forced to choose between him, on his return, and Fred Parsons. The potential match between Fred, a relatively young, avidly religious shop-keeper, and Esther would be a sensible match. Although never rich they would be secure. Esther's love of religion would be satisfied. Her son would have a respectable father, whose intense religiosity, although a little hardening, would not stop him being loving. After her affair with William became public with the passing of the months, she was forced to leave Woodview to have her child. Before leaving she is not kind to William whom she tries to make respect her by being severe. Unfortunately he interprets this as rejection on her part and runs away with a cousin of the Barfields whom he marries. Esther then has a monumental struggle of an economic and sociological nature to support her son and survive. After a succession of trials and difficulties she manages to be appointed to the post of maidservant to a respectable lady novelist. Seven years pass. William Latch and Esther meet on the street accidentally, just at the time when she has half promised herself to Fred. Despite her rational decision not to have anything to do with the man whom she feels has deserted her once, the 'sensation of love she once felt' returns. (*EW*, p. 197) Once again the physical plays a role in her decision to counteract her rational fears.

The choice she must make is not an easy one. Fred Parsons appeals to her religious sense and therefore seems more in tune with her early upbringing for which she has as romantic a memory as Mrs Barfield. William Latch, on the other hand, appeals to her physical

self, her passions, and her biological instinct. Because her relationship with Fred lacks the latter she can only be partly in love with
him. Moore writes that she 'almost' loves Fred. He is well meaning,
caring and faithful, but physically unattractive. A 'meagre, little
man', there is an innate weakness in his physique which makes him
poor competition for the engaging William. Fred's

> high prominent forehead rose above a small pointed face, a
> scanty growth of blond beard and moustache failing to hide the
> receding chin and the red-sealing-wax lips; his faded yellow hair
> was beginning to grow thin on the crown; and his threadbare
> frock-coat hung limp from his sloping shoulders. (*EW*, p. 174)

Moore's emphasis on 'limp', 'thin', 'scanty', 'receding', and 'faded'
leave little doubt about his inherited physical and emotional weakness. He is almost without passion. His caring spiritual nature,
Moore intimates, is his only consolation. This consolation makes
him more unattractive to his creator than to Esther whose natural
human warmth tends to accept a person for what he is. Moore paints
him as a little ridiculous. Fred worries about Esther's living with a
novelist because 'novels are very often stories about the loves of
men for other men's wives. Such books,' he laments, 'serve no good
purpose.' (*EW*, p. 175) The worst insult Moore can pay to an
individual is to paint him as an ignorant censor of books—such was
the tenor of his mind about those who insulted his works over and
over again. At the very moment when Fred lectures so, it is ironic
that Esther is considering living with William who is another
woman's husband, because that is the only way a divorce can be
obtained. The clever Mr Moore manages to make a definite point
about the ludicrous nature of literary criticism which ignores the
facts of life, and he does this without sacrificing the aesthetic
distance he likes to maintain as a novelist. Juxtaposing Fred's
lecture with the reality of Esther's life and at the same time including an implicit jibe at ignorant literary criticism, Moore is able to
emphasise the tenor of his novel which is true to life—this is what
life is really like. In a century which persistently reformed the lot of
the working man and woman to a certain extent, there were very
few novelists who tried to convey what life was really like for the
working classes. Considering this, Moore's novel is timely.

Moore takes pains to point out that at times a religious virginal
personality is simply the result of either not possessing strong

passions in any case, or simply not being placed in a situation or milieu which would challenge the ethical stance. Fred Parsons, we suspect, belongs to the former. When admonishing Esther to repentance he does not fail to assure her that he has never been responsible for a woman's fall. He is pure, but he is pure perhaps because his inherited physical debilitation hampers that which would be a normal physical drive. We are not at all surprised to hear of his virtue. Once again Moore is unwittingly returning to the argument so frustratingly expressed by Lancelot Smith in Charles Kingsley's *Yeast*. Lancelot continues his letter to the religious cousin who reminds us of Fred Parsons:

> Every man's destiny, as the Turks say, stands written on his forehead. One does not need two glances at your face to know that you would not enjoy fox-hunting, that you would enjoy book-learning, and 'refined repose', as they are pleased to call it. Every man carries his character in his brain. You all know that, and act upon it when you have to deal with a man for six pence; but your religious dogmas, which make out that every man comes into the world equally brutish and fiendish, make you afraid to confess it. I don't quarrel with a 'douce' man like you for following your bent. But if I am fiery, with a huge cerebellum, why am I not to follow mine?—For that is what you do, after all—what you like best. It is all very easy for a man to talk of conquering his appetites, when he has none to conquer. Try to conquer your organ of veneration, or of benevolence, or of calculation—then I will call you ascetic. Why not!—The same Power which made the front of one's head made the back, I suppose?[46]

Lancelot's opinion of his cousin is almost the same as Moore's attitude to Fred. Despite Fred's honest profession of purity (or it may be principally because of it) Esther 'did not like him any better' and was 'irritated by the clear tones of his icy voice'. (*EW*, p. 177) Where there is no passion there is no warmth—certainly Fred's good but 'icy' nature does little to appeal to Esther's passionate nature. Whilst Fred looks on his purity and virtue as fortunate Esther senses it is the result of something else. She realises many times just how good he is, but too much is missing—she cannot love him dearly after her passionate experience with William. Her relationship with Fred is, for her, strangely calm. Esther's volatile nature rarely allows her a calm approach to anything; her time with Fred left her calm but not satisfied. It is one of the few things in the novel that she does by halves—'She looked up at his face; her hand was on the gate, and in that moment she felt she almost loved him.' (*EW*, p. 178) It would be typical of Moore to place emphasis on 'almost' rather than 'loved'.

On his return, her temper is not so even with William—she has some trouble working out which of the conflicting emotions predominates. Her religious background gives her a few scruples related to the proposition he makes that they ought to live together prior to the divorce, but she knows it is the best thing for her son, unlike her predecessors who always reject the father when he returns. But she is more angry about 'living in sin' than ethically concerned, and a little frightened. When William uses the welfare of the boy as a lever to move Esther, something that she accepts herself, she flies off the handle, perhaps because she would prefer him to be less indirect. Her fear rests on the terribly real fact that he left her once, and may do so again. Despite their arguments, her realistic foreboding and her rational approach to an engagement with Fred, something instinctual tugs at her heartstrings—this is the animal in man, so important to the presentation of the hero or heroine—the attraction she feels William to be. She cannot separate his body and mind; studying one part of his personality from another is an abstract notion far away from Esther's mental or emotional scope. So despite her fears, her anger and her scruples the suggestion William makes to the effect that they live together 'brought an instinctive look of desire into her eyes'. His subsequent offer to settle £500 on Jackie and Esther, come what may, brings about a similar reaction within, 'the same look was in her eyes only modified, softened by some feeling of tenderness which had come into her heart'. (*EW*, p. 218) The sacrifice he is willing to make has a ring of truth to it—the money means a lot to her, not in the mercenary sense, but because it would provide something for Jackie, and a little ease for herself. She does try to fight the return of the full relationship and tries to think of Fred, but there is something far too corporeal in the way:

He took her in his arms and kissed her, and said, 'My own little wife'.

As he went up the area steps she remembered that he had used the same words before, and tried to think of Fred, but William's

> great square shoulders had come between her and this meagre
> little man. She sighed, and felt once again that her will was
> overborne by a force which she could not control or understand.
> (*EW*, p. 219)

The struggle between Fred and William is the outward manifestation of two parts of her own nature—her religious and moral self,
and her physical being. The situation is the ideal symbol for the
conflict within her throughout the novel. Moore feels he is being
faithful to the truth about human nature to present the physical
needs of the working girl as that part of her nature which gains
ascendancy in the face of hunger, overwork and poverty. Her
willpower is too weak. Knowing this, until she makes the decision to
live with William, she is 'whelmed in a sense of sorrow', because life
'was proving too strong for her'. (*EW*, p. 220) Moore presents the
soul in mild torment when it is faced with the knowledge of the
moral, religious sublime and its ethical demands, and the conflict
this has with physical needs and practical, pragmatic considerations. Esther dreams that she marries both men, a subconscious
way of recognising that she cannot serve two masters, even when
both are part of her deepest personality. The resultant terror of
marrying them both, of trying to do the impossible, helps her to
make the decision. It goes the way of her will, and not her moral
sensibility. One cannot help wondering how horrified Mrs Gaskell
would have been to face the defeat of the religious self at the hands
of physical desire and pragmatic reality. Esther lives in sin, without
shame once her mind is made up, then she marries William.

Physical attraction, and its power to change behaviour, is studied
by Moore through the minor characters in the novel. Esther's
turbulent time in London, her fortunate return to the man she
loves, and her decent nature all make her accepting and understanding when others' problems land on her doorstep. Her sometime fellow servant at Woodview, the Sarah who read the penny
dreadfuls about aristocratic love, falls in love with a very difficult
man. She knows that Bill Evans is not to be trusted, is often violent,
immoral and a heavy drinker. He could not be more antithetical to
the heroes she admired so avidly in her youth. Evans and Sarah live
in a *de facto* relationship. Several times his bad temper gets the
better of him. His bad luck at the races or his overindulgence at the
public house put him in a poor temper. Sarah is often thrown out of
their dirty rooms, but bad as they are she has nowhere else to go.

When he is particularly penniless Evans forces Sarah into prostitution to earn their bread. She turns to William and Esther for help, several times, promising that she will not return to him, but in every case she manages to forget her promise and does so. Esther understands the force which draws Sarah to Evans because she has experienced it herself. William is not so understanding, but continues to help the unfortunate Sarah because his wife wishes it so. William expresses his disgust on one of the occasions when Sarah returns for more help after going back to Evans when she had promised not to. 'You see,' Esther reminds him, 'she was that fond of him that she couldn't help herself. There's many that can't.' (*EW*, p. 293) Esther remembers, no doubt, the influence her powerlessness had in affecting the reunification of her husband and herself.

Sarah tries to rationalise the relationship, and especially her own reliance on a man for whom she has no respect. Again her experience mirrors Esther's:

'It wasn't so much what I believed as that I couldn't help myself. He has got that hold over me that me will isn't my own. I don't know how it is—I suppose men have stronger natures than women. I hardly knew what I was doing; it was like sleep-walking.'

Later she tries even harder to find an explanation for her lack of will:

A change of expression came over Sarah's face, and William said, 'You're surely not still hankering after him?'
'No, that I'm not. But whenever I meets him he somehow gets his way with me. It's terrible to love a man as I love him. I know he don't really care for me—I know he is all you say, and yet I can't help myself. It is better to be honest with you.'
William looked puzzled.

The naturalist is particularly anxious to accurately capture the powerful, innate drives in man. The sexual life is one of the strongest of these. Moore uses the concept of sexual attraction to reinforce the role of the instinctual life of man and woman. Esther speaks well for Moore when she reminds William of the social ramifications of the sexual. Her sense of the deterministic is also in tune with Moore's own stance in the novel—'We don't choose our lives, we just make the best of them. You was the father of my child, and it all dates from that.' (*EW*, p. 283)

Because man belongs to the animal world, and because lives are partly shaped by instinctual animal drives, the naturalistic novelist demands the right to be as coolly objective in his descriptions of these parts of life he chooses to discuss as is the scientist when he writes on the results of an experiment, or records his full observations of a particular natural phenomenon. It is this loyalty to objective observation and subsequent recording of data which encourage George Moore to include specific detail which nineteenth-century novelists had previously avoided. I have already discussed Moore's faithful presentation of what he sees as the sexual life of a young woman. That was, even in 1894, unheard of in English fiction. He breaks with another tradition when he disregards the division which had separated the medical observation from the novel. Not that he wanted to make one the other and *vice versa*. He did feel, however, that they could meet from time to time within the novel itself. In the early fifties Geraldine Jewsbury, herself an active novelist, had the responsibility of reading and reporting on potential manuscripts for one of the circulating libraries. She rejects one soundly because it does not regard the mutually exclusive nature of clinical observation and the content of fiction:

> I object absolutely to the indelicate prominence given the heroine's confinement of her first and only Baby; no author, unless a medical man writing for the faculty ought to enter into so much detail . . . and the account of the new born baby is very disagreeable and painful.[47]

Sensibilities after Geraldine Jewsbury on this topic remained largely unchanged for the remainder of the century. No doubt smelling salts would have been called for had Jewsbury read Moore's descriptions of the labour pains, the hospital, the baby's birth and breast feeding which followed it. After birth the boy is described as 'A pulp of red flesh rolled up in a flannel . . . ' (*EW*, p. 118)

Esther's love affair with William is not the only instinctual human function to be described. The birth of her son and the mother's instincts are awarded a great deal of observation. In the earlier Victorian novels where a child is born, that moment is given no

attention at all. We know of the pregnancy only by the condemnatory stand of society. Of the actual birth, the process, the pain, the
exhaustion, we learn nothing. If the sexual relationship between the
fallen woman and her partner is avoided, the birth of the child is
treated even more scantily. Moore felt that the reality of the
relationship between mother and child (*Mother and Child* had been
his first title for what was to become *Esther Waters*) could never be
well perceived by the reader without some specific descriptions of
the pain and pleasure which surrounds the birth. Despite Moore's
effort to treat this with detached naturalistic objectivity he could not
avoid the sense of mystic joy which Esther felt on the birth of her
boy.

When Esther returns to the home of her mother on leaving
Woodview, she becomes a constant source of income for her greedy
stepfather. Mrs Barfield, though saddened by Esther's impregnation, makes sure she has sufficient funds to survive in London, till
the birth of the child at least. The money is running out so quickly
that Mrs Saunders, the married name of her mother, advises her to
leave in order to keep what little she has left, and take lodgings close
to the hospital. The description of her labour in Mrs Jones's boarding house, and her confinement in the hospital, provide one of the
unique and controversial sections of the novel. It is this section
which led Mr Faux of Smith's circulating library to ban the book.
Moore does not spare the fussy ladies or apathetic gentlemen who
would rather not know about the pangs of childbirth, especially
when the child is a badge of shame, a bastard. The first labour pain
is 'a great and sudden shock—life seemed to be slipping from her,
and she sat for some minutes quite unable to move . . . ' (*EW*, p.
114) Mrs Jones is caring, helpful yet stoic, especially about
accepting the painful birth as the lot of women. She remains calm
even though the pain on Esther's face is vivid. ' "I think I am dying.
I cannot stand up, give me a chair, give me a chair!" and she sank
upon it, leaning across the table, her face and neck bathed in a cold
sweat.' (*EW*, p. 114) There is nothing extraordinary about Esther's
plight. There is nothing extraordinary in the style of Moore's rather
direct, somewhat modern, style of description, except that this is
the first time such detail is recorded in nineteenth-century fiction.
That in itself gives the section a unique value. A little truth about
childbirth is not in itself important. None the less, I think there is
sufficient historical value in it for students of literature and women's
studies to warrant some attention.

At the hospital the indignities Esther has to tolerate at the hands of several nonchalant student doctors and nurses provides one of the moments in the novel which follow the reform consciousness of nineteenth-century fiction. The single mother has to find a sub-scriber to the hospital willing to overlook her unmarried state and give her the required letter of admission. After one or two refusals Esther is fortunate to find one, only after a young warder has made Esther pay for the subscribers' addresses. The fact that Esther does not know anything about the hospital conditions prior to admission highlights the fear she feels and the dismay she encounters when she is put on display. The section speaks for itself without direct com-ment from Moore. Working-class girls have to expect treatment suited to their station:

> The students and the nurses were behind her. She knew they were eating sweets, for she heard a young man ask the young women if they would have any more fondants. A moment after her pains began again, and she saw the young man whom she had seen handing the sweets approaching her bedside.
> 'Oh, no, not him, not him!' she cried to the nurse. 'Not him, not him! he is too young! Don't let him come near me!'

The nurse tells her off for her outburst. They discuss her case beside the bed, then talk

> of the plays they had seen, and those they wished to see. She was soon listening to a discussion regarding the merits of a shilling novel which every one was reading, and then Esther heard a stampede of nurses, midwives, and students in the direction of the window. A German band had come into the street.
> 'Is that the way to leave your patient, sister?' said the student who sat by Esther's bed, and Esther looked into his clear blue, girl-like eyes, wondered and turned away for shame.
> The sister stopped her imitation of a popular comedian, and said, 'Oh, she's all right; if they were all like her there'd be very little use of our coming here.' (*EW*, pp. 115-16)

Moore takes pains to make the childbirth wholesome in comparison to this behaviour, which really is obscene. The band, sweets, novels, plays, impersonations, are far more important to the staff than the care of the patient. There is no regard for the feelings of the patient, who is, after all, experiencing something which calls for quiet trust, gentle care and genuine concern. Moore's first duty is not to reform; the deliberate attempt to emphasise the seedy nature of the staff makes the birth beautiful and wholesome by comparison—a subtle and effective way to counteract claims that including details of childbirth is indiscreet at best, shameful at worst.

A pulp of red flesh rolled up in a flannel was laid alongside of her. Its eyes were open; it looked at her, and her flesh filled with a sense of happiness so deep and so intense that she was like one enchanted. And when she took the child in her arms she thought she must die of happiness . . .
    Her personal self seemed entirely withdrawn; she existed like an atmosphere about the babe and lay absorbed in this life of her life, this flesh of her flesh, unconscious of herself as a sponge in warm sea-water. (*EW*, p. 118)

The number of metaphors and related images are few in the novel. It is no accident that Moore describes his heroine's transcendent state in terms which relate her to the lowest, and therefore most instinctual, forms of life—the sponge. The use of animal imagery continues its naturalistic purpose when Esther is seen feeding the baby whose lips are catching at 'the nipple and the wee hand pressing the white curve, like a lamb with a ewe, for all nature is akin; and Jenny watched the gluttonous lips, interested in the spectacle . . . ' (*EW*, p. 120)
    Esther is forced to leave the hospital, put her son out to nurse, and take a place as a wet nurse to Mrs Rivers's child whose life, it seems, is in the balance. Without establishing the natural link between mother to child, which Moore does so convincingly through his simple animal imagery, the wrenching of the pair by virtue of economic situation would not seem so unnatural, culpable and unfair. Mrs Rivers and Esther Waters have more in common than their aquatic names. By giving them names that relate Moore encourages a comparison. Both have just given birth, and both have an instinctive, deeply felt desire to save the life of their own child. Mrs Rivers, a member of the Mayfair set by virtue of her address, has had two wet nurses, both of whom failed. Esther, it seems, is having a more positive effect on the Rivers' child, but she cannot help pining for her own boy who is in the hands of Mrs Spires, the

only woman who will look after Jackie within her price range. Esther rails against the system which will not allow her to mother her own child. Mrs Spires, who is used to single mothers like Esther, even offers to bring about the disappearance of the child for a fee of £5. She had no idea that there were so many like her, or so many who gave up and provided the funds for Mrs Spires and all like her to murder the children for gain:

> By what right, by what law, was she separated from her child? She was tired of hearing Mrs Rivers speak of 'my child, my child, my child', and of seeing this fine lady turn up her nose when she spoke of her own beautiful boy . . .
>
> . . . yesterday the housemaid told her that the little thing in the cradle had had two wet nurses before Esther, and both their babies had died. It was then a life for a life. It was more. For the children of two poor girls had been sacrificed so that this rich woman's child might be saved. Even that was not enough: the life of her beautiful boy was called for. And then other memories swept by. She remembered vague hints, allusions that Mrs. Spires had thrown out; and, as in a dream darkly, it seemed to this ignorant girl that she was the victim of a far reaching conspiracy; she experienced the sensation of the captured animal, and scanned the doors and windows, thinking of some means of escape. (*EW*, pp. 136-7)

Moore believed quite firmly that the novel was directly responsible for the introduction of legislation in Parliament to make baby-farming an offence; he was to pride himself in the goodness it radiated. While the novel certainly does this in the form of the sacrifices Esther continually makes for her son, it also is honest enough to point to the inequities of the whole social system which encouraged those like Esther to take Mrs Spires's suggestion at face value. So Esther takes her chance and leaves Mrs Rivers as she is to leave other employers when she feels she is at the end of her tether. In each case it is her animal instinct which makes her long for escape, and which gives her the courage to move on when the future is unclear and bleak. At the place she worked after the Rivers's she was worked to the point that she is 'compelled like the hunted animal to leave the cover and seek safety in the open country. Her whole body cried out for rest . . . ' (*EW*, p. 157) Despite Moore's desire to objectively record Esther's trials he cannot help but convey a sense of admiration for her, especially when survival takes her all. She is not just a literary figure conveyed through detached observation. 'Hers is a heroic adventure if one considers it—a mother's fight for the life of her child against all the forces that civilization arrays against the lowly and the illegitimate.' (*EW*, p. 159) For a moment Moore shares the sympathy for the fallen we sense Dickens has for Nancy, Mrs Gaskell for Ruth, and Collins for Simple Sally. It is this sympathy and Esther's essential worthiness to receive it which makes the novel exude goodness, a fact which was always a source of pleasure for Moore. Whenever he was chastised for his nasty fiction he usually responded by reminding the critic of the goodness which inculcates *Esther Waters*. But whilst he shares this tradition of sympathy with the other great novelists, he takes great pains to make sure his heroine is quite unique. Following a set conventional type would result in a generalisation about one type of woman. 'No one who knows the most elementary things about human nature,' he suggests to Goodwin, 'has ever tried to generalize about women.'[48] It is precisely the Victorian wont to generalise about women, the perfect wife, the blue stocking, the fallen woman and so on, which the great novelists tried to counteract.

Esther's wholeness as an individual makes it difficult to see her simply as a type. Her temper is seen in action as often as her basic goodness. Few fallen women have attacked their impregnators with a knife as Esther does. She has a distinct sense of place, yet revolts against some class distinctions. She loves her son, but at times, especially when very tired, has trouble loving him constantly. She can be jealous and difficult. When William returns and buys Jackie expensive clothes and presents, Esther throws the yacht, bought by the father, across the room, breaking it. She feels some remorse about her initial sin, but is more worried about survival. She does not feel an early death in the river is her lot. She is an individual made up of conflicting hopes and emotions who is caught up in a world which has as much, if not more power in determining the pattern of her life as she does herself. I agree with Wolfe who writes of *Esther Waters* as a novel which 'records with unflinching and unchanging excitement the facts of life as they seed, flower and wither', but I do not agree that in it Moore 'is judging, not pitying'.[49] His presentation of a complete, well-rounded individual is done with the care of the naturalist's eye, and he judges with that, but he also pities with an English Victorian heart, even though he would never admit it. It is this combination of Naturalism and Victorianism which makes the novel less weighty and more positive than *A Modern Lover* or *A Mummer's Wife*.

Esther Waters is not the first fallen woman to gain Moore's attention. The type seemed to puzzle him early in his career. Gwynnie Lloyd in *A Modern Lover* and Awful Emma in *Confessions of a Young Man* are precursors to Esther, although neither is drawn with the sympathy Moore has for Esther. Moore would have constantly crossed the paths of prostitutes in London and Paris, and prostitutes from all walks of life from the wealthy, celebrated courtesan to the ugliest, poorest prostitute on the Strand. There are several matter-of-fact references to prostitution in the novel. Sarah, I have mentioned, is forced to become a temporary prostitute to feed Evans. There is a moment when Esther comes close to prostitution as her way out of unemployment and starvation. A young man 'in evening clothes was speaking to her. His voice was soft, the look in his eyes seemed kindly.' (*EW*, p. 165) Luckily, the man's attention is drawn elsewhere, leaving Esther to proceed unmolested. Prostitution is not discussed in the novel with horror—it is a fact of life, not an emotional wrangle. When William is very ill and being taken to hospital by his wife, they pass scenes which they have seen many times before. The Circus had its customary 'mob of prostitutes'. Mrs Dunbar, the former mistress of Esther, is referred to as a bad woman early in the novel—she is probably a kept mistress, or a sophisticated prostitute who frequents the infamous Cremorne Gardens, which were second in notoriety only to the Argyle Rooms. As a young man Moore visited both—they were his 'favourite haunts', though he claims to have been there as an observer rather than as a participant. He was well acquainted with the appearance of prostitutes. In a very real sense his novel is a sign of the times, in its reference to the prostitution and in its separation of the prostitute from the fallen woman. By separating them into two distinct categories he then has very little trouble justifying Esther's fall and recording her rise. Esther has the ability to recognise her own goodness. It is certainly confirmed by others in the novel, especially William who does his level best to make up for the suffering his wife had after her desertion. 'You're the best wife a man ever had.' (*EW*, p. 17) 'Your mother Jack is the best woman in the world.' (*EW*, p. 341) 'Your mother Jack is the best woman that ever lived.' (*EW*, p. 342) The fallen women in Moore's earlier writing have no rise—they remain degraded, without real sympathy—although the following description of Awful Emma demonstrates an awareness of the lot of the servant. When talking about Emma, Moore recognises the difference between himself and the early Victorians. 'Dickens would sentimentalize or laugh over you. I do neither. I merely recognize you as one of the facts of civilization.'[50] The difference between Emma and Esther is obvious. He does more than recognise Esther, he sympathises with her. This is not quite so noticeable in his recording of Emma:

> Emma, I remember you—you are not to be forgotten—up at five o'clock every morning, scouring, washing, cooking, dressing those infamous children; seventeen hours at least out of the twenty-four at the beck and call of landlady, lodgers, and quarrelling children; seventeen hours at least out of the twenty-four drudging in that horrible kitchen, running up stairs with coals and breakfasts and cans of hot water; down on your knees before a grate, pulling out the cinders with those hands—can I call them hands? The lodgers sometimes threw you a kind word, but never one that recognized that you were akin to us, only the pity that might be extended to a dog. And I used to ask you all sorts of cruel questions, I was curious to know the depth of animalism you had sunk to,—rather out of which you had never been raised . . . Life in your case meant this: to be born in a slum, and to leave it to work seventeen hours a day in a lodging-house; to be a Londoner, but to know only the slum in which you were born, and the few shops in the Strand at which the landlady dealt.[51]

If we look back at the earliest of his literary works, the poetry, we can find further evidence of a deep-seated concern over the fallen woman. Many have expressed surprise over *Esther Waters* as being uncharacteristic of the author. Walter Allen agrees that 'On the face of it, *Esther Waters* may seem a strange novel for Moore to have written . . . '[52] It is possible to trace through his earlier work a very definite, but often puzzled, concern for the fallen woman. In many ways *Esther Waters* is the answer to unanswered questions asked in earlier works. 'Ode to a Beggar Girl' appears in the second and last volume of poetry published by the author at his own expense. *Pagan Poems* was published in 1881. Edmund Yates in *The World* writes a review entitled 'A Bestial Bard': the work 'ought to be burnt by the common hangman, and the author whipped at a cartwheel'.[53] The poetry was not well received. It was abused to the point that Moore calls it his 'Poor little book'.[54]

In the first stanza of 'Ode to a Beggar Girl' Moore introduces his subject, whilst at the same time comparing her to the Virgin Mary with Jesus in her arms: the comparison quickly captures the young girl's fallen state. The Virgin as painted by the Italian masters is the ultimate in pure womanhood, pure to the extent of being unsullied by any sexual relationship with man. Moore does not know what to make of the girl. Is she a victim or a cause? What does her existence actually mean:

> You are very wonderful!
> There is something sphinx-like in your face,
> Something mystic in its mournfulness
> That oppresses me.
> Who are you, and what are you?
> Were you born of parents like yourself?
> Were you nursed upon a bosom
> Like the wretched infant who is sleeping
> Now amid the rags
> Wrapped around your own?
> Did you ever know a pleasant hour?
> Have you never had a glimpse of life?
> Did you ever think it fair?[85]

It is not difficult to see that Moore's talents lie elsewhere than poetry. Whilst he cannot help musing on the social difficulties encountered by the girl, there is a distance caused by the lack of individuality in her. Not that we expect a character description in poetry, but we do expect a glimpse into something about her nature, appearance, expression and the like. That she looks like a working-class madonna is all we have to go on—this tends to make her a type, something which Moore is to avoid in his later fiction. The fact that the poem makes no effort to answer any of the questions asked makes it a little frustrating for the reader. Whilst he makes an effort to rationalise her plight he can go no further than to admit she is 'nothing more/ than a dirty beggar'. He seeks some sort of meaning in her lot but finds none beyond the dirty façade which is 'as vile and commonplace/ As the thousands straying/ Daily . . . ' There is no meaning, no escape and, lost in the immensity of the numbers, no hope. The only solution lies in a quasi-romantic death, typical of the drowning of the young girl in *Three Men in a Boat* and thousands of other fallen women.

The poet reveals that the subject of the poem had been previously seen visiting her dead friend at the morgue. It is typical of the romantic melancholic poem that the persona just happens to find himself wandering about a morgue. The drowned girl has no ring on her finger. She had, perhaps, died after being deserted or was simply starving from want of clients. The person cannot see where he fits as he reflects on the dead body at peace and the living wreck—he asks the question again, puzzled by the difference between her lot and his own:

> What are you? a beggar born to nothing
> Save a large inheritance of woe,
> Whilst a dilettante poet I
> Gratify the febrile whim
> Born of pampered flesh and intellect.

He accepts the difference for what it is, feeling that her only hope lies with her dead friend, and a transcendental return to being at one with the earth:

> Death is always kindly—die!
> Think how beautiful your sister looked,
> Made angelic with peace . . .
>
> The living clay becomes
> Once again incarnate
> Of the soul of man becoming God.

The maudlin conclusion to the poem is not convincing, none the less the poet's helplessness remains vivid. Esther's life, which was to be written thirteen years later, provides some of the answers to the questions asked. Like the fallen woman in the poem above, Esther is bedevilled by heredity and environment, but the heroine from the novel possesses something which the beggar girl does not—spirit, individuality, courage, determination and sufficient patience to be able to counteract the weight and power of the social system. Moore becomes rather Victorian without really realising it by giving his heroine the will to survive the onslaught of heredity and environment. Esther's may well be 'a rough page torn out of life' (*EW*, p.

226) as much as is the beggar girl's, but like most of the fallen women of the nineteenth century the trials of the former make her larger, more impressive, more indomitable. Esther rarely sounds like a Victorian heroine ('What do it matter what people think, so long as I know I hasn't done no wrong.' (*EW*, p. 66)) but she shares more in common with Mercy and Ruth than she does with the beggar girl. The trials of Mercy, Ruth and Esther make them heroic. Although uneducated, like Nancy or Simple Sally, her experience ultimately makes her more sensitive, more understanding, better endowed with a practical common sense—'them what hasn't been through the trouble never thinks the same as them that 'as . . . ' (*EW*, p. 188) In an indirect way the novel is the pathway which the reader takes as he follows the daily life of the heroine. Vicariously he is able to intellectualise and emotionalise the troubles faced by Esther. She has a type of reality about her which, because of experiences shared with the reader, makes her one of the most memorable women in nineteenth-century fiction. She provides an answer to 'Ode to a Beggar Girl', and that answer lies in her ability to triumph over adversity whilst accepting her limitations without a continual grumble. She might well be 'like a hunted animal' but it is her human courage and working-class dignity which makes her more dynamic than the fallen madonna seen as powerless by the young dilettante poet in Paris. Esther is such a well drawn figure that her life has outlived the fame of her creator. Moore has lost much of his popularity since the Second World War. His eightieth birthday was greeted by an article in the *Times* which acknowledged him as the 'master of English letters'.[56] Few today would nominate him thus, but despite his fall from grace Esther continues to be widely read, and readily available. Whilst the dramatic version of the novel has all but disappeared, a televised version of the novel was distributed throughout the world in the 1970s. It is ironic that *Esther Waters* is almost solely responsible for Moore's reputation as a humanitarian—Susan Mitchell remembers that when she first read it she 'discovered in it not only a brain but a heart, and in spite of an extraordinary amount of evidence since produced to me of Mr Moore's want of heart, I cannot rid myself of the conviction I felt when I read that book'.[57] But he did not enjoy being accused of humanitarianism, which he argues is the refuge of the dull-witted:

All men of inferior genius, Victor Hugo and Mr. Gladstone take refuge in humanitarianism. Humanitarianism is a pigsty, where liars, hypocrites and the obscene in spirit congregate . . . Far better the blithe modern pagan in his white tie and evening clothes, and his facile philosophy. He says, 'I don't care how the poor live; my only regret is that they live at all'; and he gives the beggar a shilling.[58]

If Gladstone had forseen this railing would he, I wonder, have made such a point of supporting the novel and the novelist? Nevertheless the novel's caring portrayal of the poor belies this anti-humanitarianism—their hopes, fears, needs and limitations play a large role in the accurate recreation of working-class life to be found in the work. The novel certainly cares how the poor live. Even 'Ode to a Beggar Girl' and the presentation of Awful Emma in *Confessions of a Young Man* confirm a certain amount of caring behind the creation. Without that trait in the author they would never have been written, preparations which moved toward the creation of his masterpiece. The novel certainly shows some sort of concern for the working classes. Content of the novel which specifically studies the habits and attitudes of working-class figures certainly helps to pave the way for Lawrence and Bennett, both of whom include in their work studies of the particular problems of the non-aristocratic and non-middle-class lifestyles. *Esther Waters* is, in this respect, more influential than is normally admitted. Like his former Master, Zola, Moore found the key to faithful presentation of working-class figures through observing them at work and play, at least what little they had of it. He certainly studied people closely, and often he tells of his pre-France days in London which were spent observing the life of the city in its multifaceted aspect. He talked to Havelock Ellis about illegitimate children and the mothers' needs, when gathering information for the novel.[59] All the racing figures in the novel may have come from his father's stable. He lived in the Temple which encouraged him to brush shoulders with common folk, and though no democrat, he took an interest in their plight, perhaps far more than he ever cared to admit. In the autobiographical trilogy, *Hail and Farewell*, he remembers this contact. Sonja Nejdefors-Frisk includes details from this autobiography to support her stance that Moore had very real contact with the working-class milieu so important to the naturalistic novel:

'My poor laundress used to tell me every day . . . of her trouble, and through her I became acquainted with many other poor people, and they awakened spontaneous sympathy in me, and by doing them kindness I was making honey for myself without knowing it.' When living in a lodging-house in the Strand, Moore studied a servant there 'as one might an insect under a microscope', as he puts it. And he sometimes thought that she would make good material for a book. [60]

Observing working-class situations and attitudes at an early age, and maintaining an interest in them gave him the ability to paint a working-class canvas unlike any other novelist in the nineteenth century. His working-class characters bear no resemblance to the comic cameos of low life which abound in Dickens. The first thing that Moore insists on is the difference between middle-class reactions and working-class attitudes to the same situation. The working class in the novel do not react to Esther's fall in the same manner as their betters. The close proximity of living, the struggle for survival gave them a more pragmatic outlook than their middle-class counterparts who, like Mrs Wood in *East Lynne* and *Pomeroy Abbey*, saw the fall as a fate worse than death. The working class cannot afford to have such finely tuned, moralistic sensibilities, though Miss Rice's total acceptance of Esther, and her love for her is a reminder that one ought not to generalise about *the* middle-class attitude towards anything. That accepted, I still think there is justification in looking at the attitude of a large section of that middle class which shared Mrs Wood's determination that the fall was permanent and irrevocably disastrous for the unlucky girl. Another important point to make, before proceeding with the comparison of class attitudes, concerns the exposure and discovery of Victorian hypocrisies and double standards, which were numerous and far reaching. From Lytton Strachey on we have felt that a discovery of Victorian hypocrisy is the result of twentieth-century enlightenment and perspicacity. This may be true, but only partly true. One reason we see the age as one where hypocrisy and close-mindedness were rife is because a large number of critical Victorians recognised negative Victorian habits themselves and made sure the expositions were well published. One could think, for instance, that city slums were a nineteenth-century invention, whilst forgetting that one reason eighteenth-century poverty seems less extreme is simply because few at that time felt other than that they were natural and acceptable phenomena. If the Victorians were not so self-critical we would find it more difficult to come to grips with their social and moral problems. Moore belongs to this long tradition of self-criticism, not in the personal but in the national sense.

The novel does contain middle-class characters who possess the archetypal fear of fallen women as corrupting figures. They reject Esther with the often heard irrevocable rejection. Esther is employed by the Trubners, mother and son who together run the household. After one year of discreet behaviour her 'crime' is discovered—that she has an illegitimate son. Esther is summoned to Mrs Trubner's drawing room, knowing that her place in the house is in jeopardy, is then informed by her employer that the story is out. Esther responds in a characteristic manner: 'I've a child but that don't make no difference so long as I gives satisfaction in my work'. Mrs Trubner finds it impossible to agree with Esther, but is even more rancoured by Mrs Barfield's character reference which made no mention of the child. It is one thing to be misled by a servant— that is almost expected—but to be led astray by a member of the same class is 'most reprehensible'. Mr Trubner bursts into the drawing room unaware of the interview in progress. Espying Esther he regards her with 'a look of instinctive repulsion'. Mrs Trubner is, surprisingly enough, reasonably convinced by Esther's argument which dwells on the potential increase in Spires-like child murders when single women in that state find it impossible to get work and be given a chance. But she is unwilling to make the decision in Esther's favour, when the son refuses to take any responsibility in the final decision, but is happy to point out the normal clichés as they relate to having a fallen woman in the house. He cannot accept having 'loose women about the place'. As much as that annoys Moore, he is even more determined to show how faulty are Trubner's preconceptions about the homogeneous set of attitudes one must always expect from fallen women: they no longer deserve anything when they have chosen to forego their chastity: 'I don't see why we should harbour loose women when there are so many deserving cases'. (*EW*, pp. 157-8) When Esther leaves the house she criticises her former employers in a manner which could have been written by Wilkie Collins. 'It is a strange thing that religion should make some people so unfeeling'. (*EW*, p. 159)

But whilst condemning the heartless, habitual middle-class response typified in the Trubners, Moore is realistic enough to know the negative disasters which can be visited on a sometime respectable family which is tainted by a sexual fall. The rising middle-class or county family can suffer a terrible setback if a sexual fall is made public. Prosperous matches can be cancelled outright, and upward mobility can be put into reverse. The aristocracy can afford to flaunt every convention. When *Esther Waters* was written Bertie's relationship with Lillie Langtry was public knowledge. Middle-class families had to be far more careful. Peggy, Mary Barfield's cousin, is the young lady who finds William irresistible. Smarting under Esther's misplaced rejection he returns Peggy's advances, only to be dismissed when the affair is discovered. Peggy departs the same day, without warning, to elope with William and marry him on the continent with little or no prospects for lasting happiness. They travel to France very much in the same direction as Lady Isabel Carlyle and her seducer, Francis Levison, both of whom feature largely in Mrs Wood's *East Lynne*. For Mrs Wood the continent was the only 'refuge for such fugitives', and in one sense she is correct. Fallen couples like those above and the newly married Latches can never stay in England. Instead of the happy life they expected the Latches' affair is plagued by instability, incompatibility and Peggy's infidelity. The major point is this: not only does Peggy ruin her own social prospects, she is responsible for a threat to the social prospects of the other family members. Peggy has just eloped with William. The servants respond:

> They are just crazy about it upstairs. Ginger and the Gaffer are worst. They say they had better sell the place and build another house somewhere else. None of the county people will call on them now—and just as they were beginning to get on so well! Miss Mary, too, is terrible cut up about it; she says it will interfere with her prospects, and that Ginger has nothing to do now but to marry the kitchenmaid to complete the ruin of the Barfields. (*EW*, p. 80)

Singer is the son of the house, the nickname reflecting the sandy colour of his hair. In his righteous indignation he conveniently forgets the 'various burlesque actresses at the Shoreham Gardens' whom he 'had been after'. (*EW*, p. 44) This is the old story. His nefarious activity, if carried out with a certain amount of discretion and circumspection, is not only expected but condoned with no ill effects to Miss Mary's prospects, or the family's social security. When Mr Trubner feels Esther's continued presence in his house puts at risk his young male cousins who come to his house, it is probably not the potential act which is abhorrent to him, it is the place. His house cannot be the venue for sowing wild oats. It is this reason, and others related to it, which force Mrs Barfield to send Esther away, despite her feeling that Esther is more sinned against than sinning.

Mrs Barfield's stand is rather enlightened. On discovering Esther is seven months pregnant she is more upset about the concealment of the fact than about the sin itself. Esther, who would have enjoyed the luxury of being honest, felt she had to conceal the pregnancy so that she could earn sufficient to see her through the birth. She cannot afford, as a working-class girl, to put religious ethics before survival. 'Had I told you [before],' she reminds the hurt Mrs Barfield, 'you would have sent me away there and then. I had only a quarter's wages, and should have starved or gone and drowned myself.' (*EW*, p. 83) If Mrs Barfield is not softened by this, and I suspect she is, Esther's subsequent statement to the effect that she must think of her child even before her own conscience, definitely does. Esther, however, is never dishonest for the sake of it, nor for her own self-preservation. Mrs Barfield wants to take most of the blame away from Esther, suggesting that because Esther is led into temptation it is not her fault. The servant will not tell the mistress that which she wants to hear. Instead she tells the truth as she sees it. Mrs Barfield is speaking first:

'Can I give you a character? You were tempted, you were led into temptation. I ought to have watched over you better—mine is the responsibility. Tell me, it was not your fault.'

'It is always a woman's fault, ma'am. But he should not have deserted me as he did—that's the only thing I reproach him with; the rest was my fault—I shouldn't have touched that second glass of ale. Besides, I was in love with him, and you know what that is. I thought no harm, and I let him kiss me. He used to take me out for walks on the hill and round the farm. He told me he loved me, and would make me his wife—that's how it was. Afterwards he asked me to wait till after the Leger, and that riled me, and I knew then how wicked I had been. I would not go out with him or speak to him any more; and while our quarrel was going on Miss Peggy went after him, and that's how I got left.' (*EW*, p. 84)

Despite the honesty of her 'blunt English way' and her essential goodness, both recognised by Mrs Barfield, she must be sent away. Keeping her there is out of the question—that would be condoning lascivious behaviour at Woodview. Esther is not a contaminating influence, but would be seen as such by other county families. To soften her conscience, and because she has genuine regard for Esther, Mrs Barfield gives her what she feels is sufficient money to see her through the ordeal, and gives her a character reference, the single most important thing which will keep her off the streets.

In contrast to the middle-class attitudes well described by Moore, there is quite a different stand made by the working folk. Even though individual members of the working class adopted the finer sentiments of the middle classes in an effort to earn respectability, and perhaps as a sign of upward mobility, the general rule was to stick by a friend in trouble. When Esther must leave Woodview Sarah and Margaret express their sorrow at her departure. The scene is genuinely touching, but not over-sentimentalised:

> Esther went upstairs to pack her box, and when she came down she found all the women in the kitchen; evidently they were waiting for her. Coming forward Sarah said: 'I hope we shall part friends, Esther; any quarrels we may have had—There's no ill feeling now, is there?' . . .
>
> The babbling of so many voices drew Mr. Leopold from the pantry; he came with a glass of beer in his hand, and this suggested a toast to Sarah. 'Let's drink baby's health,' she said. 'Mr. Leopold won't refuse us the beer.'
>
> The idea provoked some good-natured laughter, and Esther hid her face in her hands and tried to get away. But Margaret would not allow her. 'What nonsense!' she said. 'We don't think any the worse of you; why, that's an accident that might happen to any of us.' (*EW*, pp. 87-8)

The working girls at the house have nothing to lose by being accepting of Esther. Their genuine pity for her plight combines with a down-to-earth honesty about her so-called fall. It could happen to anyone. Margaret does not need to surround herself with Trubner-like panegyrics about the cleansing of society through the expulsion of the sinner.

Moore continues his study of different working-class reactions to Esther's predicament by dwelling on the responses made by her mother and stepfather respectively, when she returns home to

London with all the 'grief and trouble that girls of her class have to bear . . . ' (*EW*, p. 88) By having more than one generalised working-class attitude in the novel, we tend to judge the record as more true to life. Moore does the same thing with the middle-class reaction in the novel—the Trubner response might be common, but there is always signs of enlightenment on the horizon exemplified by Miss Rice and Mrs Barfield. He gives his novel, therefore, a range of opinions which furthers the impression that it is a reliable picture of the life of the times.

Mrs Saunders, now the mother's married name, is pregnant herself. She is to die having the child at home, when Esther is in the hospital having her boy. The mother presumes, when she greets Esther in the doorway, that the girl has lost her place through losing her temper. Esther does have a passionate nature, an obvious temper, a determination and a streak of aggressiveness in her character, all of which her mother recognises. It is these very traits which help to cause her fall, yet make it possible for her to survive, and to avoid the answer taken by many of a weaker temperament. (I am astonished to read, in Susan Mitchell's recollections of George Moore, that she remembers Esther as 'refined' and 'delicate'.[61]) Mrs Saunders, who knows her daughter well, assumes that her lack of self-control has led to her presence on the doorstep. Whilst she does shed a few tears when the truth is told, she is too concerned about the general economic situation at home and about her problematic marital match to give Esther's fallen state an exaggerated shocked response. Given the difficulties she has to face, Moore does not write of the mother in a condemnatory tone. There are several young children. The older girls, aided by their more advanced siblings, work all day making cloth dogs to contribute to the income Mrs Saunders desperately needs. The dog-making recalls the old story of slave labour, required even in respectable dress-making workshops in the novels of Gaskell and Gissing. If the lot of the respectable apprentice is appalling, the working-class girl has even more to face. In this social context she cannot afford the luxury of a fine sensibility to sexual transgression. The mother, therefore, accepts Esther because she loves her but also because there is little point doing otherwise. There is little time for living, let alone time for playing fine games of social distinction. Mrs Saunders concludes, 'I don't want no telling that my Esther ain't a bad girl.' (*EW*, p. 107)

Mr Saunders, one of the more Zolaesque figures in the novel, is brushed in bold naturalistic strokes. He comes home 'sniffing the odour of the meat', which the women have bought for him out of Esther's money, 'like an animal going to be fed'. (*EW*, pp. 95-6) They intend to give him a good dinner so that he will be in a sufficiently generous frame of mind which will allow Esther to remain at home for a while. When Mr Saunders is told about his stepdaughter's pregnancy he uses the revelation as a barb with which to prod the religion so dear to his wife and Esther. 'The goody goody set are the worst. So she 'as got herself into trouble! Well she'll 'ave to get 'erself out of it.' (*EW*, p. 99) He searches for an excuse which will enable him to get rid of what he sees as one, or possibly two, new mouths to feed. He then resorts to an adopted, more typically middle-class attitude. Esther and her child cannot remain at home providing a poor example for the other children in his 'respectable' home. His scruples, however, are short-lived when it is pointed out to him that there is money to pay for the lodging. In the face of their poverty (caused, incidentally, by his intemperance) his would-be middle-class scruple disappears:

'No, I tell yer. No, I won't 'ave it! There be too many 'ere as it is.'

'Only a little while, Jim!'

'No. And those who ain't wanted 'ad better go at once—that's my advice to them. The place is as full of us that we can 'ardly turn round as it is. No, I won't 'ear of it!'

'But, Jim, Esther is quite willing to pay her way; she's saved a good little sum of money, and could afford to pay us ten shillings a week for board and the parlour.'

A perplexed look came on Jim's face.

'Why didn't yer tell me that afore? Of course I don't wish to be 'ard on the girl, as her 'ave just heard me say. Ten shillings a week for her board and the parlour—that seems fair enough: and if it's any convenience to 'er to stop 'ere, I'm sure we'll be glad to 'ave 'er. I'll say right glad, too. We was always good friends, Esther, wasn't we, though ye wasn't one of my own?' So saying, Jim held out his hand. (*EW*, p. 101)

In professing their friendship Jim has conveniently forgotten the time when Esther threw boiling water in his face. His lack of real affection in the face of social difficulty and drunkenness is one terse look at working-class coldness. There are other examples in the novel. Jenny comes to the hospital ostensibly to inform Esther of her mother's death. It takes Jenny one week from the funeral to give her sister the bad news, and when she does it is given in a matter-of-fact manner. She really comes, we discover, to ask Esther for two pounds out of her needed funds, so that she can accompany her father and family to Australia. Esther's reluctance to part with money needed for the preservation of her son cannot withstand a girl who has part of Jim Saunders in her. Without Esther's help, she threatens, prostitution will be her only option. The sad thing is that she is correct. The way of the city gives Jenny few alternatives. Prostitution is one of the few openings within reach of the young working-class girl. Moore sees prostitution more as a necessity than as a result of immoral depravity. He echoes Mrs Butler's stand earlier in the century when she reminds Frederic Harrison in a letter that

> for the lessening of this enormous evil it needs only that men of education should apply themselves earnestly to the much neglected subject of social economy; for this is not a question of natural vice so much as one of political and social economy.[62]

Esther, aware of economic necessities, gives Jenny the £2 required. We never find out if the family does travel to Australia, or if Mr Saunders spends the much-needed money at the public house. By allowing for pragmatic working-class characteristics of the type we see in Jenny, Moore is taking pains not to leave his readers with a noble-savage, romantic impression of working-class life at the end of the century. Goodness inherent in the natures of Mrs Jones, Mrs Lewis, and Esther, all single struggling women, is well balanced by the evil, necessary or otherwise, in Saunders, Mrs Spires, Bill Evans, all of whom collectively make up a Dickensian set of criminals, minus the sense of humour so characteristic of that writer. 'No world,' Moore is to write in 'Mummer Worship', 'can be so wholly pure or impure—that some proportion of vice, as well as virtue, must find its way into human life! The entire removal and abolition of either would mean death to the human race.'[63] The absence of either virtue or vice in the working classes in the novel would also mean death to the work. But whether he is looking at the vice or virtue of the members of the working class in the novel he is sufficiently fair to allow for their difficulties of survival. Even in the presentation of Saunders he is a little sympathetic: the public house is the only place he can go to escape the noise and grime of work, or the overcrowding at home. It is one of the few places he can find some sort of companionship outside the family circle. On the whole then, whilst allowing for the existence of evil in the working class, his social awareness makes him largely sympathetic.

He has even less admiration for members of the non-working classes like Mrs Rivers who demands the sacrifice of poor lives for her one Mayfair-born child. Even though her mother's instinct makes her as she is, the advantage of the power wealth provides gives her an unfair advantage. In *Esther Waters* Moore seems to have a reasonably sophisticated realisation of the realities of class structure in England at the turn of the century. His sensitivity felt for members of the working class is reminiscent of Gaskell's mill workers in *North and South* and *Mary Barton*, but it is more surprising to find in Moore. As a younger man, he was forced to leave Paris for London—problems of the poor on his Irish estate demanded his return to Britain. Then the spoiled aristocrat comes to the fore:

> That some wretched farmers and miners should refuse to starve, that I may not be deprived of my demi-tasse at Tortoni's, that I may not be forced to leave this beautiful retreat, my cat and my python—monstrous. And these wretched creatures will find moral support in England; they will find pity.[64]

With the publishing of *Esther Waters*, his understanding of class problems, especially those experienced by the poor, comes of age. His close analysis of Esther and those like her, gives him greater insight into problems endemic in poverty and want. There is even a subterranean vein of something akin to socialism both in Esther's personality and in the novel itself. Those hearing the temper tantrum in the above would never have believed it.

From time to time Esther has trouble accepting her 'betters' as such. On leaving Miss Rice, she hugs her knowing that her place forbids such familiarity. She has trouble accepting that Peggy is her superior. She has just eloped with William:

> [William] . . . had gone where she could not follow. He had gone where grand folk lived in idleness, in the sinfulness of the world and the flesh, eating and gambling, thinking of nothing else, with servants to wait on them, obeying their orders and saving them from every trouble. She knew that these fine folk

thought servants inferior beings. But they were all the same flesh and blood. Peggy wore a fine dress, but she was no better; take off her dress and they were the same, woman to woman. (*EW*, p. 76)

The conclusion of the novel has a very definite levelling effect. Woodview is crumbling and largely deserted. Mrs Barfield takes Esther once again. Both are mothers with only sons. Both are widows whose husbands' passion for horseracing had something to do with their deaths. While Mrs Barfield's social situation has been declining throughout the novel, Esther's has been rising. For a time she and William are proprietors of a reasonable business. When the women live together at Woodview they are 'more like friends and less like mistress and maid'. (*EW*, p. 357) The novel moves to the point where a human relationship is more powerful than caste.

The novel also makes very direct criticism about the fact that it is common to see two laws in England—one for the rich and one for the poor. Justice may be blind most of the time, but it does have the habit of peeking through the blindfold to discover the class of its potential victim and the amount of power he or she has. The courtroom scene at Sarah's trial is a particularly effective dramatic way to expose the lack of fairness inherent in the traditional English class structure. Sarah has stolen her master's plate and has given it to Bill Evans, who is supposed to pawn it and use the money for a bet on the horses, which, when successful will provide sufficient to redeem the pledge and leave enough for the couple to live in comfort. Evans has promised marriage on the horse's winning. As expected, Evans disappears. The judge, prior to sentencing Sarah to hard labour for eighteen months, lectures the assembly on the evils of betting:

'There is now only one more point which I wish to refer to, and that is the plea that the prisoner did not intend to steal the plate, but only to obtain money upon it to enable her and the partner in her guilt to back a horse for a race which they believed to be—' his lordship was about to say a certainty for him; he stopped himself, however, in time—'to be, to be, which they believed him to be capable of winning. The race in question is, I think, called the Cesarewitch, and the name of the horse [lordship has got three hundred on Ben Jonson], if my memory serves me right [here his lordship fumbles amid papers], yes, the name is, as I thought, Ben Jonson. Now, the learned counsel for the defense suggested that, if the horse had won, the plate would have been redeemed and restored to its proper place in the pantry cupboards. This, I venture to point out, is a mere hypothesis. The money might have been again used for the purposes of gambling . . . The vice among the poorer classes is largely on the increase, and it seems to me that it is the duty of all in authority to condemn rather than condone the evil, and to use every effort to stamp it out. For my part I fail to perceive any romantic element in the vice of gambling. It springs from the desire to obtain wealth without work, in other words, without payment; work, whether in the past or the present, is the natural payment for wealth, and any wealth that is obtained without work is in a measure a fraud committed upon the community. Poverty, despair, idleness, and every other vice spring from gambling as naturally, and in the same profusion, as weeds from barren land. Drink, too, is gambling's firmest ally.'

At this moment a certain dryness in his lordship's throat reminded him of the pint of excellent claret that lordship always drank with his lunch, and the thought enabled lordship to roll out some excellent invective against the evils of beer and spirits. And his lordship's losses on the horse whose name he could hardly recall helped to a forcible illustration of the theory that drink and gambling mutually uphold and enforce each other. When the news came in that Ben Jonson had broken down at the bushes, lordship had drunk a magnum of champagne . . . (*EW*, pp. 303-4)

William Latch is well aware of the 'old story—one law for the rich, another for the poor'. When Esther prevaricates against William's illegal betting in the bar when his health does not permit work on course, he replies by reminding her of the betting which goes on at Tattersall's and the Albert Club. He cannot see the difference. His ensuing angry dialogue answers the pedantic harangue which his lordship was wont to deliver in court:

'Why shouldn't the poor man 'ave his 'alf-crown's worth of excitement? The rich man can have his thousand pound's worth whenever he pleases. The same with the public 'ouses—there's a lot of hypocritical folk that is for the docking of the poor man of his beer, but there's no one that's for interfering for them that drink champagne in the clubs. It's all bloody rot, and it makes me sick when I think about it . . .

' "All work and no play makes Jack a dull boy", Esther. Their only pleasure is a bet. When they've one on they've something to look forward to; whether they win or lose they 'as their money's worth. You know what I say is true; you've seen them, how they look forward to the evening paper to see how the 'oss is going on in belling. Man can't live without hope. It's their only hope, and I says no one has a right to take it from them.' (*EW*, pp. 281-2)

William virtually repeats that which the narrator has previously noted in an earlier chapter. 'A bet on a race brings hope into lives which otherwise would be hopeless.' (*EW*, p. 244)

Working-class hopes, freedom and limitations are important to the meaning of the novel. The working class can only hope within a certain social framework—their dreams are the only things that are free. Esther and William have few—perhaps their only dream in the novel is to go to Egypt for a cure as Miss Mary Barfield had done. But they are not free to do so. Freedom is a luxury that Esther and her mother do not have. Seymour possesses a little and abuses it a little. The judge possesses a lot and abuses it a great deal. The novel studies the heart of England in the 1890s; its frame of reference covers a great deal: religion, morality, class differences, pleasure, human instincts, marriage, economics. The problems the novel highlights are as English as the heroine herself. It is the England of vice and virtue, in the rich and in the poor. As Professor Hough has it—Moore 'shows people behaving as they do behave'. This, in some ways, runs contrary to the tenor of nineteenth-century English fiction which so often shows people as we would like them to behave, a facet of a literary tradition which accounts for much of its greatness, and much of its poor work. It is the originality of the work which prompts Professor Hough to remark that it has 'little of the smell of English literature', therefore its naturalistic tendencies make it a 'great French novel rather than a great English novel'.[65] It may not 'smell' of English literature—I would agree—but it certainly does of England itself. Professor Hough supplies a list which belies his own argument on the lack of an English quality in his work—'it is about servants' halls, racing stables, lodging houses, and pubs . . . '[66] The point needs to be made: Moore did not write in the nineteenth-century Victorian manner, if indeed such a manner does exist *per se*, but he did write a new kind of novel which was to influence such writers as Joyce, Wolf and Bennett. They, in turn, cause ever-increasing ripples in the ocean of English fiction which are still moving past us. Who would have thought that we would owe so much to George Moore, and he to one of the most finely drawn of the late Victorian fallen women, Esther Waters? The novel 'won for English fiction a great deal of the freedom its author desired.'[67] The historical perspective proves Shaw incorrect, even though Moore's popularity is at a low ebb, when he writes that Moore has 'no heights and no depths except in certain descriptions of Ireland and certain scandalous passages . . . '[68]

Notes

1. Joseph M. Hone, *The Life of George Moore* (New York: Macmillan, 1936), pp. 25-6.

2. John Freeman, *A Portrait of George Moore in a Study of His Work* (London: T. Werner Laurie, 1922), p. 34.

3. Ibid., p. 35.

4. Ibid., p. 36.

5. J. A. V. Chapple, *Documentary and Imaginative Literature 1880-1920* (London: Blandford Press, 1970), p. 62.

6. George Moore, *Esther Waters* (London: J. M. Dent, 1962), p. 177. Hereafter, quotes from this edition will be accompanied by the abbreviation *EW* and page number, in the body of the text.

7. Geraint Goodwin, *Conversations with George Moore* (New York: Haskell House, 1974), p. 18. (This edition is a reprint of the original work, published by Jonathan Cape, London, 1940.)

8. George Moore, 'A Visit to Medan' in *Confessions of a Young Man* (London: William Heinemann, 1933), p. 243.

9. Susan L. Mitchell, *George Moore* (Dublin: Talbot Press, 1916), pp. 43-4.

10. Anthony Farrow, *George Moore* (Boston, Massachusetts: Twayne, 1978), p. 45.

11. Anne Lyon Haight, *Banned Books* (London: George Allen and Unwin, 1955), p. 69.

12. Ibid.

13. Guinevere L. Griest, *Mudie's Circulating Library and the Victorian Novel* (Bloomington: Indiana University Press, 1970), pp. 82-3.

14. Ibid., p. 83.

15. Ibid.

16. Ibid.

17. Ibid., p. 149.

18. Ibid., p. 150.

19. Ibid., p. 153.

20. Henry Blyth, *Skittles—The Last Victorian Courtesan* (London: Rupert Hart-Davis, 1970), p. 218.

21. Ibid., pp. 188-9.

22. Griest, *Mudie's Circulating Library*, p. 154.

23. Ibid., p. 208.

24. Ibid., p. 209.

25. Haight, *Banned Books*, p. 52.

26. Ibid., p. 57.
27. Ibid., p. 61.
28. Ibid., p. 71.
29. Goodwin, *Conversations with George Moore*, pp. 149-51.
30. Humbert Wolfe, *George Moore* (London: Thornton Butterworth, 1931), p. 21.
31. Ibid.
32. Freeman, *A Portrait of George Moore*, p. 111.
33. Ibid., pp. 111-12.
34. Ibid., p. 113.
35. Ibid.
36. Ibid., p. 111.
37. Charles Kingsley, *Yeast*, Vol. II, *The Works of Charles Kingsley* (London: Macmillan and Company, 1879), p. 33.
38. Ibid., p. 30.
39. Ibid., p. 14.
40. Ibid., p. 4.
41. Ibid.
42. Wolfe, *George Moore*, pp. 102-3.
43. Theophile Gautier, *Mademoiselle de Maupin* (Sydney: Dymock's Book Arcade, 1951), p. 193.
44. Goodwin, *Conversations with George Moore*, p. 150.
45. Mitchell, *George Moore*, p. 36.
46. Kingsley, *Yeast*, p. 31.
47. Griest, *Mudie's Circulating Library*, p. 154.
48. Goodwin, *Conversations with George Moore*, p. 211.
49. Wolfe, *George Moore*, p. 120.
50. Sonja Nejdefors-Frisk, *George Moore's Naturalistic Prose* (Upsala: Lundequist, 1952), pp. 127-8.
51. Ibid.
52. Walter Allen, 'Introduction' in *Esther Waters*, p.v.
53. Goodwin, *Conversations with George Moore*, p. 239.
54. Ibid.
55. George Moore, 'Ode to a Beggar Girl' in *Pagan Poems* (London: Newman, 1881), pp. 5-15.
56. Nejdefors-Frisk, *George Moore's Naturalistic Prose*, p. 36.
57. Mitchell, *George Moore*, p. 45.
58. Moore, *Confessions of a Young Man*, p. 217.
59. Nejdefors-Frisk, *George Moore's Naturalistic Prose*, p. 126.
60. Ibid., p. 127.
61. Mitchell, *George Moore*, p. 46.
62. Paul McHugh, *Prostitution and Victorian Social Reform* (London: Croom Helm, 1980), p. 21.
63. George Moore, 'Mummer Worship' in *Confessions of a Young Man*, p. 243.
64. Nejdefors-Frisk, *George Moore's Naturalistic Prose*, p. 26.
65. Graham Hough, 'George Moore and the Novel', in Graham Owens (ed.), *George Moore's Mind and Art* (Edinburgh: Oliver and Boyde, 1968), p. 168.
66. Ibid.
67. Rupert Hart-Davis (ed.), *George Moore: Letters to Lady Cunard, 1895-1933* (London: Rupert Hart-Davis, 1957), p. 8.
68. Goodwin, *Conversations with George Moore*, p. 19.

EPILOGUE

Individual dynamism in the Victorian Age was a male province. The Queen Victorias and the Florence Nightingales and the George Eliots are so few in number they become the exceptions which prove the rule. In *The Egoist* Meredith admits that a study of the unenviable position of women reveals more about the society which oppresses them than about the women themselves:

> Women have us back to the condition of primitive man, or they shoot us higher than the topmost star. But it is as we please. Let them tell us what we are to them; for us, they are our back and front of life; the poet's Lesbia, the poet's Beatrice; ours is the choice. And were it proved that some of the bright things are in the pay of darkness, with the stamp of his coin on their palm, and that some are the very angels we hear sung of, not the less might we say that they find us out, they have us by our leanings. They are to us what we hold of the best or worst within. By their state is our civilisation judged, and if it is hugely animal still, that is because primitive men abound and will have their pasture.

Hardy, Collins, Mrs Gaskell, Dickens, Trollope, Eliot, Gissing and Moore, all believed that their presentation of the fall of women is a criterion by which to judge their civilisation as a whole. The very existence of these novelists and their novels, both which recognise the goodness in Nancy, Ruth, Mercy, and Tess, affirm that whilst primitive man may masquerade in civilised costume, individual vision can penetrate the disguise and see him for what he is. The art of novelists studied here is a triumph for this vision, and a triumph for art. It is by their open minds, their sensitivity, their largeness of spirit and their individual genius that I would prefer to judge their age.

BIBLIOGRAPHY

Primary Souces

Ainsworth, William H. *Jack Sheppard*. London: Richard Bentley, 1839

Brontë, Charlotte. *Jane Eyre*. London: Penguin Books, 1978

Collins, Wilkie. *The Fallen Leaves*. London: Chatto and Windus, 1893

———.*Man and Wife*. London: Chatto and Windus, 1892

———.*The New Magdalen*. London: Chatto and Windus, 1893

Dickens, Charles. *Hard Times*. London: J. M. Dent and Sons Ltd, 1974

———.*Oliver Twist*. London: Penguin Books, 1971

———.*Sketches by Boz*. London: J. M. Dent and Sons Ltd, 1968

Eliot, George. *Adam Bede*. London: Collins (undated)

Gaskell, Mrs Elizabeth. *Ruth*. London: Smith, Elder and Company, 1906

Gautier, Theophile. *Mademoiselle de Maupin*. Sydney: Dymock's Book Arcade, 1951

Gissing, George. *The Unclassed*. Sussex: The Harvester Press Ltd, 1976

Hardy, Thomas. *Tess of the d'Urbervilles*. London: Pan Books in association with Macmillan, 1978

Hudson, Derek (ed). *Munby: Man of Two Worlds*. London: Abacus, 1974

Jerome, Jerome K. *Three Men in a Boat*. London: J. M. Dent and Sons Ltd, 1957

Kingsley, Charles. *Yeast*. London: Macmillan and Company, 1879

Lytton, Right Hon. Lord. *Paul Clifford*. London: C. J. Howell and Company, 1840

Meredith, George. *The Egoist*. London: Penguin Books, 1968

Moore, George. *Confessions of a Young Man*. London: William Heinemann Ltd, 1933

———.*Esther Waters*. London: J. M. Dent and Sons Ltd, 1962

———.*Pagan Poems*. London: Newman and Company, 1881

Scott, Sir Walter. *The Heart of Midlothian*. London: Collins, 1952

Trollope, Anthony. *An Autobiography*. London: Oxford University Press, 1950

———.*An Eye for an Eye*. London: Anthony Blond, 1966

225

——. *The Vicar of Bullhampton*. London: Oxford University Press, 1940

Trollope, Mrs Francis. *Jessie Phillips: A Tale of the Present Day*. London: Colburn, 1843

Wood, Mrs Henry. *East Lynne*. London: Collins, 1954

——. *Pomeroy Abbey*. London: Richard Bentley and Son, 1890

Nineteenth-century Criticism and Reference

Carlyle, Thomas. 'The Hero as Poet. Dante; Shakespeare'. *English Critical Essays*. Edmund D. Jones. (Ed.), London: Oxford University Press, 1971

Chapple, J. A. V. and Pollard, A. (eds). *The Letters of Mrs. Gaskell*. Manchester: Manchester University Press, 1966

Coustillas, Pierre and Partridge, Collin (eds). *Gissing: The Critical Heritage*. London: Routledge and Kegan Paul, 1972

Daily Chronicle. December 1895, rpt in Coustillas

Hart-Davis, Rupert (ed). *George Moore: Letters to Lady Cunard 1895-1933*. London: Rupert Hart-Davis

Lerner, Lawrence and Holmstrom, John. *Thomas Hardy and his Readers*. London: The Bodley Head, 1968

Lewes, George Henry. 'Ruth', *The Leader*, IV, 22 January 1853, pp. 89-91

Oliphant, Mrs. *Blackwood's Magazine*, November 1870, rpt in Page

Page, Norman (ed). *Wilkie Collins: The Critical Heritage*. London: Routledge and Kegan Paul, 1974

Saturday Review. 4 May 1870, xxix, 646-7, rpt in Smalley

——. 9 July 1870, xxx, 52-3, rpt in Page

——. 2 August 1879, xlviii, 148-9, rpt in Page

Smalley, Donald (ed). *Trollope: The Critical Heritage*. London: Routledge and Kegan Paul, 1969

Spectator. 15 February 1879, iii, 210-11, rpt in Smalley

——. 15 May 1880, liii, 627-8, rpt in Page

Swinburne, Algernon Charles. 'Wilkie Collins', *Fortnightly Review*, November 1889, cclxxi, 589-99, rpt in Page

Taylor, R. H. *The Personal Notebooks of Thomas Hardy*. London: The Macmillan Press Ltd, 1978

Thackeray, William M. 'Going to See a Man Hanged', *Frazer's Magazine*, August 1840, xxii, pp. 154-5.

The Times. 3 June 1870, p. 4, rpt in Smalley

Wood, Charles W. *Memorials of Mrs Henry Wood*. London: Richard Bentley and Son, 1894

Yates, Edmund. 'The Novels of Wilkie Collins', *Temple Bar*, August 1890, lxxxix, 528-32, rpt in Page

Twentieth-century Criticism and Reference

Ashley, Robert. *Wilkie Collins*. London: Arthur Barker Ltd, 1952

Auerbach, Nina. 'The Rise of the Fallen Woman', *19th Century Fiction*, 1980

Blyth, Henry. *Skittles—The Last Victorian Courtesan: The Life and Times of Catherine Walters*. London: Rupert Hart-Davis, 1970

Brooks, J. R. *Thomas Hardy: The Poetic Structure*. London: Elk Books, 1971

Chapple, J. A. V. *Documentary and Imaginative Literature 1880-1920*. London: Blandford Press, 1970

Collie, Michael. *The Alien Art: A Critical Study of George Gissing's Novels*. Kent: Archon Books, 1979

Collins, Philip. *Dickens and Crime*. Bloomington, Indiana: Indiana University Press, 1962

Craik, W.A. *Elizabeth Gaskell and the Provincial Novel*. London: Methuen and Company Ltd, 1975

Curtis Brown, Beatrice. *Anthony Trollope*. London: Arthur Barker Ltd, 1950

Elwin, Malcolm. *Victorian Wallflowers*. London: Jonathan Cape, 1937

Farrow, Anthony. *George Moore*. Boston, Massachusetts: Twayne Publishers, 1978

Frazer, Sir James George. *The Dying God, VIII The Golden Bough*. London: Macmillan and Company Ltd, 1920

Freeman, John. *A Portrait of George Moore in a Study of His Work*. London: T. Werner Laurie, 1922.

Gilcher, Edwin. *A Bibliography of George Moore*. Illinois: Northern Illinois University Press, 1970

Goodwin, Geraint. *Conversations with George Moore*. New York: Haskell House Publishers Ltd, 1974

Griest, Guinevere L. *Mudie's Circulating Library and the Victorian Novel*. Bloomington, Indiana: Indiana University Press, 1970

Haight, Anne Lyon. *Banned Books: Informal Notes on Some Books Banned for Various Reasons at Various Times and in Various Places*. London: George Allen and Unwin, 1955

Heineman, Helen. *Mrs. Trollope: The Triumphant Feminine in the*

Nineteenth Century. Athens, Ohio: Ohio University Press, 1979

Hollingsworth, Keith. *The Newgate Novel 1830-1847*. Detroit: Wayne State University Press, 1963

Hone, Joseph M. *The Life of George Moore*. New York: Macmillan, 1936

Howe, Irving. *Thomas Hardy*. New York: Collier Books, 1967

Korg, Jacob. *George Gissing: A Critical Biography*. London: Methuen and Company Ltd, 1965

Laird, J. T. *The Shaping of Tess of the d'Urbervilles*. Oxford: The Clarendon Press, 1975

McHugh, Paul. *Prostitution and Victorian Social Reform*. London: Croom Helm, 1980

Mitchell, Susan L. *George Moore*. Dublin: The Talbot Press Ltd, 1916

Nejdefors-Frisk, Sonja. *George Moore's Naturalistic Prose*. Upsala: Lundequist, 1952

Nield, Keith. 'Introduction', *Prostitution in the Victorian Age: Debates on the Issue from 19th Century Critical Journals*. Westmead, Hants: Gregg International Publishers Ltd, 1973

Owens, Graham. *George Moore's Mind and Art*. Edinburgh: Oliver and Boyd, 1968

Pearson, Michael. *The Age of Consent*. Newton Abbot, Devon: David and Charles Ltd, 1972

Pinion, F. B., *et al*. *Thomas Hardy and the Modern World*. Dorset: The Thomas Hardy Society Ltd, 1974

Robinson, Kenneth. *Wilkie Collins: A Biography*. London: The Bodley Head, 1951

Sadlier, Michael. *Trollope: A Commentary*. London: Constable and Company Ltd, 1945

Sharps, J. G. *Mrs Gaskell's Observation and Invention*. London: The Linden Press, 1970

Stewart, J. I. M. *Thomas Hardy*. London: Longman, 1971

Tindall, Gillian. *The Born Exile: George Gissing*. London: Temple Smith, 1974

Tracy, Robert. *Trollope's Later Novels*. London: Cambridge University Press, 1975

Walkowitz, Judith R. *Prostitution and Victorian Society*. London: Cambridge University Press, 1980

Wolfe, Humbert. *George Moore*. London: Thornton Butterworth Ltd, 1931

INDEX

44,036

Watt, George.

The fallen woman in
the nineteenth-
century English
novel

DATE			
APR 1 5 1986	NOV 2 8 2003		
MAR 7			
APR - 6 1988	APR 1 6 2004		
APR - 6 1988	DEC 0 7 2007		
APR 1 5 1988			
APR 0 2 1990			
APR 1 3 1991			
APR 0 7 1995			
DEC 2 3 1997			
DEC 0 5 1997			
NOV 1 8 2003			